T0383950

Out of Poverty
Second Edition

Out of Poverty provides a comprehensive defense of Third World sweatshops that does not put economic efficiency over people but instead explores methods of improving the welfare of those in Third World countries. The author explains how sweatshops provide the best opportunity for workers; and how they play an important role in development, leading to better wages and working conditions. Using economic theory, empirical evidence, and historical investigation, Powell argues that the anti-sweatshop movement would harm the very workers it intends to help by creating less-desirable alternatives and undermining development. Including a new chapter on the 2013 Rana Plaza factory collapse in Bangladesh, this revised and expanded second edition also explores how sweatshop wages have changed, how poverty alleviation has progressed in countries with sweatshops in the late 1990s and early 2000s, and how boycotting Uyghur forced labor in China differs from other sweatshop boycotts.

BENJAMIN POWELL is Professor of Economics at Rawls College of Business Administration, Executive Director at the Free Market Institute, Texas Tech University, and Senior Fellow at the Independent Institute. He is the coauthor of *Wretched Refuse? The Political Economy of Immigration and Institutions* (Cambridge University Press, 2020) and the Amazon best-selling *Socialism Sucks: Two Economists Drink Their Way through the Unfree World* (Regnery, 2019). His research on sweatshops has been reported in the *New York Times* and the *Wall Street Journal.*

CAMBRIDGE STUDIES IN ECONOMICS, CHOICE, AND SOCIETY

Founding Editors

Timur Kuran, *Duke University*
Peter J. Boettke, *George Mason University*

This interdisciplinary series promotes original theoretical and empirical research as well as integrative syntheses involving links between individual choice, institutions, and social outcomes. Contributions are welcome from across the social sciences, particularly in the areas where economic analysis is joined with other disciplines such as comparative political economy, new institutional economics, and behavioral economics.

Books in the Series:

Out of Poverty

Sweatshops in the Global Economy

Second Edition

BENJAMIN POWELL
Texas Tech University

CAMBRIDGE
UNIVERSITY PRESS

INDEPENDENT
INSTITUTE

Shaftesbury Road, Cambridge CB2 8EA, United Kingdom

One Liberty Plaza, 20th Floor, New York, NY 10006, USA

477 Williamstown Road, Port Melbourne, VIC 3207, Australia

314–321, 3rd Floor, Plot 3, Splendor Forum, Jasola District Centre,
New Delhi – 110025, India

103 Penang Road, #05–06/07, Visioncrest Commercial, Singapore 238467

Cambridge University Press is part of Cambridge University Press & Assessment,
a department of the University of Cambridge.

We share the University's mission to contribute to society through the pursuit of
education, learning and research at the highest international levels of excellence.

www.cambridge.org
Information on this title: www.cambridge.org/9781009505352

DOI: 10.1017/9781009505321

First published 2014
Second edition 2025

Published in association with the Independent Institute.

A catalogue record for this publication is available from the British Library

Library of Congress Cataloging-in-Publication Data
NAMES: Powell, Benjamin, 1978– author.
TITLE: Out of poverty : sweatshops in the global economy / Benjamin Powell,
Texas Tech University.
DESCRIPTION: Second edition. | Cambridge, United Kingdom ; New York, NY,
USA : Cambridge University Press, 2025. | Series: Cambridge studies in
economics, choice, and society | Includes bibliographical references and index.
IDENTIFIERS: LCCN 2024020913 | ISBN 9781009505352 (hardback) |
ISBN 9781009505321 (ebook)
SUBJECTS: LCSH: Sweatshops. | Anti-sweatshop movement – History. |
Economic development – Moral and ethical aspects.
CLASSIFICATION: LCC HD2337 .P694 2025 | DDC 331.25/6–dc23/eng/20240819
LC record available at https://lccn.loc.gov/2024020913

ISBN 978-1-009-50535-2 Hardback
ISBN 978-1-009-50536-9 Paperback

Contents

Figures

Tables

Acknowledgments

My first debt for this book is owed to David Skarbek. Now a Professor of Political Science at Brown University, he was an undergraduate student in an international economics class that I taught at San José State University in 2004. He approached me desiring to write a term paper that we might jointly be able to turn into a scholarly journal article. I suggested working on an empirical investigation of sweatshop wages. We eventually published the paper that evolved out of that project in the *Journal of Labor Research*. It was my first sweatshop-related journal article.

That initial research led to many invitations to give public lectures about sweatshops. I have given lectures to, or participated in debates in front of, civic groups, professional associations, and, mostly, college and university student groups. I resist the urge to try to name each audience I have lectured to about sweatshops because I will surely leave some out. It now numbers somewhere in the hundreds. This book is a direct result of the public lectures and the feedback I received at them. In the course of my lectures, I found myself addressing more and more aspects of sweatshops that went beyond topics I had been able to address in scholarly journal articles. Ultimately, I decided that it was time to write a book on the topic that could more fully elaborate and document the points I was making in my lectures. I am indebted to the students and faculty members who helped to arrange these many lectures and the participants, both hostile (and there were many of them) and sympathetic, who provided me with feedback over the last two decades.

The second edition of this book, like the first, draws on my prior research. I'm indebted to coauthors Matt Zwolinski, J. R. Clark, David Skarbek, Kevin Grier, Towhid Mahmood, and Linan Peng, for their contributions to that research. Chapter 8, in particular, draws heavily on work that Matt did with me and many of the ideas appearing in that chapter were initially his. Similarly, the material on Uyghur forced labor in Chapter 11 draws heavily on work Li Peng did in our coauthored research. I also thank Giancarlo Ibarguen and his staff at Francisco Marroquín University for the help they provided J. R. Clark and I in surveying workers and visiting factories in Guatemala. Some of that research appears in Chapter 5. The sweatshop wage data that was updated in this second edition draws on work I coauthored with Towhid Mahmood and the empirical analysis that forms the basis of Chapter 6 was coauthored with Kevin Grier and Towhid. I'm also grateful that the editors of the *Journal of Economic Behavior and Organization*, the *Journal of Business Ethics, Business Ethics Quarterly, Comparative Economic Studies*, the *Journal of Labor Research*, the *Independent Review*, and *Human Rights Quarterly* all saw fit to publish my research on sweatshops. Research originally appearing in those outlets makes it into parts of chapters throughout this book.

I'm grateful to the Earhart Foundation for the financial support that allowed me to write much of the first edition of this book over the course of two summers and to the Free Market Institute at Texas Tech for support writing much of the updated second edition in the summer of 2023. I thank Nicolas Cachanosky, Rick Weber, Tylor Orme, Rosolino Candela, and Audrey Redford, who provided valuable research and manuscript preparation assistance for the first edition of this book while they were working as my graduate assistants at Suffolk University, and Leonel Regalado Cardoso, who provided manuscript preparation assistance for the second edition. I also thank Linley Hall, who provided valuable professional editorial assistance for the first edition, and Amanda Smith, who helped design the cover of the second edition.

I'm grateful that Cambridge University Press Senior Editor Scott Parris and Series Editors Timur Kuran and Peter Boettke believed in this project from the beginning and encouraged me to pursue it. I also thank Kristen Purdy, who replaced Scott, and her staff for seeing the first edition through to completion, and Robert Dreesen and his staff for handling the approval and production of this second edition. I also thank Christopher Briggs, who was able to involve the Independent Institute in the publication of the second edition of this book. I also thank two of the three anonymous Cambridge University Press reviewers for valuable feedback on the manuscript for the first edition of this book and both anonymous reviewers of the proposal for the second edition. I'm indebted to Jeffery Rogers Hummel for providing valuable feedback on the historical chapter in this book and to Matt Zwolinski and Mark LeBar for helping me avoid saying anything (hopefully) that philosophers would consider stupid in the chapter on ethics. The greatest reviewing thanks go to David Skarbek and Josh McCabe, who read the entire manuscript of the first edition and provided valuable feedback that often substantially altered my presentation of the material.

Over the last two decades I have benefited from discussions with some great colleagues and graduate students at Texas Tech University, Suffolk University, and San José State University. I have also benefited from teaching about sweatshops at summer seminars hosted by the Independent Institute, the Foundation for Economic Education, the Institute for Humane Studies, and the Fund for American Studies. Susan Love Brown, with whom I lectured at a summer seminar, gave me the idea for the title of Chapter 4.

Texas Tech University's Free Market Institute has been an ideal intellectual home for me for more than a decade. I'm thankful for the great colleagues and graduate students I get to work with there on a daily basis. As always, I'm thankful to Peter Boettke, for his mentorship over the entire course of my career. Finally, I thank my wife Lisa for her love, patience, and continued support and both her and my son Raymond for putting up with endless conversations about economics.

Preface

Christian Hansen oiled the machinery and fixed the belts at the Waterhead Mills in Lowell, Massachusetts for a dozen years. The mill processed corduroy, velvet, and finished cotton goods. It ran on steam power until 5 o'clock; after that some of the machines changed over to electric power. Part of Christian's job was to change the motors over at 5 o'clock. On March 16, 1920, Christian went about his usual work routine. Shortly after 5 o'clock he threw one of the switches to turn on the electric power. The nearby compensator box hadn't been properly grounded and was leaking electricity. Christian was hit with 550 volts of electricity and died on the spot.

At about the same time Leona Gagne began working at the Cardinal Shoe Factory in nearby Lawrence, Massachusetts. She worked up to 10-hour days, sometimes 6 days per week. The pay was modest but as her son Paul recalls it, "It wasn't bad for what she did. And the money helped put my brother and I through school."

I knew Leona as "Nana." She was my great-grandmother. Christian was my step-father's great-grandfather. Yet, in the pages that follow, I'm going to defend the type of "sweatshop" jobs that Leona and Christian worked in. I will argue that the jobs are the best realistic alternative available to the workers employed in them and that such jobs are part of the very process of economic development that allows the descendants of Leona, Christian, and their counterparts toiling in Third World sweatshops today to enjoy a higher standard of living with safer, better-paying jobs.

As an economist, I'm hardly alone in making this defense and I'm not the only such economist who had ancestors who worked in sweatshops.

Another economist described the situation his immigrant mother, Sara
Friedman, was in when she arrived in the United States around the turn
of the 20th century:

> Very shortly after my mother's arrival, she started earning her own living by
> working as a seamstress in a "sweatshop." In view of the bad reputation of
> sweatshops, it is interesting that I never heard my mother make a negative remark
> about her experience. On the contrary, she regarded it as enabling her to earn a
> living while she learned English and became adjusted to the new country.[1]

Her son, Milton, would go on to teach at the University of Chicago and
win a Nobel Prize in economics. When economists, such as Milton or
I, defend the existence of so-called sweatshop jobs, it is not because of
any lack of compassion for the workers. Rather, our defense stems from
an understanding of the laws of economics. The laws of economics do
not put "profits over people." They dictate which policies will help poor
workers and which policies will harm them. If you want to help today's
Leonas, Christians, and Saras in the Third World, you should be interested in learning how economic theory relates to sweatshops. I sincerely
hope this book helps you in that endeavor.

[1] Milton and Rose Friedman, *Two Lucky People* (Chicago: University of Chicago Press,
1998), 20.

I

Introduction

Abigail Martinez earned only 55 cents per hour stitching clothing in an El Salvadoran garment factory. She worked as long as 18 hours a day in an unventilated room, while the company provided undrinkable water. If she upset her bosses, they would deny her bathroom breaks or demand that she do cleaning work outside under the hot sun. Abigail's job sounds horrible. Yet many economists defend the existence of sweatshop jobs like hers.[1]

"In Praise of Cheap Labor: Bad Jobs at Bad Wages Are Better Than No Jobs At All." Only a right-wing free-market apologist for global capitalism could ever write an article with such an appalling title. Right? Wrong. Those are the words of a darling of the left, *New York Times* columnist and Nobel Prize–winning economist Paul Krugman.[2] Krugman argues that critics have not found a viable alternative to these Third World sweatshops and that the sweatshops are superior to the rural poverty that the citizens of these countries would otherwise endure.

Krugman is not alone. After Haiti's devastating earthquake, Paul Collier, author of *The Bottom Billion*, prepared a report for the United Nations outlining a reconstruction plan for the country.[3] The development of a Haitian garment industry was central in his plan. He argued

---

[1] Facts in this paragraph were reported by Leslie Kaufman and David Gonzalez in a *New York Times* article on April 24, 2001, entitled "Labor Standards Clash with Global Reality."

[2] Paul Krugman, "In Praise of Cheap Labor: Bad Jobs at Bad Wages Are Better Than No Jobs At All," *Slate Magazine*, March 1997.

[3] "Haiti: From Natural Catastrophe to Economic Security," *A Report for the Secretary-General of the United Nations*, January 2009, retrieved from www.focal.ca/pdf/haiticollier.pdf.

I

that Haiti had good access to key markets and that "due to its poverty
and relatively unregulated labour market, Haiti has labour costs that are
fully competitive with China." Collier essentially outlined a sweatshop
model of economic development for Haiti.

Wages and working conditions in Third World sweatshops are appalling compared to the wages and conditions that most readers of this book
are likely used to. Any decent person who has witnessed poor workers
toiling in a sweatshop should hope for something better for those workers. So why have people such as Krugman, Collier, and many other
economists from across the ideological spectrum defended sweatshop
employment? These economists defended sweatshops because they are the
best achievable alternative available to the workers who choose to work
in them, and sweatshop employment is part of the process of development
that eventually leads to higher wages and improved working conditions.

How bad are the alternatives to sweatshops? In Cambodia, hundreds of people scavenge for plastic bags, metal cans, and bits of food
in trash dumps. Nicholas Kristof reported in the *New York Times* that
"Nhep Chanda averages 75 cents a day for her efforts. For her, the idea
of being exploited in a garment factory – working only six days a week,
inside, instead of seven days in the broiling sun, for up to $2 a day – is a
dream."[4] Other common alternatives are subsistence agriculture, informal sector work, begging, or even prostitution.

Recent international trade did not invent poverty. The history of
humanity is one of poverty. In most places in the world, for most of
human history, people had low incomes, worked long hours, and had
short life expectancies. Poverty has been the norm and unfortunately
still is the norm for much of the world's population. Although First
World citizens often express a desire for an end to poverty, normal
Third World rural poverty doesn't raise the sense of moral outrage
that sweatshops do.[5] People become more outraged about sweatshops
because the poor workers are toiling for our benefit. Unfortunately,
that moral outrage can lead wealthy consumers and their governments

---

[4] Nicholas Kristof, "Inviting All Democrats," *New York Times*, January 14, 2004.
[5] I continue to use "Third World" to describe the poorer countries of the world even
though it's a bit dated and out of fashion. "Developing world" is often inaccurate since
some countries are actually getting poorer and, besides, rich countries are still developing
too. I don't like "less developed" because then their problem is insolvable – some countries will always be relatively less developed no matter how rich they get. Underdeveloped
is true of all countries, even rich ones, compared to their potential. I will continue to use
Third World until someone comes up with something more satisfactory.

to take actions that, although they may assuage their feelings of guilt, make Third World workers worse off by taking away their ability to work in a sweatshop and throwing them into an even worse alternative, such as scavenging in a trash dump.

This book provides a comprehensive defense of sweatshops. This defense does not deny that sweatshops have wages far below the levels in the developed world. Nor does it deny that sweatshops often have long and unpredictable working hours, a high risk of injuries on the job, and generally unhealthy working conditions. Sweatshops also sometimes deny lunch or bathroom breaks, verbally abuse workers, require overtime, and break local labor laws. Despite these atrocious conditions, sweatshops are still in the best interest of the workers who choose to work in them.

Sweatshops that coerce their workers with the threat of violence, or get the government to do it for them, are the one type of sweatshop I condemn. That is slave labor and has no place in a moral society. That type of sweatshop cannot be defended by the economic arguments made in the remainder of this book. If a worker must be coerced with the threat of violence to accept a job, then that job is obviously not the best alternative available to that worker – otherwise they would have voluntarily taken the job.

Despite all their drawbacks to Western eyes, most sweatshops with low wages and poor working conditions are places where workers voluntarily choose to work. Rarely do employers actually use the threat of violence to obtain employees. Admittedly, workers' other options are often much worse. A starving person with no alternative employment is likely to take a very bad job, if offered one. But that doesn't change the fact that the bad job was his best option. To help sweatshop workers, more options are needed. Unfortunately, much of the anti-sweatshop movement's advocacy, if implemented, would take away the sweatshop option but will not replace it with something better that's actually attainable.

Economic theory is used throughout this book, but nowhere do I advocate "economic efficiency" as my ethical standard. The welfare of poor workers, and potential workers, in the Third World is the standard used throughout this book. Nowhere do I favor economic efficiency, the welfare of Western consumers, or profits at the expense of workers. The welfare of the worker is the end; the crucial question is the means to achieve it.[6] Any serious anti-sweatshop activist *must* be concerned with

---

[6] I'm not sure how to make this point more clearly. Most anti-sweatshop activism is undertaken in the name of improving the lives of people who work in sweatshops. Economic reasoning helps us establish whether policies or actions that are chosen as a means of

this question. Market forces motivate how firms interact with workers; thus, activists need to appreciate the role they play as a means to helping workers. Economics puts limits on people's utopias. Wishing doesn't make things so. Economic theory forces us to examine how actions taken by activists, NGOs, governments, consumers, and others will impact the incentives of businesses that employ sweatshop workers. Unfortunately, many actions for which the anti-sweatshop movement has agitated adversely impact incentives and harm worker welfare.

The next chapter introduces the anti-sweatshop movement. It's a diverse movement that includes celebrities, ministers, students, politicians, intellectuals, unions, and consumer-activists, who advocate for policies such as international labor standards and minimum or "living" wages in the name of helping workers. When a country fails to adopt their favored policies, sometimes they will advocate imposing trade restrictions against the country. In other cases, they may simply protest or boycott an individual firm or company that uses sweatshop labor.

But what effect will such actions have on the welfare of workers? To answer this question, we need to understand the economic forces that determine sweatshop wages. Chapter 3 explains how the maximum wage that workers can earn is limited by their productivity and how their next best alternative employment limits the minimum wage they will voluntarily accept. Unfortunately, many actions taken by activists do nothing to raise these two bounds; in fact, they often advocate policies that would push wages above the maximum level that employers are willing to pay. As a result, sweatshop wages don't improve for many workers. Instead, their jobs disappear. This chapter also examines what happens to the wages and employment of workers when consumers engage in boycotts to protest conditions they object to. The second half of Chapter 3 examines possible exceptions scholars have raised to the basic theory outlined in the first half of the chapter.

If sweatshop workers lose their jobs, what are their other alternatives? Are they all destined to scavenge in trash dumps? Chapter 4

helping those workers can achieve their goal. That makes much of this book a means-ends analysis. This point seems lost on philosopher Joshua Preiss who claims that the most charitable way to understand my analysis is through a global prioritarian frame. I need not, and do not, embrace any such general global prioritarian frame. The prioritizing of the welfare of sweatshop workers is done by those who undertake actions to help them. Economics helps us figure out if those actions will deliver on the goal or not. Chapter 8 will consider other philosophical ends, raised by Preiss and others, and the relationship between those ends and worker welfare. Joshua Preiss, "Freedom, Autonomy, and Harm in Global Supply Chains," *Journal of Business Ethics* 160, No. 4 (2019), 881–891.

systematically investigates how sweatshop wages compare with alternative earnings in the countries where they operate. It compares the wages in the very firms that the Western press has identified as sweatshops with poverty living standards, agricultural workers' earnings, and the average income in each of these countries. Sweatshops earnings, while low by the standards most readers are used to, usually compare quite favorably with the alternatives available for many workers in these countries. Sweatshop jobs aren't just better when compared with scavenging in trash dumps. They are better than many jobs in the countries where they are located.

Even some critics of sweatshops will admit that the wages paid by sweatshops are better than worker alternatives. Instead, they claim that the real problem is the deplorable health and safety standards in these factories. But health and safety standards, and working conditions more generally, are intimately tied to wages. Employers care about the total cost of compensating workers but care little about how that cost is divided between wages and other forms of compensation. Workers do care about that mix. As a result, firms have every incentive to make the mix of compensation match the preferences of their employees. As Chapter 5 argues, health and safety standards are low because the workers' overall level of compensation is low, and they prefer the vast majority of their meager compensation as wages. The best cure for low health and safety standards is the process of economic development that raises overall compensation.

But what about truly dangerous conditions? On April 24, 2013, the Rana Plaza factory in Bangladesh collapsed, killing 1,129 workers and injuring another 2,500. Surely cases like this illustrate that greater safety regulation would improve the lives of workers. Chapter 6 examines the Rana Plaza disaster and the actions that were subsequently taken by activists and major international brands to improve safety standards and monitoring. Economists know that there are no "free" solutions – only trade-offs. Chapter 6 argues that, while the reaction to the Rana Plaza disaster improved safety, it also cost nearly a third of the jobs that should have been created in the garment industry in subsequent years. These jobs would have been a significant step out of poverty for many workers in Bangladesh. A reasonable person could easily conclude that the overall reaction to the Rana Plaza disaster did more to harm worker welfare than to improve it.

What about the children? In 1993, US Senator Tom Harkin proposed banning imports from countries that employed children in sweatshops.

In response, Bangladeshi firms laid off 50,000 children. What was their next best alternative? According to the British charity Oxfam, many of them became prostitutes or starved.[7] Prostitution and starvation are clearly worse alternatives than sweatshop labor. Chapter 7 explains how all of the preceding arguments apply to children as well as adults and how economic growth leads to the abolition of child labor.

What about ethics? Don't workers have a "right" to better treatment or higher wages? Even if the sweatshop is the workers' best alternative, isn't it still unethical to buy their products? Chapter 8 makes an ethical case for buying sweatshop products on consequentialist grounds, while considering issues of background injustice, exploitation, and objections to the arguments used in this book by philosophers on the grounds of autonomy, the limits of choice, and global labor justice.

Anti-sweatshop activists often seem to forget that they live in countries that once had widespread use of sweatshops too. Chapter 9 provides historical perspective by examining the role that sweatshops played in the development of the United States and other wealthy countries. Sweatshops are part of the process that creates new technology and capital that eventually raise labor productivity. This process of economic growth leads to improved wages and working conditions. Although the process took more than 100 years in the United States, it can happen much more rapidly today because the world has a greater amount of capital and technology that it can export to these poor countries. Witness the rapid rise of the Asian tigers and China's growth today. Chapter 9 will also demonstrate that the level of development the United States had achieved before adopting more stringent labor standards was much greater than the level of development in sweatshop countries today. If the United States had adopted more stringent standards when it was as poor as the sweatshop countries today, it would not have grown as rapidly to achieve the high living standard it enjoys today. Finally, Chapter 9 revisits the countries that were analyzed in the first edition of this book to see how they are developing. These countries had sweatshops reported in the news between 1995 and 2010. All of them experienced significant increases in average incomes and major decreases in poverty rates. Some no longer have sweatshops reported in the most recent decade and those that do usually report sweatshop wages that are significantly higher than were reported in the previous decades. In short, with more than a decade of evidence since

---

[7] See Paul Krugman, "Reckonings; Hearts and Heads," *New York Times*, April 22, 2001.

the publication of the first edition of this book, the process of development is lifting people out of poverty in the countries identified in that edition – just as the book argued it would.

Chapters 10 and 11 describe how sweatshops can be replaced with better alternatives. Chapter 10 builds on the previous chapter by describing how the process of economic development takes place and describing the necessary enabling environment that allows a country to grow out of sweatshops.

Sweatshops may be the best option currently available for workers, but any moral person would aspire to help improve those conditions. What good can activists possibly do? Chapter 11 outlines positive steps activists can take to improve the lives of sweatshop workers. The chapter first returns to the issue of slave labor in the Xinjiang Uyghur Autonomous Region of China. It argues that there is ample evidence that the Chinese government is using violent coercion of the Uyghur people to force them to work in sweatshops and that activists can productively direct their protests against such slave labor. The chapter also considers "Ethical" branding and the role for profit or nonprofit firms in monitoring this labeling. Trade policy and immigration policy are other areas in which activism could help. All the actions outlined in this chapter would help improve the lives of poor sweatshop workers, but they will be marginal compared to the main cure.

The very process of industrialization and development, of which sweatshops are part, is ultimately the cure for sweatshops. As capital accumulates, technology improves, and workers build skills, productivity rises. As firms compete with each other for the productive workers, total compensation gets bid up. This process raises wages and improves working conditions, and it occurred in virtually all of the wealthy countries in the world today.

I have studied sweatshops for the past 20 years. In that time, I have become convinced that many well-meaning people advocate actions that are detrimental to the lives of sweatshop workers because they do not understand the economic forces that govern the creation of sweatshops and their alternatives. The remainder of this book explains these economic forces and illustrates them with the best available evidence. This book is intended for a wide audience that includes economists, other social scientists, and policymakers. It's also intended for the general public and, in particular, people who have been active in the anti-sweatshop movement and genuinely care about the welfare of impoverished sweatshop workers.

Rather than hold protests that risk cutting the process of development short by destroying sweatshop jobs, activists should instead buy products made in these factories and embrace the forces of economic development that will improve the lives of sweatshop workers. *New York Times* columnist Nicholas Kristof wrote that people need to rethink their objections to sweatshops and that "We need to build a constituency of humanitarians who view low-wage manufacturing as a solution."[8] I hope you will join this constituency by the time you're finished reading this book.

---

[8] Nicholas Kristof, "My Sweatshop Column," *New York Times*, January 14, 2009, retrieved from http://kristof.blogs.nytimes.com/2009/01/14/my-sweatshop-column/.

2

The Anti-Sweatshop Movement

The modern anti-sweatshop movement began developing in the early 1990s, but much of the activity was limited to isolated protests and individual actions. In the latter half of the 1990s, the movement developed many interrelated organizations that waged sustained campaigns against sweatshops. Most of those organizations continue their anti-sweatshop activism today. The movement contains a mix of celebrities, politicians, unions, student activists, and scholars. Some affiliate with major anti-sweatshop organizations, whereas others speak out or protest on their own.

There are significant differences between the different organizations within the anti-sweatshop movement in terms of both the changes for which they advocate and how they pursue their advocacy. However, all the major anti-sweatshop organizations have this in common: They all believe that free market competition in the global economy is not, at least alone, the best way to improve the lives of sweatshop workers. The groups vary in their opinion of exactly how the process of free market competition should be altered to improve the lives of workers. Some advocate for consumer activism through either boycotts or "Shop with a Conscience" programs. Other groups want legal mandates created and enforced that dictate living wages, health and safety standards, and working hour regulations. Some groups favor trade restrictions on countries that do not mandate and enforce these labor standards. Some groups concern themselves only with child labor, whereas others focus mostly on the freedom to unionize.

The remainder of this chapter traces the development of the major players in the anti-sweatshop movement and outlines what reforms each group wants and how it agitates for them. No attempt is made within this chapter to assess the merits of the policies they advocate; these are examined later. Rather, it provides a guide as to how those later arguments apply to individual organizations.

THE DEVELOPMENT OF THE ANTI-SWEATSHOP MOVEMENT

Although most of the modern anti-sweatshop movement has its beginnings in the 1990s, there were important predecessors. Unionization and activist campaigns for domestic sweatshops were active in the United States around the turn of the 20th century. Most important for the modern international movement, however, was the creation of the International Labour Organization (ILO) in 1919 because it continues to play an important role in the anti-sweatshop movement today.

The ILO is an organization of governments, employers, and workers and is now an agency of the United Nations. The ILO develops conventions, which are legally binding on countries that enter into ILO treaties, and recommendations, which serve as guidelines but are not legally binding. The ILO "core labor standards" conventions address the freedom of association and right to collectively bargain, the elimination of forced and compulsory labor, the abolition of child labor, and the elimination of discrimination in the workplace. The ILO's 1998 Declaration on Fundamental Principles and Rights at Work reiterated these principles; the ILO then launched a campaign to achieve universal ratification of the eight conventions in these areas.[1]

The ILO has 190 conventions and 206 recommendations that cover many other aspects of employment. Approximately 70 of the conventions and recommendations deal with occupational safety and health standards.[2] According to the ILO, it places a "special importance on developing and applying a preventive safety and health culture in workplaces worldwide."[3]

ILO conventions also mandate members to set a minimum wage (conv. 131), to limit maximum working hours to 8 in a day and 48 in a week (conv. 1), and to guarantee paid maternity leave for 14 weeks plus paid work breaks for breastfeeding (conv. 183). Conventions cover a host of other areas as well.

---

[1] ILO, Declaration on Fundamental Principles and Rights at Work, retrieved from www.ilo.org/declaration/lang--en/index.htm.

[2] Retrieved from www.ilo.org/safework/info/standards-and-instruments/lang--en/index.htm.

[3] ILO, Safety and Health at Work, retrieved from www.ilo.org/global/topics/safety-and-health-at-work/lang--en/index.htm.

Although ILO conventions are binding only on member countries who ratify them, the ILO also campaigns for more widespread acceptance of its conventions and recommendations. These conventions and recommendations have also served as focal points for many of the anti-sweatshop groups that developed in the 1990s.

The birth of the modern international anti-sweatshop movement came in 1990. In Europe, the Clean Clothes Campaign (CCC) began in the Netherlands; this coalition of consumer, labor, religious, human rights, and feminist groups agitated for better conditions in sweatshops. In the United States, the National Labor Committee (NLC) decided to make international sweatshops its signature campaign. The NLC's director, Charlie Kernaghan, one of the most influential early anti-sweatshop activists, gained notoriety for himself, and the cause of sweatshops, by going after prominent brands and celebrities with otherwise wholesome images in the media. In one famous instance, he confronted Kathy Lee Gifford on television with a Honduran garment worker who produced her line of clothes and made Kathie Lee cry (see Chapter 4). The NLC's activism helped raise awareness that would foster the creation of future anti-sweatshop groups.

The NLC primarily investigates and exposes what it believes to be human and labor rights abuses committed by US companies producing goods in the Third World. It engages in research and popular campaigns to raise awareness in the United States about these abuses and attempts to help workers abroad learn about and defend what it believes are their rights. It has issued hundreds of reports alleging abusive sweatshop activities in dozens of countries. The NLC gives workers' efforts in these countries international visibility and "press[es] for international legal frameworks with effective enforcement mechanisms that will help create a space where fundamental internationally recognized worker rights can be assured."[4]

In addition to publicizing specific conditions, the NLC also pushes for legislation. For example, the NLC wrote the 2006 Decent Working Conditions and Fair Competition Act with Senator Byron Dorgan.[5] The bill, which failed to pass, would have prohibited the import, sale, or export of sweatshop goods. Goods made under conditions that violate the core ILO standards would have been banned.

American unions were vitally important in making international sweatshops a popular issue and getting other anti-sweatshop organizations

---

[4] Institute for Global Labour and Human Rights, Mission, retrieved from www.nlcnet.org/about.

[5] Support Grows for Anti-Sweatshop Legislation, retrieved from www.nlcnet.org/alerts?id=0180.

started. Jeff Ballinger, who had headed the American Federation of Labor and Congress of Industrial Organizations' (AFL-CIO) Jakarta office and organized Indonesian workers for nearly four years, began a public campaign against Nike when he returned to the United States in 1992. The publicity he generated helped encourage groups such as Global Exchange, the NLC, and the People of Faith Network to begin anti-Nike campaigns of their own. These campaigns would also prove "most influential to the student movement" because so many schools had contracts with Nike.[6]

The AFL-CIO's anti-sweatshop activism has sometimes consisted of direct political lobbying, but much has taken the form of funding other anti-sweatshop groups. The AFL-CIO actively supported and lobbied for the Decent Working Conditions and Fair Competition Act. It claimed that the bill "offers a positive, proactive alternative to the current race to the bottom in the global sweatshop economy, one based on full respect for workers' human rights. Our goal is to create economic incentives for both corporations and governments to raise standards and protect workers' rights around the world." The AFL-CIO's own statements, however, give reason to question whether the welfare of Third World workers was really their motive. Their statement of support begins by describing how global competition is harming the American economy, and their conclusion claims the legislation will be "a powerful vehicle ... to take back our economy."[7] Chapter 3 will explore why the goals of helping sweatshop workers and "taking back our economy" in a First World country are at odds with one another.

The AFL-CIO created the American Center for International Labor Solidarity in 1997 and continues to help fund and direct the center.[8] According to its website, "the programs implemented and the partners chosen are determined solely by the Solidarity Center and the AFL-CIO."[9] Elizbeth Shuler, the AFL-CIO president, chairs the center's board, and all of the center's board members hold high-ranking positions in the AFL-CIO or other labor unions.[10]

The center's mission is to help "unions and community groups worldwide to achieve equitable, sustainable, democratic development

---

[6] Featherstone and USAS, *Students Against Sweatshops* (New York: Verso, 2002), 8–9.

[7] Retrieved from www.aflcio.org/aboutus/thisistheaflcio/ecouncil/eco8082006b.cfm.

[8] Solidarity Center, About Us, retrieved from www.solidaritycenter.org/content.asp?pl=409&contentid=409.

[9] Solidarity Center, About Us, retrieved from www.solidaritycenter.org/content.asp?pl=409&contentid=409.

[10] Solidarity Center, Board of Trustees, retrieved from www.solidaritycenter.org/who-we-are/board-of-trustees/.

and to help men and women everywhere stand up for their rights and improve their living and working conditions."[11] Specifically, the center claims that "strong trade unions must endeavor to ensure that workers are able to exercise their full spectrum of rights, including ILO core labor standards."[12] Furthermore, "all workers deserve decent jobs where they are treated with respect and dignity and paid a living wage."[13] The Solidarity Center also helps workers abroad fight for worker safety and health and assists workers in improving their conditions to meet international standards.[14]

The United Needle and Textile Workers Union (UNITE) was also active in publicizing sweatshop conditions. They probably received the most attention for their mid 1990s campaign against Guess Jeans, which got a popularity boost from the endorsement of the appropriately Luddite-named band Rage Against the Machine. As Featherstone and the United Students Against Sweatshops (USAS) note, "Such Campaigns reflected, in part, new AFL-CIO president John Sweeney's emphasis on corporate campaigns."[15]

The publicity that sweatshops were receiving created political pressure to do something. In 1996, the Clinton administration, in conjunction with a coalition of unions, apparel companies, and human rights groups, developed basic labor codes they wanted factories to meet and created the Fair Labor Association (FLA) to serve as the monitoring body and enforce the codes. Companies, universities, and individual suppliers can affiliate with the FLA. When a company or university affiliates, it must submit a list of their suppliers to be monitored by the FLA. The FLA's workplace code of conduct includes: no forced labor; no child labor; no workplace harassment; no discrimination; health and safety standards; freedom to collectively bargain; payment of local minimum wages or prevailing industry wages, whichever is higher; maximum hours of work; and overtime compensation.[16]

Companies that affiliate with the FLA commit to establishing internal systems to monitor working conditions, maintaining the code standards,

---

[11] Solidarity Center, About Us.
[12] Solidarity Center, Worker & Human Rights, retrieved from www.solidaritycenter.org/content.asp?pl=405&sl=405&contentid=420.
[13] Ibid.
[14] Solidarity Center, Safety & Health, retrieved from www.solidaritycenter.org/content.asp?pl=405&sl=405&contentid=418.
[15] Featherstone and USAS, *Students Against Sweatshops*, 9.
[16] Retrieved from www.fairlabor.org/our-work/labor-standards.

and submitting to external monitoring from the FLA. Results of FLA audits and investigations are published online, and affiliates are expected to work with suppliers to correct any violations. The FLA is funded by the fees paid by its affiliates.

The more radical anti-sweatshop critics of the FLA argued that it amounted to "self-monitoring" and was "thoroughly controlled by manufacturers."[17] This helped lead to more activism, specifically the spread of the student anti-sweatshop movement, and an alternative monitoring organization.

After a couple years of isolated and fragmented campus activities, in the spring of 1998, USAS, a coalition of anti-sweatshop groups at universities across the United States, was formed. US unions strongly supported the creation and growth of the student anti-sweatshop movement. In 1996, the AFL-CIO began a "Union Summer" program that placed college students in summer internships with unions. In this program, students began investigating their universities' connections to sweatshops. However, according to USAS:

The campus movement didn't begin in earnest until summer 1997, in UNITE's New York City offices. Ginny Coughlin, a newly hired UNITE organizer, asked UNITE's summer interns to research the connections between collegiate apparel and sweatshops for a possible campus campaign. That campaign, UNITE organizers reasoned, could complement the union's own anti-sweatshop efforts. Sensing that the FLA was helping manufacturers win the public relations battle, says Alan Howard, then assistant to the president of UNITE, "the union, to its credit, said, 'Here's a very important base that can help us deal with this offensive.'"[18]

Tico Almeida, a Duke student and one of UNITE's interns, began an anti-sweatshop campaign when he returned to campus that fall. The students succeeded in convincing the university to pass a code that required "manufacturers of Duke apparel to maintain safe, independently monitored facilities where workers were free to organize."[19] This student victory helped to inspire activists on other campuses and led to the creation of USAS the following spring.

USAS itself has also noted that it "has built strong relationships with North American unions, which are, in turn, showing remarkable dedication to the new generation."[20] They also note that many students

---

[17] Featherstone and USAS, *Students Against Sweatshops*, 10.
[18] Ibid., 11.
[19] Ibid., 12.
[20] Ibid., 97.

involved in the movement take jobs as union organizers, both in the summer and after graduation. This is important because "turnover is one of student activism's biggest curses ... because there's no way to keep graduates involved," but "USAS's strong relationship with US unions is helping the organization build domestic solidarity" and avoid the movement disintegrating after a few victories.[21] The AFL-CIO also helps fund USAS. For instance, it donated $40,000 to USAS in academic year 1999–2000 and another $50,000 the following academic year.[22]

Observers have noted that the USAS is "inseparably linked to the youthful, worldwide anti-corporate movement now visible at any display of conspicuous capitalism."[23] Their very broad and general concerns are evident from how they describe their own organization:

We envision a world in which society and human relationships are organized cooperatively, not competitively. We struggle towards a world in which all people live in freedom from oppression, in which people are valued as whole human beings rather than exploited in a quest for productivity and profits.

We struggle against racism, sexism, heterosexism, classism, ableism, and other forms of oppression within our society, within our organizations, and within ourselves. We strive to build relationships with other grassroots movements because we believe the student-labor solidarity movement is part of a larger struggle for global justice.[24]

These sweeping generalizations allow a diverse body of students who are discontent with globalization to align themselves together. As a result, views differ considerably within USAS and between campus affiliates. In general, however, most of the USAS's anti-sweatshop activity has taken the form of affiliates opposing their own campus's use of sweatshop labor to produce college-licensed apparel. Students have held protests, sit-ins, and hunger strikes, as well as taken over college presidents' offices, to convince their colleges to adopt policies ensuring that their clothes are not made in sweatshops.

As student activism increased, more universities began joining the FLA. However, the USAS thought that the FLA failed to adequately monitor factories.[25] In response, they, in conjunction with scholars,

---

[21] Ibid.
[22] Ibid.
[23] Ibid., 2.
[24] USAS, About Us, retrieved from http://usas.org/about-us/.
[25] For a general account of the difficulties of monitoring working conditions, see Jill Esbenshade, *Monitoring Sweatshops: Workers, Consumers, and the Global Apparel Industry* (Philadelphia: Temple University Press, 2004).

labor unions, and human rights groups, created the Worker Rights Consortium (WRC) in 2001. This organization set the bar higher than the FLA and focused on investigating worker complaints rather than certifying facilities as "sweat free." Student activism became focused on convincing their colleges to abandon the FLA and join the WRC.

The WRC now has 146 college and university affiliates.[26] The WRC has developed a model code that requires university suppliers to pay a living wage and comply with the United States' Occupational Safety and Health Administration's standards. Universities are encouraged, but not required, to adopt the model code when they affiliate with the WRC. The WRC will take colleges as members who have their own codes, provided that the codes protect workers in the areas of wages, hours of work and overtime compensation, freedom of association, workplace health and safety, women's rights, child labor, forced labor, harassment and abuse, nondiscrimination, and compliance with local laws.[27]

When a college affiliates with the WRC, it must provide the organization with a list of all factories that produce goods with the college's logo and their locations. The WRC then monitors these factories and works to improve conditions when they do not live up to the college's code. Although WRC does not recommend "cutting and running" as a first step when a supplier is out of compliance, it ultimately advocates ceasing to do business with the supplier if they continue to fail to live up to the code. In return for its monitoring, the WRC requires affiliates to pay 1 percent of licensing revenue, with a minimum payment of $1,500 and a maximum of $50,000.[28] Approximately 65 percent of the WRC's revenue comes from these fees; the rest comes from grants, individuals, and monitoring partners.[29]

In response to anti-sweatshop activism, the Academic Consortium on International Trade (ACIT), a group of international trade economists and lawyers, circulated a letter to college presidents urging them not to take ill-informed actions in response to student activism.[30] The consortium warned that, among other things, pushing for higher wages could hurt workers by jeopardizing jobs that pay better than other alternatives.

---

[26] WRC, Mission, retrieved from www.workersrights.org/about/.
[27] WRC, Frequently Asked Questions, retrieved from www.workersrights.org/affiliates/frequently-asked-questions/.
[28] Ibid.
[29] Ibid.
[30] ACIT, Steering Committee, retrieved from www.fordschool.umich.edu/rsie/acit/Documents/July29SweatshopLetter.pdf.

In response to ACIT's letter, Scholars Against Sweatshop Labor was created. Led by Robert Polin of the University of Massachusetts, the scholars drew up their own letter in late 2001 that was supportive of the student anti-sweatshop movement, the WRC and FLA, and the broad anti-sweatshop movement.[31] The letter was signed by 434 scholars, 73 percent of whom were economists. Although the letter recognized the merits of many points raised by the ACIT economists, it defended the monitoring organizations and disputed the evidence ACIT pointed to showing that wages in sweatshops were superior to other alternatives. Although they recognized the potential negative economic consequences of mandating high wages or workplace conditions, they argued that there was "no reason to assume that a country or region that sets reasonable standards must experience job losses" and further claimed that higher retail prices could allow improved conditions without leading to job losses.[32] Overall, the letter gave scholarly credibility to the anti-sweatshop movement and helped student activists in their lobbying of universities.

Over the last 30-plus years the anti-sweatshop movement transformed from a few individuals exposing working conditions to a large movement with many permanent well-funded organizations with organized anti-sweatshop campaigns.

CONCLUSION

The anti-sweatshop movement is a diverse group of organizations with many different specific goals and strategies, but some common themes do arise. First, many, but not all, of these organizations have ties with First World unions. Chapter 3 argues that there are good economic reasons for these ties to exist. Although the specific details of the reforms individual organizations call for may differ, most advocate for some form of a legal "living" minimum wage. Most want some government-set mandatory working conditions that include health and safety regulations, as well as regulations on working hours. Most are opposed to child labor. Most believe that, at a minimum, companies should respect and conform to local labor laws, and that these laws should become stronger. Most believe in some form of support for unionization of

---

[31] Scholars Against Sweatshop Labor, Statement October 2001, retrieved from www.peri .umass.edu/253/.
[32] Ibid.

Third World workers. Where the groups seem to differ the most is in whether they explicitly endorse trade sanctions when countries don't have regulations up to their standards or whether they will endorse boycotts when individual companies fail to live up to these standards. All these policies will be analyzed in subsequent chapters.

The anti-sweatshop groups are obviously not the only interest groups involved in shaping national and global trade policy. Multinational firms and other exporters and importers also play an important role, as do the governments in Third World countries. The World Trade Organization has resisted most attempts to incorporate labor standards into trade agreements because of opposition from Third World countries.[33] This book is not concerned with the political forces that have given rise to the current status quo in international labor policy.[34] Instead, the focus is on whether Third World workers would benefit if the status quo changed in the direction many activists desire. The remainder of the book is thus concerned with the desirability of various political equilibria, not the forces that give rise to any particular political equilibrium.

APPENDIX: OTHER ANTI-SWEATSHOP GROUPS

This appendix contains brief descriptions of some of the other major anti-sweatshop groups that were not discussed in the main text of this chapter. Readers not interested in these details can skip to Chapter 3 without any loss of continuity in the book's argument.

International Labor Rights Forum

The International Labor Rights Forum (ILRF) was engaged in anti-sweatshop activism before an anti-sweatshop movement truly existed. The ILRF runs campaigns targeting agricultural workers as well as traditional sweatshop workers. The organization promotes labor rights through public education, research, legislation, litigation, and collaboration with labor, government, and business groups.

---

[33] See Doug Irwin, *Free Trade Under Fire* (Princeton: Princeton University Press, 2002), 215–224, for a discussion of the politics surrounding the adoption of labor standards in trade agreements.

[34] For a book more focused on the political forces that shape the outcome of the sweatshop debate, see Shae Garwood, *Advocacy across Borders: NGOs, Anti-Sweatshop Activism, and the Global Garment Industry* (Sterling, VA: Kumarian Press, 2011).

One important aspect of the ILRF is its focus on including labor rights in US and global trade agreements. In 1984, it helped get the first labor rights clause inserted into a trade agreement. This clause required any country seeking preferential access to US markets to respect internationally recognized workers' rights, including freedom of association.[35] The organization also played a leading role in the adoption of the ILO convention. The ILRF has been involved in lobbying for labor provisions in many free trade agreements, including NAFTA and DR-CAFTA, as well as with bilateral trade deals with Colombia and Panama.[36]

The ILRF claims that, although free trade can promote development, "US trade agreements can create harmful downward pressure in developing world labor markets if they do not include strong and enforceable labor rights mechanisms."[37] The ILRF believes that "as long as poor labor standards exist in one country, workers everywhere will be hurt."[38] As a result, it would prefer to incorporate such labor rights "social causes" into the World Trade Organization.[39] Thus far, it has been unsuccessful in that regard and has settled for obtaining the inclusion of provisions in individual trade agreements.

The ILRF also sponsors the "SweatFree Communities" campaign. The campaign, started in 2003, lobbies state and local governments to procure their uniforms, garments, and other apparel from factories that have been certified as "SweatFree." During the campaign's first 7 years, 9 states, 40 cities, 15 counties, and 118 school districts adopted their "SweatFree" policy.[40]

USLEAP

The U.S. Labor Education in the Americas Project (USLEAP) is a non-profit organization that promotes respect for the rights of workers in Latin America. It advocates for a global economy in which all workers are treated fairly, paid a living wage, and are respected by corporations and governments. USLEAP's main contribution to the anti-sweatshop

[35] ILRF, Mission Statement, retrieved from www.laborrights.org/about-ilrf.
[36] ILRF, Creating a Sweatfree World: Changing Global Trade Rules, retrieved from www.laborrights.org/creating-a-sweatfree-world/changing-global-trade-rules.
[37] Ibid.
[38] Ibid.
[39] Ibid.
[40] SweatFree Communities, About Us, retrieved from www.sweatfree.org/about_us.

movement is its "Sweatshop (Maquiladora Worker) Project," through which it works with a wide range of groups and unions, including the International Textile, Garment, and Leather Workers Federation; the AFL-CIO's Solidarity Center; Maquila Solidarity Network; SweatFree Communities; USAS; and the WRC. USLEAP links North American codes of conduct, monitoring, and student anti-sweatshop activities to specific campaigns in Central America and Mexico, where it directly engages companies at the request of workers in the region.[41] Originally it was technically an independent nonprofit organization, but USLEAP's board tended to be dominated by officials from a variety of unions. When the first edition of this book was published, Tim Beaty of the International Brotherhood of Teamsters was the Vice Chair of USLEAP, and 10 of the 16 USLEAP board members were union officials. USLEAP became part of the ILRF in 2013.[42] The current president of the ILRF's board of directors, Ashwini Sukthankar, is a union official with Unite Here.[43]

Maquila Solidarity Network

The Maquila Solidarity Network was created in 1994 to work with women's and labor rights organizations in Mexico, Central America, and Asia. Similar to other groups, the Network advocates for a locally determined "living wage" and believes that governments should set and enforce regulations for decent working conditions.[44] Although it has many of the same objections to sweatshops as the above groups, and opposes the use of child labor, the Maquila Solidarity Network explicitly says that it does not advocate boycotting goods produced by child labor or calling for unilateral government action to impose trade sanctions on countries that use child labor.[45]

41 USLEAP, Sweatshop (Maquiladora Worker) Project, retrieved from www.usleap.org/about-us/projects-and-initiatives/sweatshop-maquiladora-worker-project.
42 International Labor Rights Forum, USLEAP: Justice in the Americas, retrieved from https://laborrights.org/programs/usleap.
43 International Labor Rights Forum, GLJ-ILRF Board of Directors, retrieved from https://laborrights.org/about/team.
44 Maquila Solidarity Network, Questions about Sweatshops, retrieved from http://en.maquilasolidarity.org/FAQ/sweatshops?SESS89c5db41a82abcd7da7c9ac60e04ca5f=qadsupha9gfn9ido9jdcqllo90#9.
45 Maquila Solidarity Network, Child Labour: Do's and Don'ts, retrieved from http://en.maquilasolidarity.org/node/662?SESS89c5db41a82abcd7da7c9ac60e04ca5f=qadsupha9gfn9ido9jdcqllo90.

STITCH

STITCH is less of a public advocacy group than many of the other organizations in the anti-sweatshop movement. In 1994, after attending a Guatemalan labor conference, a group of North American women decided to form a women's solidarity network, which resulted in the founding of STITCH in 1998. STITCH mainly supports the leadership capacity and skills of women workers in Latin America through workshops, program exchanges, publications, and formation of alliances with them.[46]

Organizations Abroad

Although much of the anti-sweatshop movement is located in North America, a few European organizations are worth briefly examining. The CCC was one of the earliest anti-sweatshop organizations. Based in the Netherlands, the CCC is an alliance of organizations in 45 countries with members including trade unions and NGOs.[47] The organization educates and mobilizes consumers, lobbies companies and governments, and provides solidarity support to Third World workers.[48]

The CCC believes that governments should pass legislation that supports labor standards and sanctions those companies and governments that do not. It believes these standards should include the ILO's core labor standards as well as "the right to a living wage based on a regular working week that does not exceed 48 hours; humane working hours with no forced overtime; a safe and healthy workplace free from harassment; and a recognised employment relationship with labour and social protection."[49] Although it supports government regulation, the CCC does not support boycotts that put workers' jobs at risk.[50]

The UK-based War on Want has a "Love Fashion Hate Sweatshops" campaign. Similar to the CCC, it doesn't support boycotts, recognizing that they lead only to further job losses, but does support government regulation.[51] It claims that "real change can only be achieved through

---

[46] STITCH, Who We Are and What We Do, retrieved from www.stitchonline.org/whowhat.asp.

[47] Clean Clothes Campaign, Who We Are, retrieved from https://cleanclothes.org/about.

[48] Ibid.

[49] Clean Clothes Campaign, FAQs, What Are ILO Conventions and Core Labour Standards, retrieved from www.cleanclothes.org/about-us/faqs#15.

[50] Clean Clothes Campaign, FAQs, retrieved from www.cleanclothes.org/about-us/faqs.

[51] War on Want, Love Fashion Hate Sweatshops, retrieved from www.waronwant.org/campaigns/love-fashion-hate-sweatshops.

government regulation that protects the rights of workers supplying UK companies." Specifically, it agitates for regulations that would guarantee workers a living wage, decent working conditions, and the right to form a union.

Also based in the UK is a separate Students Against Sweatshops organization that demands an end to child labor, unsafe conditions, forced overtime, and harassment of female workers, and calls for a living wage, reasonable hours, independent trade unions, and safe working conditions.[52]

[52] Students Against Sweatshops, Stamp Out Sweatshops! Retrieved from www .studentsagainstsweatshops.org.uk/about.html.

3

The Economics of Sweatshop Wage Determination

Critics point out working conditions in sweatshops that any citizen in the developed world would find deplorable. The anti-sweatshop movement suggests many laws, regulations, and consumer activist tactics, in the hope of improving the lives of sweatshop workers. Sentiments such as those expressed by Sheri Davis, a former graduate student at Ohio State University and participant at a USAS rally, are common: "Everybody wants to have a living wage. Everybody wants to be able to take care of themselves and their family. Everybody wants to retire and feel good, enjoy life. Breathe. Live. Eat. You know, the regular shit. We're not asking for nothing extra special."[1] Unfortunately, wishing doesn't make it so.

Each law, regulation, or activist activity impacts the incentives of companies who hire sweatshop workers. Some of these actions may help sweatshop workers. Unfortunately, others will have unintended secondary consequences that impact employer incentives and, as a result, leave already poor sweatshop workers even worse off. Activists need to understand the market forces that determine wages to understand which policies can help workers and which will hurt them.

HOW ARE WAGES DETERMINED?

Wages and working conditions in sweatshops are set by the same factors that set wages and working conditions in wealthier countries: supply and demand. The wages and conditions are determined by bidding

[1] Featherstone and USAS, *Students Against Sweatshops*, 39.

between employers and potential employees. Employers often make the offer, but potential employees are free to accept the offer or reject it. If employers can't attract enough workers at the wage they are offering, they will need to raise the wage to convince more workers to choose to work for them. But they will not continue raising their wage offers indefinitely.

A worker's productivity limits the maximum amount an employer will pay them. Economists call this the worker's marginal revenue product. Simply put, an employee who generates $2 per hour of revenue for the employer, that would not have been generated if that employee was not working there, has a marginal revenue product of $2 per hour. The maximum wage an employer would be willing to pay that worker is $2 per hour. At a wage of $2.01 per hour, the employer is losing one cent for every hour that employee works. A profit-maximizing business doesn't hire workers who increase their losses.

Just because a worker can create $2 per hour of revenue doesn't mean that an employer would like to pay them that much. Ideally, from the employer's perspective, they would like to pay workers zero and pocket the entire $2 per hour as profit. But few people, even in very poor countries, are willing to work for nothing. To convince a worker to accept a job, the employer must offer them more than whatever that worker can make at what the worker perceives as their next best alternative. Workers compare the available wages, working conditions, hours, and so on, and choose the offer that they think is in their best interest.

These two factors determine the bounds within which wage bargaining can occur. The upper bound is limited by the worker's productivity. The lower bound is limited by the worker's next best alternative. The actual wage must fall somewhere between these two bounds.

In practice, these bounds are often very close together. When an area contains more than one sweatshop, the amount of revenue a worker could generate by working at any one of them is closely related to the amount of revenue that they could generate in another sweatshop. If an employer offers them wages far below their productivity, the employee can find another firm who would profit by offering them higher wages. For many workers, their next best alternative to working in one sweatshop is working in another sweatshop. As a result, wages are bid up to approximately the worker's marginal productivity. In some situations, such as where factory jobs are few, the gap between productivity and the worker's next best alternative can be larger.

If activists want to help sweatshop workers, they need to advocate for things that will raise sweatshop workers' productivity and give them more alternatives. In short, policies need to raise these upper and lower bounds. Economists have found that approximately 70–80 percent of the variation in wages across nations can be attributed to differences in productivity.[2] Thus, the main focus of activists needs to be on raising the upper bound by increasing productivity. Advocating any policy to raise wages that doesn't raise these bounds risks raising workers' compensation above their productivity and thus unemploying the workers that the activists were trying to help.

IMPACT OF ACTIVISTS' ACTIONS

Anti-sweatshop activists are often unaware of the basic economics of wage determination. As a result, they advocate policies or pursue courses of action that harm sweatshop workers. Legal minimum or "living" wages are one such policy endorsed by many of the groups described in the previous chapter.

Passing a law that mandates higher pay does nothing to make workers more productive, nor does it create new alternatives to bid workers away from their current jobs. Legal minimum wages simply outlaw potential gains from trade between employers and workers. Paraphrasing liberal Nobel Laureate Paul Samuelson, it does a potential sweatshop worker, who can create $2 per hour of value, no good to know that by law he must be paid $3 per hour if that very law keeps him from getting a job.[3]

A legal minimum wage of only one cent per hour is unlikely to unemploy even the least skilled workers. But it also would have no effect because wages would be higher to begin with. In some instances, a minimum wage could fall between the upper and lower bounds for particular workers and, as a result, raise their wages without unemploying them. But any minimum wage likely to positively affect those workers will almost certainly also raise the legal minimum above another, less-skilled worker's productivity and thus result in them being laid off. These laid-off workers end up employed in less-desirable alternatives.[4]

---

[2] See Doug Irwin, *Free Trade Under Fire* (Princeton: Princeton University Press, 2002), 210.

[3] Samuelson's quote was, "What good does it do a black youth to know that an employer must pay him $2 an hour if the fact that he must be paid that amount is what keeps him from getting a job?" Samuelson, *Economics*, 9th ed. (New York: McGraw Hill, 1973), 393–394.

[4] Another unfortunate outcome that results from legal minimum wages above market clearing levels is that workers waste resources competing to be the ones who get the remaining jobs. This competition could take the form of queuing or investing in wasteful quality signals. In either case it leaves the laborers poorer on net. For a classic reference see Yoram Barzel, "A Theory of Rationing by Waiting," *Journal of Law and Economics* 17 (1974), 73–95.

Skeptics may respond that they do not see much evidence of the minimum wage causing unemployment in the United States. In fact, studies do find evidence of minimum wage–related unemployment among US workers, but the effect is usually on a small segment of society that is young, a racial minority, and lacks a high school education. The reason is simple. Minimum wage laws in the United States are set at rates that are low enough, relative to productivity, that they are well below most people's upper and lower bounds.[5] A high minimum wage relative to productivity, however, can have a major effect.

The first federal minimum wage law in the United States illustrates what happens when a minimum wage is set well above productivity levels. The Fair Labor Standards Act set the US minimum wage at 25 cents per hour in 1938. At the time, the average wage in the United States was 62.7 cents per hour, so most workers were unaffected. However, the law also applied to Puerto Rico, a poorer, less developed, US territory.[6] Many workers in Puerto Rico were earning only 3–4 cents per hour. The result was massive business bankruptcy and high unemployment in Puerto Rico. Imposing minimum wages in Third World sweatshop-using countries today at rates similar to those we have in the United States would have similarly disastrous consequences.

Advocates for minimum wages in Third World countries likely would respond that they realize they can't impose a minimum wage as high as the one in the United States. Instead, they advocate a lower minimum wage that is often based off the local cost of living. But that begs the question, "Why not mandate a higher wage?" If activists believe that mandating higher wages can result in workers earning more without unemploying others, and they care about the workers, why wouldn't they want a higher minimum wage? Implicitly those who push for "not-too-high" minimum wages recognize the unemployment impact a legal minimum can have. Unfortunately, even at very low levels, a minimum wage large enough to have any positive effect for a few workers will also unemploy others.

A critic might argue that companies that employ sweatshop workers, or those that subcontract to them, often make millions of dollars. Such companies are not going to close because of a low minimum wage

---

[5] Another reason we don't see larger unemployment effects is that employers compensate by decreasing worker benefits on other margins. Hourly employees may find their hours cut or restaurants that used to let employees have free meals may now charge for them, and so on.

[6] On the 1938 minimum wage in Puerto Rico, see Simon Rottenberg, "Minimum Wages in Puerto Rico," *The Economics of Legal Minimum Wages*, edited by Rottenberg (Washington, DC: American Enterprise Institute, 1981), 327–339.

that raises their cost a little bit. This objection ignores the fact that all economic decisions are made on the margin. Companies don't face only the decision of whether to stay in business or to close. They choose how much to produce and what mix of capital, low-skilled workers, and high-skilled workers to use. If a company is maximizing its profits, it employs each of these factors of production up until the point that the revenue from the last (marginal) unit of each of them equals its cost.

A minimum wage increases the relative cost of low-skilled labor compared to high-skilled labor and capital. Rather than passively accepting lower profits, a profit-maximizing company responds to a minimum wage law by decreasing the amount of low-skilled labor it uses and replacing it with higher-skilled workers and capital. In the context of sweatshops, this could take the form of firing some workers and replacing them with machines, while keeping other workers. Alternatively, a firm could move from a less productive country to a more productive one where higher labor costs are offset by higher labor productivity. Both of these actions may help some workers but will harm the least productive and poorest ones. Firms may also balance the increased pay with cuts to other forms of compensation such as health and safety conditions, for which activists often advocate regulations to improve. This topic will be discussed in Chapter 5.

Economists have done much empirical work studying the effects of minimum wage laws. People skeptical of the standard economic argument presented here typically point to an infamous 1995 book by economists David Card and Alan Krueger, which empirically argued that the negative employment impact of minimum wage laws was small to nonexistent.[7] Economists have found problems with Card and Krueger's study and much empirical work has been done since their analysis. Economists Kevin Murphy, Donald Deere, and Finis Welch summarized the problem with generalizing from Card and Krueger's analysis:

Each of the four studies examines a different piece of the minimum wage/employment relationship. Three of them consider a single state, and two of them look at only a handful of firms in one industry. From these isolated findings Card and Krueger paint a big picture wherein increased minimum wages do not decrease, and may increase, employment. Our view is that there is something wrong with this picture. Artificial increases in the price of unskilled laborers inevitably lead to their reduced employment; the conventional wisdom remains intact.[8]

[7] David Card and Alan Krueger, *Myth and Measurement: The New Economics of the Minimum Wage* (Princeton: Princeton University Press, 1995).

[8] Donald Deere, Kevin Murphy, and Finis Welch, "Sense and Nonsense on the Minimum Wage," *Regulation* 18, No. 1 (1995), 47–56.

In the nearly 30 years since Card and Krueger's study, the vast majority of empirical studies have found that the minimum wage does lower employment. Economists David Neumark and William Wascher survey the vast literature studying the effect of the minimum wage in their book.[9] They find that the bulk of the empirical evidence accumulated over the last 20 years indicates that the minimum wage reduces employment for the least skilled workers and lowers their earnings. In short, the Card and Krueger study is an outlier, not the norm.

Most of the empirical research on the minimum wage discussed here, including Card and Krueger, examine the effects of minimum wages in the United States or other wealthy countries where sweatshops are not located. However, there is a large literature examining the effect of minimum wages in poorer countries. David Neumark, along with fellow economist Luis Felipe Manguia Corella, recently surveyed the 61 papers, most published since 2000, examining the impact of minimum wage in developing countries.[10] On average, these papers found significant negative employment impacts of minimum wages. The magnitudes varied significantly and not all papers found negative effects. However, the minimum wages studied in the articles varied substantially in how binding they were relative to market wages, how strongly they were enforced, whether they applied to the formal or informal sectors, and whether they focused specifically on the employment effects on low-wage workers. Neumark and Corella find that, across all these studies, the data shows that the impact of a minimum wage is more likely to be negative, and larger in magnitude, when the minimum wage is binding, enforcement is stronger, it applies to the formal sector, and it examines the effect on low-wage workers. In short, the best evidence in the empirical economics literature studying minimum wages in poorer countries indicates that enforcing or increasing minimum wages in settings where sweatshops are most likely to operate is precisely where minimum wages harm workers most.

One study looked specifically at a case where minimum wages were raised to combat sweatshops. In response to anti-sweatshop activism and the US government's threat to remove special tariff privileges, if human rights issues were not addressed, the Indonesian government

---

[9] David Neumark and William Wascher, *Minimum Wages* (Cambridge, MA: MIT Press, 2008).

[10] David Neumark and Luis Felipe Manguia Corella, "Do Minimum Wages Reduce Employment in Developing Countries? A Survey and Exploration of Conflicting Evidence," *World Development* 137 (2021), 1–23.

made increasing the minimum wage a central component of its labor market policies in the 1990s. The real value of the minimum wage more than doubled between 1989 and 1996. What happened to manufacturing employment? Ann Harrison and Jason Scorse estimated that a doubling of Indonesia's minimum wage was associated with a decrease in employment of between 12 and 36 percent. They also found that wage increases led to plant closures among small exporters. They conclude that "the significant negative impact on employment needs to be seriously considered in any campaign to increase the mandated minimum wage or to increase compliance with the minimum wages."[11]

Activists also use boycotts to attempt to improve pay and working conditions in sweatshops. Their logic is straightforward. If consumers voluntarily cease purchasing products, or activists can persuade stores to stop stocking products, that were made by workers who didn't have high enough wages or safe enough working conditions, then companies will improve pay and conditions so that they can sell their products. Unfortunately, activists miss the secondary consequences of boycotts that end up harming workers.

Boycotts necessarily decrease the quantity demanded for the targeted goods in the short run. This could lead profit-maximizing firms to decrease the wages of workers making the targeted goods or to lay off workers. Boycotted firms need fewer workers, since they do not need to make as many goods because of the decreased demand. Furthermore, a boycott decreases the upper bound of compensation because it impacts the amount of revenue an employee creates. When a boycott lowers the demand for a good, firms must cut prices to clear the market. But lower prices for the final good mean that the same effort and physical productivity on the part of a worker results in less revenue for the company. As a result, workers' marginal revenue product decreases through absolutely no fault of the employee. That means that the upper bound a firm is willing to pay an employee falls. Thus, boycotts harm workers through both decreased wages and decreased employment, while they are in effect.

---

[11] Ann Harrison and Jason Scorse, "Multinationals and Anti-Sweatshop Activism," *American Economic Review* 100, No. 1 (2010), 263. Curiously, Harrison and Scorse go to great lengths to cast anti-sweatshop activism in the most favorable light. Most of the paper emphasizes how they do not find any *additional* unemployment effects from anti-sweatshop activism beyond the unemployment effect of the minimum wage. Yet it is anti-sweatshop activism that was in large part responsible for increasing the minimum wage.

However, if firms capitulate to a boycott quickly, the boycott is strategic, and consumers rapidly resume purchases, a boycott could, in principle, succeed in getting the desired outcome before firms adjust employment or wages. Furthermore, some scholars have argued that many contemporary boycotts are not boycotts in the traditional sense of a withdrawal of purchases but are rather threats of boycotts or media-centric campaigns aimed at tarnishing a corporation's image more than decreasing corporate sales.[12] To the extent boycotts are of this style, and don't ultimately decrease demand for the targeted good through the tarnished corporate image, they have the potential to affect change without harming workers in the short run. However, sweatshop boycotts are a little different than other types of media-centric boycotts because the action triggering the boycott is the wages and working conditions of the sweatshop employees. Any capitulation to boycotters' demands necessitates changes to factors such as wages and working conditions that could decrease employment in sweatshop factories, even when the boycott itself does not impact consumer demand. Capitulating to activist demands raises the cost of low-skilled labor relative to its substitutes: capital and higher-skilled workers. As a result, the long-run effect of the boycott, similar to a minimum wage, will be to improve the lives of some relatively more productive workers and to throw the less productive workers into worse alternatives. Thus, sweatshop boycotts carry a "double risk" of harming innocent workers. They could harm them through decreased demand during a boycott and they also could harm some workers by "succeeding" in getting the firm to cease sourcing from factories paying low wages, or that have bad working conditions, but at the expense of employment opportunities that were previously the least bad option for those sweatshop workers.

The anti-sweatshop activism that motivated the Indonesian minimum wage increases mentioned earlier in this chapter is a good illustration of how even media-centric boycotts can harm workers. The campaign began because of research led by Jeff Ballinger, who was working for the AFL-CIO in Indonesia documenting that factories producing for Nike paid the lowest wages among Indonesian export sector factories. Ballinger publicized his findings in an article entitled "The New Free-Trade Hell: Nike's Profits Jump on the Backs of Asian Workers" for *Harper's Magazine* in 1992 and followed up with an appearance

---

[12] See Monroe Friedman, "The Ethical Dilemmas Associated with Boycotts," *Journal of Social Philosophy* 32, No. 2 (2001), 232–240.

discussing his claims on CBS. Ballinger's own organization, Press for Change, as well as other groups like Global Exchange, and the National Labor Committee, followed up by creating an international campaign to pressure Nike, and to a lesser extent also Reebok and Adidas, to change the conditions in their Indonesian suppliers' factories. Harrison and Scorse write, "The campaign against Nike, Adidas, and Reebok in Indonesia was essentially a media campaign, which operated … through contacts with newspaper columnists, magazine writers, TV shows, and other outlets."[13] They document the success of this media campaign in generating coverage by observing the change in the ratio of articles about the Indonesian economy in global news outlets that mention sweatshops. They note that "the ratio of the number of articles on sweatshops or child labor relative to articles on general economic issues on Indonesia in major world newspapers increased from zero to a high of 10 percent of all articles at the peak in 1996."[14]

The media pressure campaign was successful in generating changed practices within Nike. Nike developed a new Code of Conduct for labor practices for supplier factories just as this media campaign began.[15] However, the Code of Conduct was not fully implemented at these Indonesian factories until 1995–6 at the height of the media pressure campaign.[16] During that period, the Code of Conduct was implemented through Nike's production division, with monitoring done by Ernst & Young. Nike decided instead to set up a dedicated labor practices department by 1996. As Murphy and Matthew note in their business school case study of Nike,

> The decision to set up the labour practices department came at a time when Nike was facing growing media and activist pressure about working conditions in its Asian footwear and apparel factories. Activist use of the Internet to disseminate critical reports about Nike was of particular concern. According to Dusty Kidd [the head of the labor practices department], there was a lot of discussion within the company about how best to respond to the criticism.[17]

Similarly, Harrison and Scorse report that "as a result of activist pressure, these firms [Nike, Adidas, and Reebok] were induced to sign codes

[13] Harrison and Scorse, "Multinationals and Anti-Sweatshop Activism," 249.
[14] Ibid., 249–250.
[15] David Murphy and David Matthew, *Nike and Global Labour Practices: A Case Study Prepared for the New Academy of Business Innovation Network for Socially Responsible Business* (London: New Academy of Business, 2001), 6.
[16] Ibid.
[17] Ibid., 7.

of conduct pledging to raise wages and improve working conditions in factories producing their products."[18]

The boycott of Nike, and Indonesian suppliers more generally, appears to be a best-case scenario for a sweatshop boycott. The campaign was media-centric, rather than focused on reducing sales during the boycott (in fact, Nike sales were growing at this time), and both the targeted firm and the source country government implemented reforms desired by the activists. However, we also need to answer the second empirical question of how the implementation of reforms impacted the workers they were supposed to help.

As mentioned, Harrison and Scorse found "large, negative effects of the minimum wage increases on aggregate manufacturing employment" caused by the government's capitulation to activists demands.[19] However, Harrison and Scorse also attempted to isolate the impact of targeted anti-sweatshop activism, rather than national-level minimum wage policy. They take advantage of the fact that the media-centric boycotts were targeted at Nike, Adidas, and Reebok and that the suppliers for these firms were geographically clustered. They employed a difference-in-differences methodology to compare wage and employment growth in Textile, Footwear, and Apparel (TFA) plants, in districts with subcontractors for these footwear firms, against the wage and employment growth of TFA firms in other districts. This methodology attempts to control for factors that affected the TFA industry overall (including the minimum wage increases), to isolate the effect of the activism on targeted firms. They find wage growth in districts with targeted firms was as much as 30 percent higher in large foreign-owned exporting firms.[20] Although they found that activism did cause the exit of small firms, unlike the national increase in the minimum wage, they did not find that targeted anti-sweatshop activism caused decreased employment in targeted districts.

However, a new study by economist Ryo Makioka, published in the *Review of Development Economics*, argues that the firms in districts with Nike, Reebok, and Adidas suppliers differed from the firms in other TFA districts on both observable and unobservable characteristics.[21] Observable characteristics can be controlled for in Harrison

[18] Harrison and Scorse, "Multinationals and Anti-Sweatshop Activism," 247.
[19] Ibid., 248.
[20] Ibid.
[21] Ryo Makioka, "The Impact of Anti-Sweatshop Activism on Employment," *Review of Development Economics* 25 (2021), 630–653.

and Scorse's study, but their methodology assumes that the firms in targeted and untargeted districts are alike on unobservable character-istics. To account for unobservable differences, Makioka employs a synthetic control methodology. This method better matches targeted firms to untargeted firms, based on their trends prior to the advent of anti-sweatshop activism, to create a better counterfactual to evalu-ate activism-impacted targeted firms against. Unlike the earlier study, Makioka finds that employment decreased by 29.8 percent in firms tar-geted by activists. Makioka explains this main result:

The estimate can be interpreted as the effect of the anti-sweatshop movement through firms' increasing compliance with minimum wage regulations, offering voluntarily higher wages, and maintaining higher working standards, because having a similar log employment over the pretreatment periods implies that the treatment and control groups are similar in terms of both observed and unob-served determinants, including minimum wages.[22]

Any wage gains, for workers who keep their jobs, from increases in the minimum wage or targeted anti-sweatshop activism must be weighed against the losses experienced by workers who lose their jobs as a result of this activism. Taken together, the abovementioned studies indicate that national minimum wage and targeted activism each led to nearly one-third less employment in the firms they affected. The first edition of this book reported that more than half of the people in Indonesia were living on less than $2 per day (purchasing power adjusted), and roughly 20 percent were living on less than $1.25 a day, at the time of this activism, while workers in firms targeted by anti-sweatshop activists, and identified in the media, paid approximately $6 per day (purchasing power adjusted).[23] This indicates that the numerous sweatshop workers displaced by activists' actions had a high probability of ending up sup-porting themselves with jobs that provided living standards significantly below those provided by sweatshop jobs.

Trade sanctions and embargos have consequences similar to those of boycotts, but there are important differences. When activists push for trade sanctions against countries with lower wages or worse working conditions, they are advocating for a government policy that prohibits the purchase of products made in sweatshops, or makes it more difficult for anyone who might want to do so. With a boycott, only the voluntary actions of some potential consumers decrease demand. Others are still

---

[22] Ibid., 642.
[23] See the 2014 edition of *Out of Poverty*, 55–57.

free to buy the targeted products. Thus, trade sanctions can lead to a bigger decrease in demand for sweatshop goods than boycotts and thus often harm workers even more.

Trade sanctions are often aimed at changing government policies in poorer countries, whereas boycotts are aimed at convincing companies to change their policies. If trade sanctions are effective, governments create new laws mandating minimum wages or working condition standards that affect many firms. Unfortunately, this means that many more Third World workers are harmed if the trade sanction causes a change in government policy compared to a boycott, because the higher-mandated compensation will affect many firms, rather than just the one targeted by a boycott. If a trade sanction is not effective at convincing a government to change its policies, as is often the case, the sanction tends to remain in place for an extended period of time, resulting in a long-term decrease in demand for products made in these countries, thus harming workers. Sometimes, even when it becomes obvious to nearly everyone that a trade sanction is not going to cause another country to change its policies, and that the sanction harms poor people in the country, the sanction remains.[24] Witness the United States' 60-plus-year embargo against Cuba.

When activists call for minimum wages, boycotts against firms with low wages or poor working conditions, or trade sanctions against countries with sweatshops, they are taking actions that will harm many of the very workers they intend to help. Many of these activists argue for such policies because they are simply ignorant of the basic economics of how sweatshop wages are determined and how their favored policies would interact with market forces. However, not all critics of sweatshops are so ignorant.

UNIONS AND SWEATSHOPS

Unions, at their best, collectively bargain to raise the wages and improve working conditions for their members. Thus, they are operating in the bargaining range between the upper and lower bounds of compensation and trying to secure wages closer to the upper bound rather than

[24] Kimberly Elliott, Gary Hufbauer, and Barbara Oegg report that since 1970 only one out of five times the United States has unilaterally imposed trade sanctions has succeeded in achieving their objective. "Sanctions," *The Concise Encyclopedia of Economics*, edited by David Henderson (2008), retrieved from http://econlib.org/library/Enc/Sanctions.html.

the lower. However, as we've already seen, the bulk of the variation in wages across countries is driven by differences in productivity – the upper bound. So, even successful union bargains, which improve wages on the margin, are unlikely to do much to lift workers out of poverty in low-productivity countries with sweatshops. Furthermore, unions are more likely to lower worker productivity than raise it and thus can lower the upper bound of compensation. Worse yet, the main way unions achieve better wages for members is through "closed shop" restrictions that limit competition from other would-be employees, who are not union members. That might be good, on the margin, for workers in the unionized firm but, from a poverty alleviation standpoint, it excludes other poor people from escaping even worse poverty in the informal or agricultural sector by moving into factory work. Even at its best, unionization isn't likely to do much to alleviate poverty in countries with sweatshops. But it gets worse.

A union's job is to bargain with employers to secure better wages and working conditions for union members. Why, then, have so many unions taken up the cause of Third World sweatshop workers? Most of these workers aren't union members. However, the AFL-CIO, UNITE, and other union-funded organizations have argued for laws, regulations, or trade restrictions, supposedly to improve conditions for these workers.

The unions would have us believe that they are advocates for labor generally and that they are helping Third World workers out of solidarity.[25] But union members pay dues to benefit themselves, not for charity. The reality is that unions use the mantra of "helping sweatshop workers" to improve wages and working conditions for their much wealthier First World union members.

Unions understand the economics of wage determination. They understand that if one raises the cost of unskilled labor in Asia and Latin America, by mandating minimum wages or costly health and safety benefits, employers will demand a smaller quantity of that labor. What will they replace it with? Sometimes machines. But another substitute for low-cost, low-productivity labor is high-cost, high-productivity labor. When fewer garments are sewn in Honduras, more will be sewn

[25] Some scholars actually seem to believe this too. Philosopher Joshua Preiss took issue with my treatment of unions in the first edition of this book because it ignored the "broader social and political purpose" of unions. He seems to favorably view the fact that unions push for laws mandating higher pay and better working conditions for nonunion members, as if these unions were helping these nonmembers rather than harming them (as explained in this chapter). Preiss, "Freedom, Autonomy, and Harm in Global Supply Chains."

in the United States, by workers who are members of UNITE and other unions. The greater employer demand for US garment workers helps unions increase their membership and bargain for higher wages and better working conditions for *their* members.

The protectionist nature of the anti-sweatshop movement is lost on many activists.[26] Sue Casey, a USAS activist, reported an "uncomfortable moment when a UNITE official, presenting USAS with an award, thanked the student organization 'for helping us in our struggle *against imports*.' Since USAS goes out of its way not to take protectionist positions, Casey says, 'that really stunk'" (emphasis in original).[27] Similarly, Tico Almeida, the student who helped start the student anti-sweatshop movement at Duke, laments, "Some media would later use the union relationship as 'proof' that the student anti-sweatshop movement had protectionist intentions, but a 'Made in the USA' provision – whether in corporate or university codes of conduct – has never once been proposed by the students."[28] "Made in the USA" requirements or explicit intentions are not necessary to make actions taken by USAS and other groups protectionist measures. As outlined in Chapter 2, USAS lobbies colleges to join the WRC, which requires codes that mandate, among other things, creating their own minimum wages and following local minimum wage laws. The effect of these actions is to drive garment production from the Third World to the First World. Regardless of intent, the economic incentives created by USAS actions create protectionist outcomes that benefit First World unions.

The "Shop with a Conscience Consumer Guide" provides a graphic illustration of how a seemingly non-protectionist-motivated policy generates a protectionist result. The International Labor Rights Forum, SweatFree Communities, and Sweatshop Watch jointly sponsor the guide, which lists firms selling products that have been made in factories the guide has deemed "sweat-free." These sweat-free sources are either unionized or run as worker cooperatives, have healthy and safe working conditions, offer wages and benefits that will "lift workers' families out of poverty," and treat the workers with "respect, dignity,

---

[26] And apparently some professional philosophers. Joshua Preiss writes, "In many cases, the goals of labor activism are not only to further wages and working conditions of union members, but also to further the condition of workers generally... a central goal of much union activism has frequently been to raise the pay and better the working conditions of non-union workers." Preiss, "Freedom, Autonomy, and Harm in Global Supply Chains," 883.

[27] Featherstone and USAS, *Students Against Sweatshops*, 17.

[28] Ibid., 16.

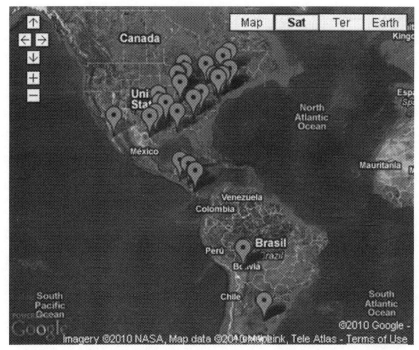

FIGURE 3.1 Location of factories supplying the "Shop with a Conscience Consumer Guide"

and justice."[29] Forty-one factories met these criteria and were certified. As Figure 3.1 shows, 29 of these factories were located in the United States and Canada; only 11 were located in Latin and South America, and a single factory (not shown) was in Asia. Although consumers might feel they were "shopping with a conscience," they were mostly buying products made by wealthy First World union workers, while decreasing the demand for products made in poorer countries and thus harming the employment prospects of the poorer Third World workers.

The unions masquerade publicly as friends to sweatshop workers. But the reality is much more devious. They intentionally advocate policies that will harm those very workers, and naïve young activists end up acting as tools that help the unions achieve their protectionist goals.[30]

[29] SweatFree Communities, Our Criteria, retrieved from www.sweatfree.org/shopping_suppliercriteria.

[30] This is not unlike the motives for the labor regulation passed during the Progressive era in the United States. Economist Thomas Leonard argues that labor legislation whose public rational was to help women or children was really motivated by the desire to limit their

As economist David Henderson says, "Someone who intentionally gets you fired is not your friend."[31] Contrary to their claims, First World unions are no friends of sweatshop workers.

AN ILLUSTRATION OF ECONOMICS
IN ACTION: THE BJ&B CAMPAIGN

The BJ&B factory, owned by the Korean firm Yupoong and located in the Villa Altagracia export processing zone in the Dominican Republic, was a major producer of baseball hats for Nike, Reebok, the Gap, and other major companies.[32] It employed more than 2,000 workers in 2001, but under harsh conditions. Workers were agitating for a union and UNITE helped them gain publicity and allies with USAS. The FLA and WRC conducted audits and issued reports. The publicity eventually forced BJ&B to recognize the union in 2003 and enter into an agreement that would "give workers a 10 percent wage increase, educational scholarships, paid holidays, and the establishment of a workers' committee to deal with health and safety concerns at the factory."[33] The agreement was "hailed by many as a sign of the success of transnational organizing, particularly the strategic role played by USAS in exerting pressure on universities to take action through the WRC."[34]

The activists' victory was short-lived. Soon the economic forces described in this chapter began asserting themselves. Yupoong threatened to close the factory and shift its production to overseas plants when the agreement was renegotiated just a year later in 2004. Activists again pressured the factory to negotiate and it stayed open, but it began laying off workers. Finally, in 2007, Yupoong closed the BJ&B plant because it was no longer competitive. The plant closure was really just the final nail in the coffin for the workers. The workforce had already shrunk from 2,000, before activists pressured the factory, to only 234 at the time of its closure.

labor force participation so that they would not compete with males. See, for example, "Protecting Family and Race: The Progressive Case for Regulating Women's Work," *American Journal of Economics and Sociology* 64, No. 3 (2005), 757–791.

[31] David R. Henderson, "The Case for Sweatshops," Hoover Institution, Stanford University, February 7, 2000, retrieved from www.hoover.org/news/daily-report/24617.

[32] Unless otherwise cited the facts in this section are from Shae Garwood, *Advocacy across Borders: NGOs, Anti-Sweatshop Activism, and the Global Garment Industry* (Sterling, VA: Kumarian Press, 2011), 180–185.

[33] Ibid., 181.

[34] Ibid.

In 2010, the location of the BJ&B factory became the site of one of the anti-sweatshop movement's big "success" stories, the Altagracia Project. The Altagracia Project "was set up to operate as a model factory, showcasing that a factory could pay a living wage (three times the average wage for garment workers in the region), respect workers' rights to join a union, and at the same time turn a profit."[35] The factory succeeded in selling its products at more than 600 college campuses throughout the United States.[36] However, seven years after its founding the company still hadn't made a net profit in a single year.[37] Even if it continues to stay in business, it is hard to judge the net effect of activist activity in the Villa Altagracia region as anything other than a horrible failure. BJ&B provided the best available alternative for 2,000 people a little over a decade ago. Activists' actions raised the cost of labor and cost all of those workers their jobs. The Altagracia Project employed only 120 people a decade later, when the first edition of this book came out, and it appears that it employs only 130 people in 2023.[38]

The laws of economics are clear. When the cost of labor increases, companies use less of it. Even this supposed "success story" of the anti-sweatshop movement is not immune from these forces, and activists' actions ultimately made the vast majority of affected workers worse off.

SCHOLARLY OBJECTIONS TO STANDARD SWEATSHOP ECONOMICS

Not all of the people who oppose sweatshops but understand the basic economic logic of wage determination are union demagogues. A growing scholarly literature challenges whether standard supply and demand analysis can be applied accurately to Third World sweatshops.[39]

---

[35] Ibid., 185.

[36] Alta Gracia, "What Is a Living Wage?" Retrieved from http://altagraciaapparel.com/story.

[37] Sarah Adler-Milstein and John M. Kline, *Sewing Hope: How One Factory Challenges the Apparel Industry's Sweatshops* (Oakland, CA: University of California Press, 2017).

[38] Alta Gracia Apparel, retrieved from https://en.wikipedia.org/wiki/Alta_Gracia_Apparel.

[39] Notable examples in this literature include Denis G. Arnold and Norman E. Bowie, "Sweatshops and Respect for Persons," *Business Ethics Quarterly* 13, No. 2 (2003), 238; Denis Arnold and Laura Hartman, "Moral Imagination and the Future of Sweatshops," *Business and Society Review* 108, No. 4 (2003), 427. Denis Arnold, "Philosophical Foundations: Moral Reasoning, Human Rights, and Global Labor Practices," *Rising above Sweatshops: Innovative Approaches to Global Labor Challenges*, edited by Laura Hartman, Denis Arnold, and Richard E. Wokutch (Westport, CT: Praeger, 2003), 79; John Miller, "Why Economists Are Wrong about Sweatshops and the

Scholars have challenged whether the background conditions that are necessary to make trade mutually beneficial are present in Third World countries. They have also attempted to identify economic mechanisms that would allow wages to be increased without causing unemployment. Finally, some have recognized the inherent unemployment effects of minimum wages but have argued that welfare gains to remaining workers more than offset the harm caused to those workers who lose their jobs. The remainder of the chapter considers, and ultimately rejects, these arguments.

THE NECESSITY OF COMPETITIVE MARKETS

The most basic point made by defenders of sweatshops is that workers' voluntary choice to accept sweatshop employment demonstrates that sweatshops are the best alternative available to them. Therefore, activists shouldn't advocate policies that could jeopardize these jobs. Critics have challenged whether this choice demonstrates that sweatshops provide the best jobs and whether conditions and wages cannot be improved, without jeopardizing the jobs, on the grounds that the underlying conditions are not the type of competitive markets described in economics textbooks. Arnold and Hartman argue,

> Free markets ... generate many benefits; but their ability to generate those benefits presumes certain fixed conditions. For example, transactions among workers and employers optimally satisfy the interests of each only if there is a free flow of information, the transaction is truly voluntary, people are able to make rational decisions about their self-interest, and there are many buyers and sellers (e.g. no potential for exploitative monopoly exists).[40]

Let's examine each of these conditions. The free flow of information improves economic efficiency. But information itself is not free. When

---

Antisweatshop Movement," *Challenge*, January/February (2003), 97; Robert Pollin, Justine Burns, and James Heintz, "Global Apparel Production and Sweatshop Labor: Can Raising Retail Prices Finance Living Wages?" *Cambridge Journal of Economics* 28, No. 2 (2004), 153–171; Denis Arnold and Laura Hartman, "Beyond Sweatshops: Positive Deviancy and Global Labour Practices," *Business Ethics: A European Review* 14, No. 3 (2005), 208; Denis Arnold and Laura Hartman, "Worker Rights and Low Wage Industrialization: How to Avoid Sweatshops," *Human Rights Quarterly* 28, No. 3 (2006), 676–700; Denis G. Arnold and Norman E. Bowie, "Respect for Workers in Global Supply Chains: Advancing the Debate over Sweatshops," *Business Ethics Quarterly* 17, No. 1 (2007), 139; and Denis Arnold, "Working Conditions: Safety and Sweatshops," *The Oxford Handbook of Business Ethics*, edited by George Brenkert and Tom Beauchamp (New York: Oxford University Press, 2010), 635.
[40] Arnold and Hartman, "Beyond Sweatshops," 208.

Arnold and Hartman elaborate, they write that workers "may not be able to make a fully informed choice because of their lack of information about what lies ahead. Furthermore, such labor choices, once made, can be difficult to undo when additional information is learned 'on the job.'"[41] This is a fact of life in all markets. It's always impossible to know what lies ahead, and there are often transaction costs for reversing course once new information is obtained.

Arnold and Hartman are holding up an unreasonable standard of "perfect competition" that never exists in any real-world market and that assumes away the very problems the market must solve. Only in the end state of perfect competition is all information fully known. The real competitive market process is about discovering opportunities for gains from trade. Bidding by buyers and sellers reveals information about people's willingness to supply and demand all products, including labor. This very market process discovers the previously unknown knowledge.[42] Rather than a flaw of markets, the lack of perfect information is one of the essential reasons we need markets.

Cases of outright fraud, in which employers intentionally disclose false information to employees, are more complicated. If the transaction cost of changing jobs is low, and the fraud easy to detect once one is on a job, then the market can sort the situation out easily, and the workers we observe still on the job are demonstrating that it is their best alternative. For example, job risks account for one-third of manufacturing quit rates in the United States.[43] The same process can work in sweatshops if employees find themselves in jobs that are riskier to their health and safety than was advertised to them.

In cases where transaction costs are high and the fraud is not easy to detect, the market would have a harder time sorting it out. Even in this case, however, in the long run, information from disgruntled workers can spread, which will help others to make better choices, and even eliminate the harmful business practice by making it unprofitable because of the negative impact on the firm's reputation.

As a general rule, outright fraud should be illegal. In practice, identifying harmful fraud can be difficult. In some cases, government-mandated wages or working conditions may push total compensation above the level

---

[41] Ibid., 209.
[42] See Friedrich Hayek, "The Use of Knowledge in Society," *American Economic Review* 35, No. 4 (1945), 519–530.
[43] Kip Viscusi, Joseph Harrington, and John Vernon, *Economics of Regulation and Antitrust*, 4th ed. (Cambridge, MA: MIT Press, 2005), 836.

at which employers can profitably employ workers. In such a situation, advertising conditions that comply with the law, when the de facto conditions do not, may be beneficial for employees. I discuss the case for violating labor laws in Chapter 5. There is also a gray area around failure to disclose information compared to outright misrepresentation of it. Here it would depend on what local implicit contract custom is, which can vary considerably between countries. Things that US workers might expect to be disclosed, workers in poorer countries might not expect. For example, disclosure of working with a chemical that causes cancer in 70-year-olds might be expected in the United States but not in a country where the life expectancy is only 50 years. As I argue in Chapter 5, in many instances, providing poor working conditions is better for workers than mandating better conditions. Some may argue that workers have a 'right' to better conditions but the ability of workers to waive their 'right' to such better conditions is important for their own well-being. Whether that waiver comes after disclosure or with the norm of nondisclosure is of secondary importance.

Defenders of sweatshops assume that transactions are voluntary. John Miller has written that although sweatshop employment may be superior to the informal sector, this does not "suggest that these exchanges between employers and poor workers with few alternatives are in reality voluntary... Rather, these exchanges should be seen as 'trades of last resort' or 'desperate' exchanges that need to be protected by labor legislation regulating such things as limits on hours, a wage floor, and guaranteed health and safety requirements."[44] Arnold and Hartman, like Miller, write that preconditions for efficient markets are not met because "workers may agree to labour under poor conditions, but only because they have no other option for securing income."[45] Their objections relate to what economist Michael Munger has termed "euvoluntary exchange," or truly voluntary exchange. Munger argues for an exchange to be truly voluntary (1) there must be conventional ownership of items by both parties, (2) there must be the conventional capacity to transfer and assign this ownership to the other party, (3) there must be the absence of regret, for both parties, after the exchange, (4) neither party is forced by a threat, and (5) neither party is coerced in the sense of being harmed by failing to exchange. It is point number five that Arnold, Hartman, and Miller are saying is absent in sweatshops, and thus the exchange is not truly voluntary. As the next chapter will argue, the alternatives to sweatshop

---

[44] Miller, "Why Economists Are Wrong," 101.
[45] Arnold and Hartman, "Beyond Sweatshops," 209.

employment are often much worse and, as a result, workers feel like they must take offers of sweatshop employment. But Munger does not go wrong where these sweatshop critics do. He explains,

Exchanges that are not euvoluntary are generally welfare improving, and they improve the welfare of the least well off most of all. The confusion that arises in judging exchanges that are not euvoluntary is understandable, but unfortunate. The observer, seeing the degree of inequality, or desperation of one of the parties to a potential exchange, is actually perceiving a disparity in levels of welfare of the respective BATNAs, or "Best Alternatives to a Negotiated Exchange" [next best alternatives to trading]. This disparity is a consequence of differences that come before exchange is contemplated, and are not caused by the exchange.

But the confused observer seeks to help the less well off party by out-lawing the exchange. The observer, believing that the party should not have to exchange on such terms, blunders in and dictates that the party should not be allowed to exchange on such terms. The problem is that this ensures that party is marooned at his grossly inferior BATNA, an outcome that access to exchange could have avoided.[46]

Lacking other good options does not change the fact that choosing the sweatshop job demonstrates that it is the worker's best alternative. True coercion takes away options by restricting the worker's choice set. Adding the option of working in a sweatshop expands the choice set. Adding governmental restrictions on what employers can offer workers, like Miller advocates, uses the threat of government coercion to take away some options, and that can throw workers into worse alternatives.

I do not assume that all people are always some version of a neoclassical "*Homo economicus.*" People tend to choose what is in their best self-interest. It is impossible for outside observers to know the subjective trade-offs made by other human beings.[47] Sweatshop workers have much more local knowledge of their particulars of time and place than First World scholars and activists do, and those workers certainly have the incentive to choose what is best for themselves.[48] I know of no systematic reason why their 'rationality' should be questioned.

Arnold has also written that defenders of sweatshops "assume that multinational corporations always act with instrumental practical

[46] Michael Munger, "Euvoluntary or Not, Exchange Is Just," *Social Philosophy and Policy* 28, No. 2 (2011), 211.
[47] See Edward Stringham, "Economic Value and Costs Are Subjective," in *Handbook on Contemporary Austrian Economics*, edited by Peter Boettke (Cheltenham: Edward Elgar, 2010), 43–66.
[48] A point recognized by Arnold himself in his discussion of moral imagination. See Arnold, "Philosophical Foundations," 79.

reason aimed at self-interested profit maximization. Such a view is empirically inaccurate."[49] Unfortunately, he merely asserts that the view is empirically inaccurate; he does not offer any proof. A corporation's job is to maximize shareholder value, and this includes the present value of the future stream of profits – not just short-run profits. Thus, profit maximization leaves plenty of room for ethical branding or other sweatshop improvement policies that may decrease short-run profits but enhance long-run profitability through brand image. Citations of companies pursuing such policies do nothing to undermine the general profit maximization model.

This doesn't mean that companies have discovered all possible ways to maximize long-run profits. Competition is itself a discovery procedure.[50] When Arnold and Hartman document voluntary innovations that companies have made in worker health and safety, they perform a valuable service that is part of the market's discovery process.[51] But just because not every innovation has been discovered by the market process doesn't make corporations any less rational.

Finally, Arnold and Hartman question whether markets are beneficial if the number of buyers and sellers is small. In fact, elsewhere Arnold specifically singles me out: "Defenders of sweatshops, such as Matt Zwolinski and Benjamin Powell, assume that such labor markets are competitive, but it is not clear that such an assumption is warranted. In many nations employers have monopsony power over the workers."[52] But many buyers and sellers need not be present for markets to produce efficient results.

If there is freedom of entry, a monopoly (monopsony) can produce results identical to a competitive market. If employers systematically pay workers less than their marginal revenue product, then new firms have an incentive to enter the market and bid the workers away from the underpaying firm because in the process they will earn above-normal profits. As a result, even a single firm, when threatened with entry by other firms, pushes wages toward workers' marginal contribution to revenue.[53]

---

[49] Arnold, "Working Conditions," 637.
[50] See Friedrich Hayek, "Competition as a Discovery Procedure," in *New Studies in Philosophy, Politics, Economics, and the History of Ideas* (Chicago: University of Chicago Press, 1978).
[51] Benjamin Powell, "In Reply to Sweatshop Sophistries," *Human Rights Quarterly* 28, No. 4 (2006), 1031–1042, praises Arnold and Hartman on exactly this point.
[52] Arnold, "Working Conditions," 651.
[53] Economists refer to this as contestable markets theory. There is also a large experimental economics literature that shows small numbers of buyers and sellers achieve results that approximate what a perfectly competitive market is supposed to achieve.

What if freedom of entry does not exist? Countries with sweatshops often suffer from numerous government regulations and interventions into the market. Even if a government regulation prohibits or raises the cost of entry, an individual sweatshop is better than none at all. If the single sweatshop disappeared, the labor market would be restricted even more. Rather than protest the sweatshop, inefficient regulations that inhibit the market process should be opposed.

Arnold and Hartman have mistaken *sufficient* conditions to ensure competitive markets generate beneficial results for *necessary* conditions. As economist Peter Boettke explains, "The 'invisible hand' solution does not emerge because the mainline economist postulates a perfectly rational individual interacting with other perfectly rational individuals within a perfectly structured market, as many critics suppose."[54] Instead the beneficial outcomes generated by the "invisible hand" process emerge "through the reconciliation process of exchange within specific institutional environments. It is the 'higgling and bargaining' within the market economy, as Adam Smith argued, that produces social order."[55]

EFFICIENCY WAGES

Some scholars argue that the existence of efficiency wages means that firms can raise wages without unemploying workers. An efficiency wage is an above-market-rate wage paid to employees in order to induce greater productivity from the employees. Arnold and Hartman write, "there is evidence to support the claim that positive MNC deviants who voluntarily pay employees a living wage (or a 'fair wage') will achieve increases in worker productivity and loyalty. The most obvious ways in which wages affect productivity are captured by nutrition models of efficiency wages."[56] Yet nutritional needs cannot justify efficiency wages from profit-maximizing garment firms.

Malnourished workers are less productive, so employers should want to pay enough to ensure productivity. Arnold and Hartman state that because workers will spend income on other family members, firms may need to pay a worker two to four times the amount necessary to meet the worker's minimum daily caloric intake. The increased productivity

---

[54] Peter Boettke, *Living Economics: Yesterday, Today, and Tomorrow* (Oakland, CA: The Independent Institute, 2012), xvii.
[55] Ibid.
[56] Arnold and Hartman, "Beyond Sweatshops," 217.

from an efficient diet may not offset the increased cost of paying two to four times the cost of that diet, however. More importantly, when the difference between malnourished and healthy worker productivity does justify paying enough to ensure a minimum caloric intake, firms can more efficiently provide those calories through free or subsidized meals at work. Although Arnold and Hartman grant that this is a possibility, it is in fact almost always the case.[57] An efficiency wage is not necessary to improve caloric intake because workers will spend some portion of their earnings on things other than their own food; thus, employers can almost always provide the calories directly at a lower cost.

Arnold and Hartman also claim that "a second economic model [of efficiency wages] emphasizes the gift-exchange nature of employment relations, as opposed to the pure market exchange of such relations. On this model, employees who are compensated at rates significantly higher than the wages demanded by the market are seen as making a gift to workers, who reciprocate with greater productivity and greater loyalty."[58]

A gift-exchange style efficiency wage may be necessary when the labor market is tight and monitoring employee productivity is difficult. If a firm pays an above-market wage in these cases, then the employees have something to lose if they are caught underperforming, thus they will work harder. Monitoring employee productivity is simple in most sweatshop jobs, and most such jobs exist in labor markets that have substantial unemployment or underemployment in informal sectors. Absent these two key characteristics, Arnold and Hartman are wrong to assume that an employee will work harder because higher wages are seen as a "gift" from the employer. Employees already work as hard as they are going to because labor market alternatives are poor and monitoring of workers is intense.

Paying efficiency wages may sometimes maximize profits. However, the conditions necessary for efficiency wages to improve productivity are not widespread in Third World sweatshops. When they are present, managers have every incentive to adopt them voluntarily. There

---

[57] Arnold and Hartman, "Worker Rights," 46. See Benjamin Powell and Ryan Murphy "Nutritional Efficiency Wages and Unemployment: Where's the Beef?" *American Journal of Agricultural Economics* 97, No. 2 (2015), 405–413, for a discussion of why nutritional efficiency wages are not likely to ever be a cause of equilibrium unemployment in real-world markets and a model showing the few theoretical exceptions where nutritional efficiency wages could cause unemployment and the lack of empirical relevance for these theoretical exceptions.

[58] Arnold and Hartman, "Beyond Sweatshops," 218.

is no reason to believe that pushing for legally mandated higher wages will result in higher productivity in most sweatshop jobs because they become efficiency wages, and thus the standard economic model that predicts higher wage mandates will lead to lower employment still holds.

PASSING COSTS ON TO CONSUMERS

Scholars have also claimed that increased compensation may not lead to lower employment because firms may be able to pass costs on to the consumer: "Increased labor cost may be offset by the value added to the good insofar as consumers demonstrate a preference for products produced under conditions in which the rights of workers are respected."[59] Certainly, some consumers value ethically produced items by an amount great enough to justify sweatshops paying higher total compensation. If these consumers do not decrease their quantity of purchases when prices for ethically produced goods are higher than those of other goods, then a decrease in employment is not necessary. Some companies have employed this strategy successfully. But how widespread is consumer demand for ethically produced goods?

Robert Pollin and coauthors have argued that doubling the wages paid to apparel workers in Mexico would add 1.6 percent to the retail price of men's casual shirts, which is within the amount a survey suggested US consumers would be willing to pay for goods produced under "good" working conditions rather than sweatshop conditions.[60] However, what US consumers say they would be willing to pay is a poor substitute for actual market transactions. Ultimately, the market process must discover the demand, just like for any other product. Experimentation in production methods and marketing by different firms will be necessary. Results from surveys should be made available to companies to encourage them to consider if giving workers better wages or conditions would enhance the demand for their product. However, all consumers of sweatshop goods are unlikely to value ethically produced goods by enough to justify industry-wide higher compensation. Only through the market's competitive process can the companies and products capable of implementing this strategy be found. Ethically conscious consumers can best voice their opinions by buying ethically produced products when given the opportunity. Chapter 11 discusses voluntary ethical branding in greater detail.

[59] Arnold and Hartman, "Worker Rights," 29.
[60] Pollin, Burns, and Heintz, "Global Apparel Production."

COST CUTTING IN OTHER AREAS

Sweatshop critics have also claimed that increased wages, when not off-set by efficiency wages or increased consumer demand, may be "readily absorbed as an operating expense" or "balanced by internal cost-cutting measures."[61] The first is highly unlikely. If a company can relocate to another country to avoid the increased wages, a profit-maximizing firm need not "absorb" the higher operating expense. Furthermore, wages are not a fixed cost. They are a variable cost, that is, one that varies with the quantity of a good produced. Sweatshop labor is often paid an hourly rate or a rate per unit of output. Economics is a science that deals with marginal adjustments. Raise the marginal variable cost of labor, and firms do not have to make an all or nothing choice of "continue the same quantity of production with a lower profit" or "don't produce at all." Instead, they can vary the quantity they produce. Faced with higher marginal labor costs, firms will optimize profits by cutting back production to the point at which the new higher marginal cost equals their marginal revenue. This will decrease the quantity of labor they demand.

Arnold and Hartman posit that even if firms cannot absorb the cost of higher wages as an operating expense, they could still cut costs in other areas to compensate. They suggest decreases in the number of home country managers or cuts in "executive perks."[62] But if these things were adversely affecting profits, wouldn't companies already be cutting costs?[63] Firms are not known to leave profits on the table intentionally. Companies will cut these costs if and when doing so is beneficial. Academics are unlikely to be more aware of a company's unnecessary costs than the actual company, which has a profit incentive to find these inefficiencies. Furthermore, even in cases in which costs exist that potentially could be cut, nothing ties these cuts to increases in worker wages. A profit-maximizing firm would not increase worker wages just because it found a cost to cut elsewhere. Either it is efficient to pay workers more because of consumer demand for ethically produced goods or efficiency wages or it is not. If it is not efficient (in the profit-maximizing sense) to pay workers more, then finding other areas of inefficiently high costs does not make it desirable to trade one inefficiency for another from a firm's perspective. The firm would simply eliminate the existing inefficiency.

---

[61] Arnold and Hartman, "Worker Rights," 29.
[62] Ibid., 29–30.
[63] Interestingly, chief executives and their perks fit the model of efficiency wages much more closely than assembly workers.

ACCEPTING A LOWER RATE OF RETURN

Scholars have suggested that the cost of increased wages could be borne by owners via a lower return on equity: "In such cases, the costs of respecting workers must be regarded as a necessary condition of doing business. The point should not be problematic for any manager who recognizes the existence of basic human dignity."[64] However, it is likely to be very problematic. A higher return on equity attracts more capital to a given industry or business. Even an executive concerned with human dignity faces this constraint. A lower return on equity will limit the number of factories that firms can open and hence will limit job creation in the impoverished countries where sweatshops exist because raising the needed capital to open new factories will be harder. Appeals to human dignity will work only to the extent that they create greater value in the minds of consumers for the products that are produced. Even owners who believe they should accept a lower return on equity to be ethical will face the financing constraints of the market and will be limited in the number of jobs they can create.

DOES OVERALL WORKER WELFARE IMPROVE DESPITE JOB LOSSES?

The impact on sweatshop workers' welfare, and the welfare of other poor people in the countries where sweatshops are located, is the standard used to evaluate the desirability of various laws, policies, and activists' actions throughout this book. The economic theory and empirical evidence reviewed earlier in this chapter indicate that enforcing higher minimum wages or engaging in boycotts will lead some workers to lose their jobs and be thrown into less-desirable alternatives. The welfare of those workers is clearly harmed. But that fact, by itself, does not establish that overall sweatshop worker welfare is harmed. Instead, any gains to workers who keep their jobs must be weighed against the losses to any workers who lose their jobs to evaluate how a policy impacts worker welfare.[65]

---

[64] Arnold and Hartman, "Worker Rights," 30.

[65] Philosophers Mathew Coakley and Michael Kates attempted to argue that weighting gains to workers who keep their jobs against losses to workers who lose their jobs would result in finding that sweatshop regulation improves overall worker welfare. See Mathew Coakley and Michael Kates, "The Ethical and Economic Case for Sweatshop Regulation," *Journal of Business Ethics* 117 (2013), 553–558. However, they made numerous errors in their analysis. This subsection of the chapter does not delve into their many mistakes but instead takes their key insight and then applies

It would not be complicated to evaluate how a minimum wage impacts worker welfare if it was set high enough to cause all sweatshop workers to lose their job. Nor would it be difficult to evaluate if a minimum wage led to no job loss, perhaps because of one of the above mechanisms, and yet led to wage increases for at least some workers. Unfortunately, most minimum wages, and other policy changes, fall somewhere in between, making our task more complicated. So, let's start by using economic theory to figure out who is most likely to bear most of the burden of the cost of a minimum wage in order to understand how employment will generally be impacted.

How much of the burden of a higher wage mandate is borne by which parties affected by the mandate depends on the relative price sensitivities of workers, firms, consumers, and capital owners. Economists call these price sensitivities "elasticities." More elastic parties are more price-sensitive and adjust their behavior a lot to avoid increased costs. Less elastic parties change their behavior less in response to any price increase or decrease. The major relevant factor in thinking about relative elasticities, in the case of sweatshop wage mandates, is the ability of affected parties to escape negative consequences for themselves by switching to substitutes.

Minimum wages, and many other labor market regulations, are determined at the national level. Sweatshops are often owned by domestic subcontractors producing for major multinational brands. If, for example, the Indonesian government increases the minimum wage, thus increasing costs for the domestic producers, those producers can't pass costs on to multinational buyers because these buyers have a wide range of countries that they can source apparel from. A multinational buyer's tie to any one country can be broken easily by placing orders elsewhere – either in other Third World countries with cheaper labor or in countries that have higher-cost but more productive workers. Even in the short run, multinational buyers are highly price elastic because they can easily and quickly switch suppliers. Furthermore, capital is mobile. A minimum wage that increases Indonesia's cost of labor will result in firm closure (or a slowdown in firm growth) and capital flows will move away from Indonesia and toward other countries where factories will locate in the medium and longer run.

more realistic economic theory to trace out how to assess how regulations impact overall worker welfare. For a more detailed critique of their claims, see Benjamin Powell, "Sweatshop Regulations: Tradeoffs and Value Judgements," *Journal of Business Ethics* 151, No. 1 (2018), 29–36.

Sweatshop workers, on the other hand, do not have many ways to adjust their behavior. They need to work because they are desperately poor and trying to feed, clothe, and shelter themselves and their family members. Taking their labor out of a country that increases its minimum wage, like Indonesia, and moving to another country where minimum wages are lower, or to a First World country where they can be more productive, is not an option for the vast majority of workers due to the strict immigration restrictions in most destination countries that make legal immigration nearly impossible for most of the global poor (more on immigration restrictions in Chapter 11). Exiting the labor market, through either migration or not working, is simply not an option for the vast majority of workers in countries where sweatshops locate. As we'll see in the next chapter, these sweatshops usually pay better than work in other sectors of these economies. So, for workers, the quantity of labor they supply the apparel industry is not price-sensitive (elastic) in the relevant range.

When labor supply is not very price-sensitive and labor demand is more price-sensitive, any mandate, such as a minimum wage, that raises the cost of labor will cause large decreases in the quantity of labor demanded, relative to any increased benefits workers who keep their job might receive. The simplest way to assess the impact on short-run overall worker welfare, in the case of the minimum wage, is to add up the dollar gains to workers who kept their jobs and received a pay increase (keeping in mind that not all workers who keep their jobs were previously earning less than the minimum) and comparing that to the wages lost by the workers who lose their jobs.[66] The price sensitivities (elasticities) of labor suppliers and employers in sweatshop markets indicates that this calculation is highly likely to indicate losses that are greater than gains. However, elasticities are ultimately empirical phenomenon and can vary from one market to another or over time. Furthermore, "worker welfare" also must consider any long-run effects that any regulations might have on slowing economic development that impact workers in future years. The long-run effects of both sweatshops and regulation will be explored in later chapters of this book. The next chapter turns to the next piece of the puzzle by examining how sweatshop wages compare with the available alternatives workers are likely to find themselves in if sweatshop employment ceases to be an option.

---

[66] There are philosophically reasonable and compelling alternatives to counting dollar gains and losses equally for those who keep their jobs and those who lose their jobs that would require losses to be weighed more heavily than gains. These alternatives are explored in the appendix to this chapter.

CONCLUSION: TEXTBOOK ECONOMICS RECLAIMED

Demand curves slope down. Anyone who has ever taken a principles of economics class has heard that lesson many times. Sweatshop labor is no exception. Sweatshop critic John Miller summarized the position of sweatshop defenders by writing, "Their proposition is as simple as this: 'Either you believe labor demand curves are downward sloping, or you don't'... Of course, not to believe that demand curves are negatively sloped would be tantamount to declaring yourself an economic illiterate."[67] Although Miller himself believes that the economic defense of sweatshops is wrong, after considering the arguments put forth by him and other scholars critical of sweatshops, I have found their arguments lacking. Their supposed exceptions to the basic economic model do nothing to overturn the economic defense of sweatshops.

Sweatshop employers will employ fewer workers if the cost of hiring them rises. Workers choose to work in sweatshops because they deem them to be their best available option. Thus, mandating higher wages will involuntarily throw some of these workers into worse alternatives. This naturally leads us to ask, "How much better are the sweatshop jobs compared to the alternatives?"

APPENDIX: PHILOSOPHICAL CONSIDERATIONS
IN MEASURING WORKER WELFARE

Economic science can establish the trade-offs associated with policy changes. But economic science, by itself, is incapable of establishing the desirability of any policy. To establish the desirability of an economic policy an ethical judgment must be rendered in light of the trade-offs established by economics.

Sweatshop regulations decrease economic efficiency. Any regulation that changes relative prices in a way that doesn't reflect the real scarcity of resources necessarily creates deadweight losses that shrink the economic pie.[68] But efficiency is, itself, a normative standard that needs ethical justification. It counts the income of everyone, rich and

---

[67] Miller, "Why Economists Are Wrong," 107.

[68] If relative prices were failing to reflect the real scarcity of resources, it is possible, in theory, for a regulation to change relative prices to better reflect relative scarcities and thus eliminate deadweight losses and increase the economic pie. Advocates of sweatshop regulations have not made any convincing case that their preferred regulations could fall into this category.

poor, the same. Implicitly, it assumes a dollar of income generates the same amount of human welfare regardless of who receives it. Although there are good arguments in favor of using economic efficiency as a welfare standard, in the context of the debate surrounding the regulation of sweatshops, I have chosen to argue exclusively in terms of the welfare of sweatshop workers, and other poor people, in the Third World. This standard, in the spirit of value-free economics, embraces the ends of the anti-sweatshop activists – the welfare of the world's poor – and asks if the proposed means, sweatshop regulations, promote that end.

However, the "welfare of sweatshop workers and other poor people in countries where sweatshops are located" is not something that is straightforward to measure. Welfare, or utility as most social scientists would refer to it, is not interpersonally comparable, and all values gained and lost are subjective to those experiencing them. Any time that we measure gains to the winners compared with losses to the losers we are necessarily moving beyond the scope of what economic science is capable of establishing. We can measure dollar gains to winners compared to dollar losses for losers, just like we measure efficiency, but that does not directly translate into utility or welfare if those dollars are worth more to some people than to others. Despite these limitations, let's proceed to explore some aspects of "worker welfare" with these important caveats in mind.

Does Everyone Count Equally?

Should the income gains to the sweatshop workers who remain employed simply be netted against the income losses to those who lose their jobs and the other poor workers who face lower incomes because of competition from the newly unemployed sweatshop workers? If standard economic efficiency was our baseline, the answer for most economists is clear – yes. But the whole point of using "third world worker (and potential worker) welfare" as a welfare standard explicitly rejects counting the welfare of all equally. It ignores the welfare of capital owners and First World consumers.

Is there a break point where the welfare of some people counts for nothing and the welfare of all of the rest counts equally? Once one uses a welfare standard that explicitly excludes any welfare gains or losses to the relatively rich, one is implicitly adopting a standard where the welfare of the least well-off people matters more. If one embraces a strong Rawlsian position, that only values the welfare of the least well-off, then clearly sweatshop regulations would be undesirable. Sweatshop regulations cause income losses for the poorest of the poor through layoffs, while the remaining sweatshop workers, who, as we will see in the next chapter, are relatively better-off, experience gains. But one need not embrace a fully Rawlsian position for such considerations to impact how one judges welfare gains and losses from sweatshop regulation.

Once one rejects counting everyone's welfare equally, one does not have to take the polar opposite position that only the welfare of the least well-off counts. Perhaps, a more consistent line of reasoning would conclude that any gains or losses matter more the poorer the person experiencing them is? That standard could justify excluding the welfare of the rich people residing in the First World. But, since sweatshop workers usually have much higher living standards than many of the people living in the countries where they operate, such a standard would also have to weigh the income losses for those who become unemployed (and those who they then compete with in non-sweatshop labor markets) more heavily than the gains to those workers who remain employed after the regulation is implemented.

A complimentary line of reasoning might posit that a given dollar of income would generate more utility the lower the income of the person receiving it is. If this is assumed, then the income losses for the poor who are harmed by sweatshop regulations would again count more heavily than the income gains for those who remain employed. Welfare, as measured this way, could decrease even if total income in the poorer country increased because of sweatshop regulation.

It only seems logical to count the income losses for the poorest more heavily than any income gains for the relatively better-off workers, once one has already abandoned counting the income (or welfare) of everyone equally, by excluding gains or losses of the relatively rich in the First World.

When Do People Count?

What is the appropriate time horizon for evaluating costs and benefits? It would be odd to employ any welfare standard that cares about the world's poor today but not their welfare a year from today. Similarly, why shouldn't their welfare, and their children's welfare, be counted 20 or 30 years or more down the line. It is obviously appropriate to use a discount rate to discount future costs or benefits, compared to those achievable today. Chapters 9 and 10 will argue that the process of economic development has been the most important factor in improving sweatshop working conditions and lifting workers out of poverty. Those chapters argue that sweatshop regulations slow, and can even halt, that process of development. Even if there were small short-run welfare gains that could be achieved through some regulation, those gains would have to be compared with any slowing of the dramatic overall changes in living standards achieved through economic development. It would seem that at most plausible discount rates, any decreases in economic development because of sweatshop regulations would likely create welfare losses that dwarf any gain that could possibly be achieved in the short run.

Where Do People Count?

If a minimum wage increase is mandated in Indonesia, which poor workers' welfare counts? Just Indonesians? Philosophers Mathew Coakley and Michael Kates point out that when factories relocate, in response to an increase in the Indonesian minimum wage, some might relocate to other poorer countries. Thus, measuring only Indonesian worker welfare misses the welfare gains to other poor workers who should also count.[69] Fair enough. But embracing this line of reasoning has other important implications.

First, given the trade-offs and welfare considerations outlined in this chapter, honesty requires advocates of, say, an Indonesian minimum wage increase to explicitly admit that they favor a minimum wage increase because they weigh the benefits it will create for poorer Bangladeshi workers more highly than the losses suffered by Indonesians. I know of no anti-sweatshop scholar who has admitted this trade-off and embraced it.

Second, if promoting the welfare of Bangladeshi workers is the goal, what welfare standard dictates that it should come at the expense of other poor, but slightly better-off, Indonesian workers? Wouldn't one instead favor imposing harsher anti-competitive restrictions on even wealthier workers in the First World? Perhaps an international ban on producing apparel in the First World? Then, both poor Bangladeshi workers and poor Indonesian workers would benefit, rather than harming workers in one of these countries for the benefit of workers in the other.

[69] Coakley and Kates, "Ethical and Economic Case for Sweatshop Regulation," 555.

Some advocates of sweatshop labor might mistakenly take this argument as a case for international sweatshop regulations that proportionately impact all Third World countries rather than regulating sweatshops on a country-by-country basis. An international regulation that eliminated the ability of firms to secure greater profits by moving between Third World countries, in order to avoid the cost of sweatshop regulations, would only lead to greater substitution of First World workers and capital for Third World workers. Thus, an international regulatory regime may lead to less switching of production between Third World countries, but it would also cause greater welfare losses to the poor than when a single Third World country regulates sweatshops, when employing any welfare standard that takes into account all of the workers in the Third World.

Final Thoughts

There is no single objective scientific way to measure "welfare." Such measurements are more art than science. A measure of welfare can always be constructed in such a way that the person constructing it can reach whatever conclusion they desire. But not all art is equal. Good art incorporates the science that establishes the trade-offs that policies confront. Good art should have compelling reasons anytime it weighs the gains and losses to people differently. In the case of sweatshop regulation, it is certainly plausible to weigh the income changes to the poor more heavily than the income changes to the wealthy. But once that is done, it would seem that good art should also weigh the income changes to the extremely poor who lose their sweatshop jobs more heavily than the changes to the less poor sweatshop workers who keep their jobs. Good art recognizes both current costs and benefits and future costs and benefits and discounts accordingly.

The rest of this book will argue that, once the trade-offs associated with sweatshop regulation are correctly understood, most (all?) renderings of a reasonable standard of "worker welfare" should lead one to conclude that such regulations harm the welfare of the very people they are intended to help.

4

Don't Cry for Me Kathie Lee

How Sweatshop Wages Compare with Alternatives

The national media spotlight focused on sweatshops in 1996 after Charles Kernaghan of the National Labor Committee accused Kathie Lee Gifford of exploiting children in Honduran sweatshops. He flew a 15-year-old worker, Wendy Diaz, to the United States to meet Kathie Lee. Kathie Lee exploded into tears and apologized on the air, promising to pay higher wages.

Should Kathie Lee have cried? Wendy reportedly earned 31 cents per hour. Assuming that Wendy worked six days per week for 10 hours per day, which is not uncommon in a sweatshop, she would have earned $967 over the course of a year. That translates into approximately $2.75 per day to live on. Yet, in 1996, more than 15 percent of Hondurans lived on less than $1 per day, and nearly 30 percent lived on less than $2 per day. Wendy's income was not just higher than that of people in extreme poverty; it was $262 above the average income in Honduras that year.

Wendy Diaz's message should have been, "Don't cry for me, Kathie Lee. Cry for the Hondurans not fortunate enough to work for you." Instead, all too often, people in the United States compared 31 cents per hour to US alternatives, not Honduran alternatives. But US alternatives are irrelevant. Unfortunately, no one is offering these workers green cards. The real question is how the jobs compare with other domestically available alternatives.

When economists have defended sweatshops, they have often compared a sweatshop job to a much worse alternative such as prostitution, scavenging, or agricultural work. This chapter systematically examines sweatshop wages and compares them to the relevant available alternatives.[1]

[1] Benjamin Powell and David Skarbek, "Sweatshop Wages and Third World Workers: Are the Jobs Worth the Sweat?" *Journal of Labor Research* 27, No. 2 (2006), was the

THE SWEATSHOP JOBS

Sweatshops were described in the introduction to this book as places with pay well below levels in the developed world, where hours are often long and unpredictable, where there is a high risk of injury on the job, and where working conditions are generally unhealthy. Other characteristics might include a lack of lunch or bathroom breaks, verbal abuse, mandatory overtime, or the breaking of local labor laws. Although this general description encompasses much of what people think of when they hear of a "sweatshop," it doesn't get us very far in developing a specific list of sweatshops to compare with available alternatives.

No nice, neat international database of "sweatshop jobs" is available to download and compare with the alternatives. Indeed.com doesn't have a "sweatshop" category either. Using the above criteria to identify sweatshops leaves us with more questions than answers. Just how low does the wage have to be for the factory to be considered a sweatshop? How many of the poor working conditions must be present, and how bad do those conditions have to be? Should we stick only to cases in which ILO core labor standards are broken? Or only to cases in which local labor laws are broken? Ultimately, any line set would be a bit arbitrary and would open the door for accusations of defining sweatshops in such a way as to bias the result when they are compared with other alternatives.

As an alternative to creating a set definition of a sweatshop and then identifying firms that qualify, this chapter uses popular news sources to identify sweatshops. We used the EBSCOhost database and searched for the phrases "sweatshops AND wages," and synonyms for these such as replacing "wages" with "salaries" or dollar signs, in English-language newspapers around the globe. The criterion for inclusion in our dataset was simple: Every time a reporter referred to a factory in a Third World country as a "sweatshop," and reported wages in the same article, it was included in our dataset.[2] The one exception to this criterion was if it was

---

first research to systematically compare sweatshop jobs with their alternatives. The first edition of this book followed the same methodology and updated their data with instances of sweatshops through 2010. This edition follows these same methods for the most recent decade using data and calculations from Towhid Mahmood and Benjamin Powell, "No Sweat? Living Standards and Sweatshop Wages in Developing Countries," *The Independent Review* (2024).

[2] We eliminated stories reporting sweatshop wages in countries in Europe as well as in the North America as what is considered a "sweatshop" in developed countries is considerably different, in terms of the absolute level of wages and working conditions, from those termed a "sweatshop" in less developed countries.

apparent that firms, or governments, were using the threat of violence to coerce workers into working in a sweatshop. These are instances of slave labor and there is no reason to believe that these jobs might be superior to other available alternatives. If they were, companies wouldn't need to threaten violence to convince workers to take and keep the jobs. Slave labor sweatshop jobs, and how appropriate responses to them differ from normal sweatshop jobs, are analyzed in Chapter 11.

This empirical method of identifying sweatshops has one main advantage: It includes every newsworthy instance of a job in the Third World that someone in the First World has thought deplorable enough to call a sweatshop. Thus, the sample is not biased to exclude either the worst of the worst or the best of the worst. However, this method does have three drawbacks. The first limitation stems from our limited ability to know how the reported wages were calculated. The wages are mostly reported in US dollars, British pounds, or euros, while they were rarely reported in the local currencies the workers were actually paid with. Thus, we do not know the methods used by the reporters to convert local wages into those which they reported. In this chapter, all wages are reported in dollars for comparison purposes. When wages were quoted in currencies other than dollars in our primary sources, they were converted into dollars using the applicable exchange rate of the date the article was published. Furthermore, the wages were mostly reported in either hourly, daily, weekly, or monthly rates. Yet workers are sometimes paid in piece rates and the assumptions made by reporters converting them into rates reported by work duration are unknown. Although these limitations decrease the precision of the data, they should not systematically bias the data in any particular direction.

The news sources themselves are representative of the industry in general, with high-circulation mainstream papers and magazines from around the English-speaking world included in our data. However, a second drawback to our method is that, to the extent that reporters search for more sensational stories to generate media traffic, they may overreport on the most extreme sweatshops, while underreporting about more typical sweatshops. To the extent this happens, it would bias the findings to understate how well sweatshops compare with the relevant alternatives.

The third limitation stems from the sources used by the news reporters. Reporters often interview anti-sweatshop activists and use these activists' claims to report the wages paid by sweatshops. To the extent that activists want to illustrate how poorly paid sweatshop work might be, they may choose to use the least charitable way to convert piece rates to hourly rates, or to reference the wages of the poorest paid worker in a firm rather than a more representative worker. This bias may lead reports to understate typical sweatshop wages, and thus, our comparisons in the subsequent section might be considered lower-bound estimates. However, as we will see, even with these potential biases, sweatshop wages often compare favorably with the relevant alternatives.

There were 62 unique cases of reported sweatshop wages across 14 less developed countries from 2010 through 2019. The previous edition of this book found 85 unique cases of sweatshop wages reported between 1995 and 2010. This chapter compares sweatshop wages to the alternatives over the most recent decade. Chapter 9 makes use of the earlier data to examine how sweatshop earnings have evolved over the recent decades. All the reported sweatshops included in this chapter are located in either Asia or Latin America, except for Mauritius. Table 4.1 contains these cases of reported sweatshops, their wages, and,

TABLE 4.1 *Sweatshop wages, in US dollars, reported in the press, 2011–2019*

Country	Year	Firm/company	Per	Reported wage
Bangladesh	2012	Adidas	Hour	0.25
Bangladesh	2012	Walmart	Hour	0.18
Bangladesh	2013		Hour	0.24
Bangladesh	2013		Month	40
Bangladesh	2013		Month	52
Bangladesh	2013		Month	32
Bangladesh	2013		Day	1
Bangladesh	2013		Month	38
Bangladesh	2013		Month	37
Bangladesh	2013		Month	64
Bangladesh	2013		Month	37
Bangladesh	2013	Primark, The Edinburgh Woollen Mill, Oliver, Haggar, and Bootlegger	Hour	0.2
Bangladesh	2013	Smart Fashion Export	Hour	0.13
Bangladesh	2013	Walmart and Gap	Hour	0.06
Bangladesh	2014		Month	68
Bangladesh	2015		Hour	0.39
Bangladesh	2015	Russell Brand	Hour	0.38
Bangladesh	2016	Gildan	Hour	0.4
Bangladesh	2017		Month	113
Bangladesh	2017	Tesco and Asda	Hour	0.34
Cambodia	2013		Month	74

TABLE 4.1 *(cont.)*

Country	Year	Firm/company	Per	Reported wage
Cambodia	2013		Month	80
Cambodia	2013		Hour	0.45
Cambodia	2013		Month	75
Cambodia	2014		Month	80
Cambodia	2015	H&M	Hour	0.65
Cambodia	2016	H&M	Month	180
Cambodia	2018		Hour	0.83
China	2011	Adidas	Hour	0.51
China	2012	Golden Bear	Hour	0.5
China	2013		Hour	1.26
China	2013		Month	192
China	2014		Hour	1.25
China	2015		Hour	1.5
China	2016		Hour	0.53
China	2016	Apple	Month	312.99
China	2017		Hour	1
El Salvador	2013		Month	187
Haiti	2013	Gildan	Day	6.96
Haiti	2014	Gildan Activewear	Day	5.3
Haiti	2015		Day	4.71
Haiti	2015	Gildan	Hour	0.6
India	2012		Day	1.26
India	2013	Modalu London	Hour	0.27
Indonesia	2011		Day	2
Indonesia	2011	Nike	Hour	0.5
Indonesia	2012	Nike	Hour	1.42
Indonesia	2013		Month	120
Indonesia	2016	Nike	Day	3
Indonesia	2018	Adidas	Hour	1.27
Mauritius	2014	Compagnie Mauricienne de Textile (CMT), Topshop, Next, and Urban Outfitters	Hour	0.99
Myanmar	2013		Month	53
Myanmar	2015		Month	90
Nicaragua	2015	Gildan	Hour	0.75
Pakistan	2013		Hour	0.52
Pakistan	2014		Hour	0.53
Pakistan	2015		Month	39.71
Philippines	2015		Day	6.7
Philippines	2017		Day	5.6
Sri Lanka	2016	Ivy Park	Day	6.17
Vietnam	2013		Hour	0.53
Vietnam	2014		Hour	0.28

when available, the associated multinational brands. However, sweat-shops are often subcontractors selling to major multinational brands, so in many cases the articles did not identify which multinational the sweatshop was producing for.

As is evident from the table, the wages paid in these sweatshops are deplorably low by US standards. Hourly pay ranged from a low of six cents per hour in Bangladesh to a high of only $1.50 per hour in China. Unfortunately, when many people in the First World see these wages reported in the press, they conclude that these must be "bad" jobs. As the remainder of this chapter will demonstrate, nothing could be further from the truth. Although these wages are low by First World standards, they are high compared to what can be earned in many of the jobs available in the countries where sweatshops are located.

COMPARING SWEATSHOP WAGES WITH DOMESTIC ALTERNATIVES

As bad as sweatshop jobs are, of course they look good when compared with dire alternatives such as prostitution, begging, or starvation. But in most cases, people who lose their job in a sweatshop won't end up in these dire alternatives. If anti-sweatshop activism leads to job losses in targeted sweatshops, the relevant alternative for many of these workers could be a return to informal sector work, and the associated poverty living standards, or agricultural employment. Sweatshop jobs need to be compared with these common alternatives.

Widespread extreme poverty is common in many countries where sweatshops are located. The World Bank tracks data on the percentage of a country's population that lives on less than $2.15, $3.65, and $6.85 per day. Of course, because a dollar will buy more in one country than it will in another, the World Bank adjusts the figures for purchasing power parity (PPP), so that the figures it reports represent the same standard of living across countries. As Figure 4.1 illustrates, a large portion of the population in countries with sweatshops lives in extreme poverty.

More than 10 percent of the population lives on less than $3.65 per day in all the countries where sweatshop wages are reported except for Mauritius and Vietnam (where 9.5 percent of the population lived on less than $3.65 per day). Roughly 40 percent of the population lived on less than the $3.65 per day standard in more than a third of the countries. Extreme poverty is most prevalent in Bangladesh, Haiti, and India, where more than half the population lives below this standard. At the relatively

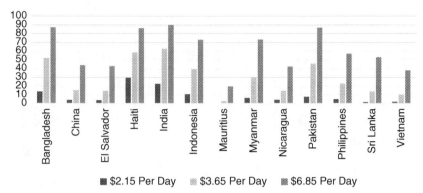

FIGURE 4.1 Percentage of population living on less than $2.15, $3.85, and $6.85 per day (PPP)

higher $6.85 per day wage, more than 40 percent of the populations lived below this standard in more than three-quarters of the countries.

To compare living standards provided by sweatshops with these extreme poverty thresholds, the sweatshop wages reported in Table 4.1 were converted to average daily income and adjusted for PPP. A 60-hour, 6-day work week was assumed to calculate annual income based on the reported wages and then divided by 365 to get average daily income. The 60-hour estimate was used because most of the articles do not report hours worked. Out of the 62 unique cases, 13 reported daily working hours, but only 6 of those also included the number of days worked. These articles report an average of 10.8 hours per day worked and, for those that specified the number of days, an average of 63 hours worked per week. An additional eight articles simply reported weekly working hours that averaged 55.1 hours. Twelve articles in total mentioned the number of days worked, and all but one reported six days, the exception being seven days. We choose the 60-hour assumption to calculate comparisons because it is a focal approximate midpoint for the roughly quarter of the cases where we have some indication of the number of hours worked. These wages are reported in Figure 4.2.

Contrary to claims that sweatshop "workers are still being paid a poverty wage" by activists like Jim Keady, the sweatshop jobs studied here compare quite favorably to the abject poverty in these countries.[3] The average annual wage in reported sweatshops was more than the

---

[3] Jim Keady, "When Will Nike 'Just Do It' on the Sweatshop Issue?" *Huffington Post*, October 2, 2009.

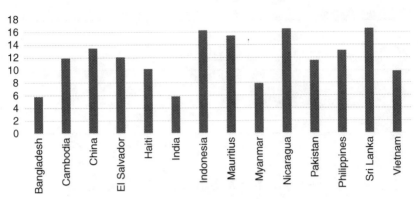

FIGURE 4.2 Average sweatshop earnings per day (US dollars, PPP)

$6.85 poverty threshold in every country except Bangladesh and India, where the living standards of 87 and 89 percent of the populations, respectively, fail to exceed this threshold. The average sweatshop living standard was $5.81 per day in Bangladesh and $5.83 in India, while more than half of the populations in both countries lived on an average of less than the $3.65 per day.

These averages are not obscuring the very low pay in some sweatshops relative to extreme poverty standards. Out of the 62 reported sweatshop cases, only one reported a daily wage less than $2.15 and only four reported daily wages between $2.15 and $3.65. Out of those five cases, four are in Bangladesh, where more than 50 percent of the population made less than $3.65 a day. The other individual sweatshop wage reported below $3.65 was in India, paying $3.62 and barely missing the cutoff, while more than 60 percent of the population lives below that standard.

Sweatshop earnings overwhelmingly lift their workers above common poverty living standards in the countries where they operate if their workers are only supporting themselves. When sweatshop workers are young and childless, or children themselves, as both are common, directly comparing their earnings to poverty standards is a good indication of a sweatshop worker's living standards. However, in cases where some portion of their wages support other dependents, these comparisons overstate their living standards.

A return to agricultural sector employment is a common alternative available for many displaced sweatshop workers. In most of the countries where sweatshops were reported, a large share of the population works in agriculture. Workers in the ready-made-garment industry, where sweatshops operate, are often women from rural areas where

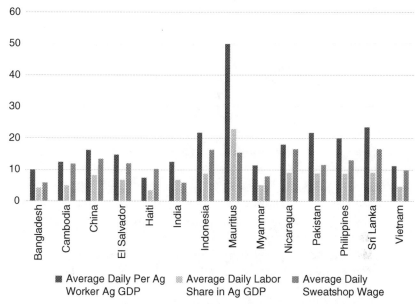

FIGURE 4.3 Alternative daily wages in agriculture (US dollars, PPP)

agricultural work is common.[4] More than 40 percent of the population works in agriculture in Bangladesh, Cambodia, India, Myanmar,
Pakistan, and Vietnam. Only 2 countries, out of 14 with sweatshops
reported, have less than 25 percent of the population employed in agriculture. Figure 4.3 compares the same daily sweatshop wage estimates
above with potential agricultural earnings. Unfortunately, there is not
systematic data on labor's share of output specifically within the agricultural sector across these countries, so an upper- and (more accurate)
lower-bound estimate are reported. The first bar for each country in
Figure 4.3 reports the daily dollar value of output per worker in agriculture. This number is simply the total dollar value of agricultural GDP
divided by the number of agricultural workers and then converted to a
daily rate. If there were no other factors of production, such as land and
physical capital, earning a return in the agricultural sector, this would
represent earnings for the workers. However, obviously land and physical capital, and other factors of production, do earn a return in agriculture. The second bar for each country multiplies the value of agricultural

---

[4] Faisal Ahmed, Anne Greenleaf, and Audrey Sacks, "The Paradox of Export Growth
in Areas of Weak Governance: The Case of the Ready Made Garment Sector in
Bangladesh," *World Development* 56 (2014), 258–271.

output per worker by labor's share of total GDP in each country. To the extent that labor earns a similar percentage of agricultural output as it does in other sectors, this measure roughly captures daily agricultural wages. To the extent that agriculture is more labor-intensive and is relatively undercapitalized, actual wages would be higher than this estimate; thus, it is a lower-bound estimate. Of our two estimates, this second one is closer to actual agricultural worker earnings.

Average sweatshop earnings are higher than average agricultural earnings in 12 of the 14 countries when agricultural earnings are estimated by adjusting for labor's share of the output. In those 12 countries, sweatshop earnings exceeded agricultural earnings by an average of 86 percent. In Cambodia, Haiti, and Vietnam, sweatshop earnings averaged twice the level of agricultural earnings. Pakistan had the smallest gap between sweatshop earnings and agricultural earnings among those 12 countries at 30 percent. Agricultural earnings exceeded average sweatshop earnings only in Mauritius and India. Mauritius is a relatively rich outlier among the countries in our sample and will be discussed further later in the chapter. Agricultural earnings in India exceeded average sweatshop earnings by 14 percent – the smallest difference in earnings among the 14 countries. Overall, sweatshop wages compare favorably with earnings in agriculture.

Although earnings in a targeted sweatshop usually exceed extreme poverty standards or agricultural earnings, it is also useful to compare these earnings with average living standards to see how far short, if at all, the sweatshop earnings fall compared with average income per capita.

To make this comparison we converted reported daily earnings into annual income assuming a 6-day work week and wages reported as weekly or monthly were multiplied by 52 and 12, respectively. Hourly data was converted using four different assumptions about the number of hours worked per week: 40, 50, 60, or 70 hours. Of course, long working hours are one of the characteristics of sweatshops, so the 60- and 70-hour work week estimates are the most relevant, based on the subset of these articles that reported hours worked. Since sweatshop wages were reported across nine years, we averaged the per capita GDP reported across each year a sweatshop was reported in that country, weighted to account for years when multiple sweatshops were reported.[5]

---

[5] For example, if there are two sweatshops reported in 2012, one in 2015, and another one in 2017 for a country the average GDP is calculated by adding the per capita GDP for the country in 2012 twice, for 2015 once, and for 2017 once and dividing the sum by four.

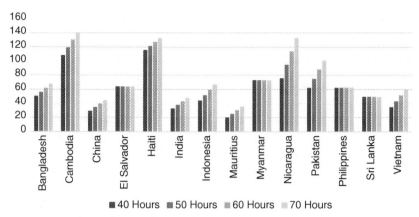

FIGURE 4.4 Annual sweatshop earnings as a percentage of average income, by country

Figure 4.4 reports the average annual sweatshop earnings as a percentage of per capita GDP for each country. Although the results are less dramatic than when compared with abject poverty, sweatshop jobs still compare well with the average income in most of these countries. Although average income per capita might be a high bar to compare sweatshop earnings with, in Cambodia, Haiti, Nicaragua, and Pakistan sweatshop jobs earn more than average GDP per capita, with realistic assumptions about the number of hours worked. It's no wonder that Paul Collier endorsed a sweatshop model of development for Haiti after a disastrous hurricane struck in 2010. In Bangladesh, El Salvador, Indonesia, and Myanmar sweatshop workers earn between 60 and 80 percent of the average income, while sweatshop workers in China, India, the Philippines, Sri Lanka, and Vietnam workers all earn about 40 to 60 percent of the national average.

The only remaining country, Mauritius, where sweatshop workers earn only about 20 percent of average GDP per capita, is an outlier among these countries in that it has considerably higher living standards than the rest of them, with GDP per capita averaging more than $18,000. In the case of Mauritius, the reported sweatshops were employing immigrants from Bangladesh, India, and Vietnam. Although low by Mauritian standards, the reported sweatshop earnings were high by the standards of these migrants' origin countries, averaging 164 percent of Bangladesh's average income, 113 percent of India's, and 81 percent of Vietnam's.

China, although not an extreme outlier like Mauritius, has lower sweatshop earnings as a percentage of average income than most of the other countries. Many of these sweatshop workers are Chinese, but, in China, internal migration plays a role in depressing the statistics. China has large income inequalities between regions and the massive movement of people from low-productivity rural areas to large cities that have sweatshops has spurred China's development.[6] In the years since market reforms began, more than 260 million migrants moved from rural to urban centers in China. If Chinese sweatshop earnings were compared with average earnings in rural inland provinces, where many of the workers migrate from, rather than the national average, the result would look much like what we see for the international migrants to Mauritius.

It's worth noting that the low average incomes in these countries do not reflect the median wage job since the average income is pulled upward by the small portion of the very rich people in these countries. It's also important to keep in mind that just because a job falls below average, doesn't mean it is a bad job *for the worker who chooses it*. By definition, many of the jobs in any economy must pay less than the average job. The key, as explained in Chapter 3, is that workers choose the best alternative available to them. These comparisons illustrate that not only are sweatshop jobs the best available for the individual worker but, in many cases, are better than alternatives available to the vast majority of the people in the country where the reported sweatshop is located.

CONCLUSION

Working in a sweatshop producing clothes for Kathie Lee Gifford raised Wendy Diaz's standard of living above that of many Hondurans who earned less than $2 per day. In fact, Wendy earned more than the average Honduran that year. The Kathie Lee Gifford case is not an outlier. It is the norm.

Workers in firms accused of being sweatshops almost universally earn more than common extreme poverty standards. However, large portions of the population in each of the countries where sweatshops are located live on less than these poverty thresholds. Similarly, sweatshop earnings exceeded average agricultural earnings in 12 of the

---

[6] See Bradley Gardner, *China's Great Migration: How the Poor Built a Prosperous Nation* (Oakland, CA: The Independent Institute, 2017).

14 countries where sweatshops were reported. It's no surprise that people often leave rural farms for factory work. Working in a sweatshop in four of these countries results in workers earning more than their average national income, and sweatshop earnings in the rest of the countries aren't drastically below average. In short, these sweatshop jobs pay wages that aren't just superior to earnings from begging or prostitution. They pay better than many of the other opportunities available to sweatshop workers and make these workers better off than many of their fellow countrymen.

If the wages are superior to other opportunities, then activists might naturally ask if they should turn their attention to improving other working conditions instead. Let's turn to that question now.

5

Health, Safety, and Working Conditions Laws

Sweatshop critics are often more upset about the conditions under which the workers toil than they are concerned about the wages the workers are paid. Sometimes sweatshop critics even admit that the wages are better than alternative available employment and make the working conditions their sole focus.[1]

A November 2012 factory fire in Bangladesh sparked worldwide outrage over safety conditions. The Tarzeen factory, which made clothes for Walmart and Disney, was denied a renewal of its fire safety certificate the previous June because of safety violations but it continued operating without the certificate. Then tragedy struck when a fire ripped through the eight-story building killing 112 garment workers who were trapped inside. Subsequent investigations found that a quarter of the factories operating in the industrial zone where Tarzeen was located lacked fire safety certificates. The executive director of the Bangladesh Center for Worker Solidarity, Kalpona Aktar, spoke what many felt when she said, "These factories should be shut down."[2] But, as tragic as this fire was, is she right? Would workers be better off if factories that don't comply with safety standards are prohibited?

Critics are correct that working conditions in sweatshops are often horrid compared to those in the United States. Fires like the one at

---

[1] For instance, Bama Athreya, from the International Labor Rights Fund, admitted that wages in sweatshops were typically higher than in domestic industry but argued that the working conditions need to be addressed in a public debate with me at Grand Valley State, December 1, 2008.

[2] Associated Press, "Factory in Bangladesh Lost Fire Clearance before Blaze," *New York Times*, December 7, 2012, retrieved from www.nytimes.com/2012/12/08/world/asia/bangladesh-factory-where-dozens-died-was-illegal.html?_r=0.

Tarzeen are an extreme case, but other conditions are also poor. Workers can be at risk of on-the-job injuries from dangerous machines. Sometimes air quality is poor and could lead to long-term health problems. The ILO estimates that 6,300 people die every day, more than 2.3 million per year, as a result of occupational accidents or work-related diseases.[3] Sometimes it is the other general working conditions that are bad. Factories may be crowded, dirty, and hot. Hours can be long, breaks short or nonexistent, overtime mandatory and unpredictable. Vacations, paid or otherwise, might not be allowed. Six-day work weeks are common, and some people work seven. Often, legally mandated benefits are not provided.

As bad as working conditions are in sweatshops, much like wages, the conditions in alternative employment are often worse. For example, although conditions in Cambodian sweatshops can be poor, the alternative of scavenging in the Phnom Penh garbage dump is much worse. *New York Times* columnist Nicholas Kristof reports that the dump is a "Dante-like vision of hell. It's a mountain of festering refuse, a half hour hike across, emitting clouds of smoke from subterranean fires."[4] Yet small barefoot children scavenge for old plastic cups that they can sell for five cents a pound. Kristof interviewed 19-year-old Pim Srey Rath, who was scavenging in the dump. She said, "I'd loved to get a job in a factory. At least that work is in the shade. Here is where it is hot." Thirteen-year-old scavenger Neuo Chanthou, whose sister lost part of her hand when a garbage truck ran over her, sums up the situation concisely by saying, "It's dirty, hot, and smelly here. A factory is better."

Activists again must be careful not to advocate for changes that may eliminate lousy sweatshop working conditions and throw workers into even worse conditions elsewhere. Dan Viederman, the CEO of Verité, an NGO "committed to ensuring that people in factories and farms work under safe, fair, and legal conditions," makes an argument that is typical of anti-sweatshop activists. He wrote, "I'm always amazed to come across opinion pieces that claim sweatshops are good for workers."[5] Why? Because sweatshop defenders "don't mention whether or not there are minimum standards that the job should meet. This is a

[3] ILO, Safety and Health at Work, retrieved from www.ilo.org/global/topics/safety-and-health-at-work/lang--en/index.htm.
[4] Nicolas Kristof, "Where Sweatshops Are a Dream," *New York Times*, January 14, 2009.
[5] Dan Viederman, "Any Job Is a Good Job? Think Again," *Huffington Post*, February 18, 2011.

pretty massive oversight."[6] Viederman claims to solve the problem for us: "Luckily for the pro-sweatshop crowd, there are already widely accepted ways of deciding whether a job is good enough, and whether kids are acceptable employees, so they won't have to think too hard about these complicated problems. These are the international standards of the International Labor Organization."[7] Rather than accept Viederman's suggestion, I invite you to think hard about these complicated problems. The remainder of this chapter examines whether mandating ILO working condition regulations would improve the lives of sweatshop workers or not.

Chapters 3 and 4 focused mostly on how wages were determined and how sweatshop wages compared with alternative employment. But when workers choose to work for a firm, they obviously also take working conditions into account too. Employees care about how much they are paid but also whether their job is safe and the conditions pleasant. Thus, a dangerous job, all else equal, demands a higher wage to attract workers.[8]

Consider dangerous professions in the United States. Jobs in fishing, mining, and truck driving all pay well considering the typical level of education of the workers. But all are relatively dangerous professions compared to US alternatives.[9] As a result, they must pay more to attract enough workers. However, the level of safety in these jobs is much higher in the United States than it is in other countries. In mining, for instance, the death rate per ton of coal extracted is 100 times lower in the United States than it is in China.[10] If the US conditions were as unsafe as the Chinese conditions, wages would need to go even higher to attract workers. Thought of differently, relatively wealthy workers in the United States "buy" better safety conditions by sacrificing wages. Relatively less productive Chinese workers cannot afford that level of safety.

Some critics of sweatshops want to separate the analysis of wages from the analysis of working conditions.[11] Some will admit that mandating higher wages may result in unemployment but want to maintain that

---

[6] Ibid.

[7] Ibid.

[8] Michael Moore and Kip Viscusi, *Compensation Mechanisms for Job Risks* (Princeton: Princeton University Press, 1990).

[9] See Tom Van Riper, "America's Most Dangerous Jobs," *Forbes*, August 13, 2007, retrieved from www.forbes.com/2007/08/13/dangerous-jobs-fishing-lead-careers-cx_tvr_0813danger.html, for a list of the most dangerous professions in the United States.

[10] Tyler Cowen and Alex Tabarrok, *The New Principles* (New York: Worth, 2009).

[11] Arnold and Hartman, "Worker Rights," is an example.

health and safety can be improved without unemploying workers. This is not true. The two are jointly determined.

Compensation can be paid directly as wages or indirectly as benefits, which may include health, safety, comfort, longer breaks, and fewer working hours. Some indirect payments can raise worker productivity. Obviously, employing healthy workers who can perform their jobs positively impacts profits. Some firms may choose to provide subsidized lunches, health care, and on-the-job safety that increases worker productivity. In fact, it is in firms' best interests to contribute indirect compensation that raises productivity. However, if these benefits cost more than the revenue gain from increased productivity, then firms do not increase their profits by providing these forms of compensation. In these cases, the firm regards such benefits as costs that come off their bottom line, just like wages. A profit-maximizing firm is indifferent to compensating workers with pay or with health, safety, leisure, and comfort benefits of the same cost, when productivity is unaffected. The firm simply cares about the overall cost of the total compensation package.

Workers, on the other hand, do care about the mix of compensation they receive. When overall compensation goes up, workers are more likely to desire more nonmonetary benefits. Comfort and safety are what economists call "normal goods" for most people. Workers demand more of these goods as their income increases. Unfortunately, many workers have low productivity, so their overall compensation level is low. Ask yourself, if you were desperately trying to feed, clothe, and shelter yourself and your family, what portion of your compensation would you want in wages versus better working conditions. Their dire circumstances lead sweatshop workers to demand most of their meager compensation in wages and little in health or safety improvements. This is why US miners "buy" more safety than Chinese miners.

This presents a problem for those who wish to separate safety and working conditions from pay. Both are limited by the same factor – the worker's marginal revenue product. Firms are indifferent about whether to pay monetary wages or in-kind benefits after adjusting for those benefits that improve productivity. Workers do care about the mix. As such, firms' profit incentive causes them to provide the mix of benefits and wages that their average worker desires to attract the best employees possible. If employers offer a mix of compensation and working conditions that does not match employee preferences, then firms are paying more for the compensation than the value the employee attaches to the overall compensation. A profit-maximizing firm can adjust the mix and lower its cost while still giving employees the same level of satisfaction. This means that the mix of compensation is really driven by employee preferences (limited by their overall productivity), not by the preferences of multinational corporations or their subcontractors.

Scholars have found plenty of empirical evidence that supports this economic theory. Economists Pavel Yakovlev and Russell Sobel studied injury rates in 353 industries in the United States from 1977 to 1989. Because firms face higher wages and injury-related costs when safety is low, it "means that labor is relatively more costly than capital in these industries once the cost of injuries is factored in. This gives firms an incentive to find and adopt new capital and technologies that reduce worker exposure to danger and lead to lower injury rates over time."[12] Empirically, this is just what they find. Industries that had higher injury rates tended to employ more capital relative to labor over time and injuries went down as a result because fewer workers were exposed to risks and those who remained exposed faced lower levels of risk.

Economist Price Fishback also found that compensating differentials played a role in worker pay when regulations were few and sweatshops were more prevalent in the United States.[13] He surveyed the literature on turn-of-the-century labor markets. At the time, common law entitled worker's families to compensation if they died on the job. Most families received that compensation without going to court and the death benefit averaged about a half-year's income.[14] To supplement the relatively low post-fatality benefit, workers in jobs with a higher risk of death were paid higher wages. Depending on the industry, the higher wages paid to workers implied that they valued their lives between approximately $38,000 and $1.5 million (in 2020 dollars).[15] Furthermore, Fishback finds that, just as theory predicts, when "workers' compensation laws raised post-accident benefits, wages adjusted downward."[16]

[12] Pavel Yakovlev and Russell S. Sobel, "Occupational Safety and Profit Maximization: Friends or Foes?" *Journal of Socio-Economics* 39, No. 3 (June 2010), 435.

[13] Price Fishback, "Operations of 'Unfettered' Labor Markets: Exit and Voice in American Labor Markets at the Turn of the Century," *Journal of Economic Literature* 36, No. 2 (June 1998), 722–765.

[14] Ibid., 735.

[15] Ibid. These dollar amounts are not the actual extra wages employees receive. They instead take into account the probability of a fatality and the extra wages received to see what price the workers themselves implicitly put on their lives when they agreed to the job with a risk of death.

[16] Ibid., 735–738.

What about sexual harassment in sweatshops? Numerous anti-sweatshop groups claim that female workers face sexual harassment ranging from verbal harassment to demands of sexual favors. For example, Bangalore ActionAid worker Malagi Christopher has heard terrible stories of harassment.[17] The *Daily Mail* reports that he's heard about a supervisor asking a woman for a condom and to sleep with him. "Another asked a girl, when she went to the toilet, if he could join her. Other women have been shown obscene photographs. They are often too scared to refuse the men's demands."[18] Similarly, Claudia Molina, a young Honduran worker, reported that her supervisors harassed the workers. "Sometimes they touch our breasts or buttocks, especially late at night, when we are sleepy."[19]

If the risk of sexual harassment is part of the working conditions at a factory, then firms have to offer higher wages to attract workers. This is precisely what Professor Joni Hersch found when studying US labor markets. She examined sexual harassment claims and wages by industry and found that women were paid higher wages in industries in which they were at a greater risk of sexual harassment. She concluded that workers receive a wage premium for exposure to the risk of sexual harassment "in much the same way that workers receive a wage premium for the risk of fatality or injury."[20] In short, the analysis of sexual harassment on the job is much the same as the analysis of other working conditions. Laws that effectively eliminate sexual harassment would lower wages. If employees desired this, then market forces would remix the compensation package to minimize harassment, while lowering wages. Claudia Molina, for example, earned $30 per week, which doesn't sound like a lot, but it amounts to an annual income of more than double the Honduran average. Some amount of that wage premium is likely a compensating differential for a greater risk of harassment.

Activists naïvely assume that demanding better working conditions will improve the lives of workers. Unfortunately, they are wrong.

---

[17] ActionAid is an anti-poverty organization with a variety of campaigns. Though far from their only focus, they are often critical of sweatshops.

[18] Natalie Clarke, "The True Price of the £6 Dress," *The Daily Mail*, September 13, 2007, retrieved from www.dailymail.co.uk/femail/article-481538/The-true-price-6-dress.html.

[19] Anne-Marie O'Connor, "The Plight of Women around the World; Central America; Labor: Sweatshops Meet U.S. Consumer Demand," *The Atlanta Journal Constitution*, September 3, 1995.

[20] Joni Hersch, "Compensating Differentials for Sexual Harassment," *American Economic Review Papers and Proceedings* (May 2011), retrieved from http://papers.ssrn.com/sol3/papers.cfm?abstract_id=1743691.

Improving working conditions raises firms' cost of hiring labor. The firm can respond to demands for improved working conditions in one of three ways. First, just as when higher wages are mandated, the firm can cut back on the number of workers it employs, which throws some workers into worse alternatives. Second, depending on the particular demands, the firm may improve some working conditions while making other conditions worse. For example, when confronted with demands for increased safety, the firm may compensate by requiring longer hours. Third, when working conditions improve, the firm can lower the wage necessary to attract employees.[21] The first of these responses is obviously bad for workers, but the second two are as well because the mix of compensation is largely driven by employee preferences. Reshuffling the mix makes workers worse off. Calls from First World activists to improve working conditions are really attempts to impose the preferences of First World activists at the expense of the preferences of the very workers they are supposedly trying to help. This is precisely what I found when my coauthor, economist J. R. Clark, and I interviewed sweatshop workers in Guatemala.[22]

A SURVEY OF GUATEMALAN SWEATSHOPS

The National Labor Committee (NLC) investigates and exposes human and labor rights abuses committed by US companies producing goods in poorer countries. It has issued hundreds of reports alleging abusive sweatshop activities in dozens of countries. The NLC identified four Guatemalan firms as sweatshops between 2006 and 2009.[23] Two of the factories, Dong Bang and Fribo, closed before we could survey workers. In 2010, we surveyed a sample of workers from the remaining two factories, Sam Bridge S.A. and Nicotex.

Sam Bridge employed more than 1,000 workers and exported clothing to the United States with Briggs New York, Koret, JM Collection, and Pantalogy labels and produces uniforms for United Airlines. Sam

---

[21] For one example, see Robert Stern and Katherine Terrell, who find that raising the cost of labor through more stringent standards, particularly in developing countries where productivity is very low, leads to less employment, production, and income. "Labor Standards and the World Trade Organization," Discussion Paper No. 499 (paper presented at RSIE, University of Michigan, Ann Arbor, 2003).

[22] J. R. Clark and Benjamin Powell, "Sweatshop Working Conditions and Employee Welfare: Say It Ain't Sew," *Comparative Economics Studies* 55, No. 2 (2013), 343–357.

[23] A fifth firm, Legumex, was also identified by the NLC. We did not include Legumex in our study because it is an agro-industrial plant rather than an apparel producer.

Bridge was founded in 1993 and is located a short distance outside of Guatemala City on the Pan-American Highway.[24] Nicotex employed approximately 320 workers. About 80 percent of their production was for Briggs New York and the remaining 20 percent for Lane Bryant. It was opened in 2007 and was located in Mixco, a suburb of Guatemala City. Nicotex closed shortly after we surveyed its workers.

The NLC's complaints about Sam Bridge include inadequate wages, long work hours, unpredictable overtime, penalties for workers who refuse overtime, arbitrary production goals, verbal abuse of workers, limiting water and bathroom breaks, not paying severance to fired workers, and inadequate ventilation, lunch facilities, and medical care. The NLC succinctly summarized its view, writing, "Sam Bridge is definitely a sweatshop."[25] It released a report in February 2009 alleging that Nicotex was a harmful sweatshop. The list of complaints was similar: long and unpredictable hours, verbal abuse, inadequate wages, not paying bonus wages on time, not enrolling and paying for mandatory health care for all workers, and not giving mandated paid vacations. The NLC summarized its view, writing that there are "Illegal sweatshop conditions at the Nicotex factory."[26]

In May 2010, we surveyed a sample of 35 workers at each factory.[27] The NLC reports had complained that prior corporate audits were laughable: "Management chooses the workers who will speak with corporate auditors, and for this they pick the newest, youngest and most timid workers who do not know much about the factory and who are most frightened about being fired. This guarantees a short but shallow interview."[28] To avoid this problem, we did not obtain permission from either company to survey their workers. We hired a local firm, Aragón & Asociados, to randomly survey a subset of workers off company property.[29] The surveys were conducted before the factory opened,

[24] It was originally named Sam Lucas and again changed its name to SAM SOL but ownership has remained the same.
[25] Institute for Global Labour and Human Rights, "Alert – Violation of CAFTA at Sam Bridge SA Guatemala," October 21, 2007, retrieved from www.nlcnet.org/alerts?id=0072.
[26] See Institute for Global Labour and Human Rights, "Women Exploiting Women," February 25, 2009, retrieved from www.nlcnet.org/reports?id=0535, for their original report.
[27] Surveys were completed over a period of three days from May 19 to May 22.
[28] Institute for Global Labour and Human Rights, "Women Exploiting Women."
[29] Aragón y Associates is headquartered in Guatemala City. Founded in 1972, they have conducted more than 5,000 research studies that have analyzed or gathered the opinions of more than 2.5 million people across Central America, the Caribbean, and South America.

when workers left for lunch, and when they left the factory to go home. Complete anonymity was guaranteed to each worker who completed a survey. Our method allowed us to obtain more honest responses than we would have obtained had we gained approval from the companies. It also limited our sample to 35 workers at each firm because of the amount of time we felt we could survey workers without drawing undue attention. We have no reason to believe that the subset of workers we interviewed is not representative of the larger population of workers based on the demographic data and work experience of our interviewees.

The average worker we surveyed was 30 years old, while the youngest was 20 and the oldest 54 years old. Slightly more than half (52.9 percent) of our sample were males, and the average worker had worked for their company for 3.8 years, with the newest employee only having been on the job for two months, while the most senior had been there for 16 years. More than 61 percent of the people surveyed worked on the production line as apparel machine operators. An additional 8.5 percent each worked in product inspection, packing, or in a supervisory role.[30] Another 7 percent worked in pressing, while 6 percent worked in some other capacity. These numbers were fairly consistent across both Sam Bridge and Nicotex.[31]

The NLC complained that Sam Bridge employees had to work long hours – often 55 to 60 hours in a week, which includes mandatory overtime. The workers we surveyed estimated they worked 52 hours a week. Only 12.5 percent of workers desired to work longer hours. More importantly, 97 percent of workers said they would not be willing to earn less in order to have fewer hours. The hours may be long, but the workers are poor and desire the hours to earn more to help feed and clothe their families.

The NLC complained that Sam Bridge managers would curse and humiliate workers. The NLC reports that the supervisors taunt the workers, shouting: "Do you have garbage for brains?"; "Why can't you reach the goal… You're all like shit, like piss water"; and "It's easier to work with animals than you. You're good for nothing." However, when asked, "How would you rate how fairly the managers treat you," all the employees we surveyed reported chose "fairly" or "very fairly."

---

[30] Excluding the six employees who worked in some form of supervisory role doesn't significantly change any of our below results.
[31] The exceptions were that all of our supervisory workers and most packers worked for Sam Bridge, while most inspectors and pressers worked for Nicotex.

The NLC reported that managers told Sam Bridge employees that they only needed to use a bathroom once per 10-hour shift, but 91 percent of the workers surveyed reported they could go to the bathroom any time they wanted, and 6 percent said they could go up to four times per day. Only 3 percent of workers reported being limited to two bathroom breaks.

Other complaints by the NLC include a lack of fans, an inadequate medical clinic, and a lack of adequate space for employees to have lunch. Yet all the employees we surveyed reported that they were satisfied with their job. Most tellingly, all workers surveyed reported that they were unwilling to earn less to have more pleasant working conditions, and 97 percent were unwilling to earn less for safer working conditions.

The NLC complained that Nicotex had long mandatory overtime hours, and alleged it failed to register all of its workers for mandatory health care through the Guatemalan Institute of Social Security and that Nicotex was cheating workers out of their paid vacation. In addition to the legal 44-hour work week, "overtime work is common, obligatory and excessive, which is a violation of Guatemalan law. It is common for the women to be forced to work 20 to 25 hours of overtime a week."[32] Furthermore, "The workers are never notified of overtime in advance. Rather, management decides, often just 30 minutes before the shift's end, instructing the workers that they must stay."[33] Our survey revealed that Nicotex workers were averaging just over 59 hours a week. Importantly, nearly 83 percent of workers surveyed said they would not be willing to reduce the number of hours worked if it resulted in lower pay. In fact, 20 percent said they would like to work more hours. We also asked workers if they would be willing to accept lower pay if their employer made their hours more predictable. Nearly 86 percent said they would not.

Guatemalan law requires all employers to enroll their workers in the Guatemalan Institute of Social Security, which provides health and pension benefits. When workers are enrolled, 4.83 percent is deducted from their wages, and the employer contributes an additional 10.67 percent of their wages. When workers' payments are up to date, they have access to special hospitals and clinics. The NLC claims that Nicotex enrolled only 20 percent of its workers at any one time to avoid making larger contributions. As a result, workers could not depend on being in the

[32] Institute for Global Labour and Human Rights, "Women Exploiting Women."
[33] Ibid.

enrolled minority and often would not have access to health care. We asked workers if they would be willing to accept lower pay in order to have health insurance; only 20 percent were.

Guatemalan law requires every worker to be guaranteed 15 days' paid vacation after they have worked for a firm for one year. The NLC alleged that "no worker at Nicotex has had a single day's paid vacation since the factory opened in November of 2007."[34] When asked to honor legally mandated vacation time, supervisors reportedly responded, "Forget it. Nicotex never rests. If you feel tired, then resign and go to your home. There you can sleep. The gates are wide and open. If you go, we will replace you in five minutes."[35] We asked workers if they would be willing to earn less to have paid vacation. Nearly 69 percent of workers were unwilling to give up any pay for vacation.

Employees at both firms were asked if they would be willing to accept lower wages to improve any of 10 working conditions. Some of these questions addressed specific NLC complaints at one firm or the other and some were more general. Table 5.1 summarizes their answers. On 8 of the 10 questions, when both firms are averaged together, more than 90 percent of the workers answered, "No." Paid vacation was the most popular improvement, but even here more than 81 percent of the workers answered that they wouldn't sacrifice any wages for vacation. Nearly 65 percent of workers surveyed answered that they were unwilling to give up any wages for improved conditions across the board for all 10 questions.

The complaints against Nicotex were released in February 2009. In August 2009, Nicotex signed an agreement with the Guatemalan Center for Studies and Support for Local Development (who had coauthored the complaint with the NLC) to improve conditions.[36] We asked workers to answer our survey based on how conditions were before the agreement was reached in our earlier questions. Next, we asked questions about how things have changed since the agreement.

According to the NLC, the agreement ensures that "the workers have won the right to healthcare. Significant health and safety improvements have been implemented. All overtime will be voluntary. Vacation time and pay will be honored. And workers are guaranteed their right

---

[34] Ibid.
[35] Ibid.
[36] The agreement can be found here: Institute for Global Labour and Human Rights, "Major Worker Rights Victory in Guatemala," October 13, 2009, retrieved from www.nlcnet.org/alerts?id=0022.

TABLE 5.1 *Desirability of the mix of compensation*

Are you willing to work for lower pay if your employer …	Nicotex		Sam Bridge		Total	
	Yes	No	Yes	No	Yes	No
Reduced the number of hours you have to work	17.1%	82.9%	2.9%	97.1%	10.0%	90.0%
Made your hours more predictable	14.3%	85.7%	2.9%	97.1%	8.6%	91.4%
Gave you more bathroom breaks	2.9%	97.1%	2.9%	97.1%	2.9%	97.1%
Gave you longer lunch breaks	5.7%	94.3%	2.9%	97.1%	4.3%	95.7%
Made your working conditions more pleasant	17.1%	82.9%	0.0%	100.0%	8.6%	91.4%
Made your working conditions safer	5.7%	94.3%	2.9%	97.1%	4.3%	95.7%
Provided health insurance	20.0%	80.0%	8.6%	91.4%	14.3%	85.7%
Gave you paid vacation	31.4%	68.6%	5.7%	94.3%	18.6%	81.4%
Treated you more fairly	20.0%	80.0%	0.0%	100.0%	10.0%	90.0%
Reduced the risk of sexual harassment	0.0%	100.0%	0.0%	100.0%	0.0%	100.0%

to defend their legal, women's and labor rights."[37] Other provisions include greater access to water and bathroom breaks and less verbal abuse from supervisors.

We find evidence that Nicotex compensated for the demanded improvements along the margins that economic theory predicts. Twenty-six percent of workers saw their hours reduced, yet, before the reforms, 83 percent of workers said they would be unwilling to work fewer hours if it meant earning less. We also asked workers if their pay had been reduced and 14 percent reported it had. Nicotex also dealt with the higher cost of labor by employing fewer workers. Eighty-three percent of workers reported that fewer people worked for Nicotex in May 2010 than before the agreement with the NLC.

[37] Ibid.

When asked a general question, "Have your working conditions improved [since the agreement]," only 31 percent answered yes while 69 percent said they had not. It's not clear whether Nicotex simply didn't implement the agreed-on changes or whether it had and workers viewed the change as net lack of improvement, because Nicotex compensated on other margins. However, we also asked employees: "Overall, how do you feel about your conditions [since the agreement]?" Fewer than 3 percent answered "much more satisfied," and only 17 percent answered "more satisfied." The most frequent response, given by 49 percent of the workers, was "the same." However, 31 percent of workers reported that they were "less satisfied" with their overall conditions since the agreement. This is some indication that Nicotex did implement reforms but that the reforms satisfied the preferences of the NLC at the expense of the preferences of the Nicotex employees.

In a follow-up visit in April 2011, we learned that Nicotex had closed in the year since our survey. Whether the closure was related to increased costs resulting from the NLC agreement or whether it was due to other economic forces is not possible to determine.

On net, these two surveys support the theory articulated earlier in the chapter. Working conditions may be poor by US standards, but the mix roughly reflects employee preferences given their overall low level of productivity.[38] I followed up these surveys by personally visiting Sam Bridge and meeting with the owner. His statements revealed that, as theory predicts, he was indifferent to the mix of compensation he had to pay workers but only cared about his total cost of labor compensation.[39]

---

[38] A survey of sweatshop workers in El Salvador similarly found that workers generally had improved their working conditions (as well as their wages) compared to their prior employment. David Skarbek, Emily Skarbek, Brian Skarbek, and Erin Skarbek, "Sweatshops, Opportunity Costs, and Non-Monetary Compensation: Evidence from El Salvador," *American Journal of Economics and Sociology* 71, No. 3 (2012), 539–561.

[39] I followed up these surveys by visiting Sam Bridge and meeting with the owner/director, MyungChul Kim, April 27, 2011. I asked him if he would be willing to give paid vacation if the workers were willing to accept less in wages. He replied, "People need money, not vacations. Guatemala is very poor." When asked about shortening the hours his employees worked, he responded that the workers desired the hours but that he would like to avoid paying overtime because it costs him more money but he has to use overtime because of the late penalty clauses attached to US orders. When asked directly if he cared whether he paid a worker the equivalent of $4 an hour in wages or whether he paid $3 in wages and $1 in other benefits, not surprisingly, he answered that it did not matter to him.

Both of these cases, but Nicotex in particular, highlight a problem that occurs when worker preferences conflict with local labor laws. Should firms respect the laws or deliberately break them?

BREAKING LOCAL LABOR LAWS

Thus far I have argued that minimum wage laws or health and safety requirements will increase the cost of labor and lead to the employment of fewer sweatshop workers. But if new labor regulations are bad for workers because they lead to unemployment and shift compensation away from their preferred mix, shouldn't the enforcement of existing labor regulations be bad for precisely the same reason? Other defenders of sweatshops such as Gordon Sollars and Fred Englander, who grant that managers of companies have moral obligations not to tolerate or encourage violations of the law, thus seem to hold an inconsistent position.[40] A more consistent view, according to Arnold and Bowie, "would seem to be that MNE [Multinational Enterprise] managers have duties to ignore local labor laws, ignore working conditions, and pay the lowest possible wages, so long as none of these practices deterred employees from working in MNE factories."[41]

Arnold writes that although defenders of sweatshops must "either deny or tacitly approve the widespread violation of labor laws that take place in global sweatshops," it is nevertheless "difficult to justify widespread violations of the law."[42] This argument is best conceived as a *reductio ad absurdum*. Because the pro-sweatshop argument, if followed to its logical conclusion, entails that managers have a duty to ignore local labor laws, and so on, and because managers clearly do not have these duties, the pro-sweatshop argument clearly must be unsound.

This challenge is an important one. If the violation of labor laws is required by the pro-sweatshop argument and is unjust, then the pro-sweatshop argument will need to be modified or abandoned. If, on the

[40] Actually, what Gordon Sollars and Fred Englander actually say is that "MNEs or their managers have duties not to tolerate or encourage violations of *the rule of law*" (emphasis added) in "Sweatshops: Kant and Consequences," *Business Ethics Quarterly* 17, No. 1 (2007), 115. Arnold and Bowie assume that violations of existing statutory law are tantamount to violations of the rule of law. I will allow this assumption for the sake of the present exposition but will return to distinguish the rule of law from statutory law later in this chapter.
[41] Arnold and Bowie, "Respect for Workers," 139.
[42] Arnold, "Working Conditions," 638.

other hand, the violation of labor laws is justifiable, then it is incumbent upon defenders of sweatshops to provide an argument for this claim.

Arnold is correct to claim that the same logic that underlies the opposition to increased legal regulation of sweatshops also counts against the enforcement of certain existing regulations by the state, as well as the compliance with certain existing regulations by sweatshops. The essence of the response is that the violation of labor laws by sweatshops is indeed sometimes justifiable if we evaluate the laws based on how they impact worker welfare.

For example, a minimum wage set above worker productivity would clearly harm local laborers. In countries where labor's marginal revenue product is $2 per hour, and $3 per hour is the minimum wage, respecting local labor laws will leave workers unemployed or push them into informal sector jobs. No one should recommend compliance with this local labor law if worker welfare is their goal.

Of course, this does not mean that all violations of labor laws by sweatshops are permissible. Some labor laws prohibit actions that defenders of sweatshops can, consistent with their pro-sweatshop position, hold to be indefensible on moral and economic grounds. The opposition to forced labor, for instance, is not only consistent with the logic of the pro-sweatshop position but arguably a presupposition of it. Sweatshops therefore should comply with laws that prohibit forced labor, not because such laws make forced labor illegal but because forced labor would be immoral and decrease worker welfare regardless of its legal status. Furthermore, it is sometimes in workers' interest for firms to comply with even bad laws, when the costs of noncompliance would be excessively high. Suppose, for instance, that a country has a law stipulating a minimum wage above the market-clearing wage for a certain form of unskilled labor. The standard position of defenders of sweatshops is that such a law is a bad law insofar as it tends to lead to greater unemployment among unskilled laborers. Nevertheless, if the law is enforced, perhaps by the imposition of monetary fines on noncompliant firms, a firm might have decisive moral and economic reason to comply with it, because doing so might be necessary to remain in business and to continue employing any labor at all. In complying with the minimum wage law, the firm may be forced to employ less than the optimal number of workers, but it would be even further from the optimal number if the firm was forcibly shut down by government enforcement efforts.

Defenders of sweatshops are therefore not logically committed to approving of all labor law violations, but the logic of our position does push toward the approval of some such violations. What makes the difference? Some scholars have suggested that the defense of sweatshops, and the case for violation of labor regulations, is based solely on the value of "economic efficiency."[43] But this is a mistake. No serious academic defense of sweatshops has ever been based primarily on the idea of economic efficiency, and thus, to the extent that the arguments given by such persons logically commit them to approving of the violation of labor regulations, that approval must be based on some other value.[44]

That value is the very same one endorsed by most critics of sweatshops: the welfare of people in the Third World.[45] Defenders of sweatshops should endorse the violation of labor laws when that violation would benefit people living in the Third World.[46] But if defenders of sweatshops base their position on the same basic value as that embraced by opponents of sweatshops, what explains the difference in their conclusions?

[43] See, for instance, Arnold and Bowie, "Sweatshops and Respect," 228 ("The intentional violation of the legal rights of workers in the interest of economic efficiency is fundamentally incompatible with the duty of MNEs to respect workers"); Arnold and Hartman, "Beyond Sweatshops," 212 (on the need to move the sweatshop debate "beyond the entrenched, polarized, political narrative of economic efficiency versus increased regulatory protection for workers' rights"); Arnold and Hartman, "Worker Rights," 690 ("Those who are genuinely interested in the welfare of the citizens of developing nations ought to demand that MNCs and their contractors respect local labor laws, rather than excusing those MNCs that violate local laws in the name of economic efficiency").

[44] Arnold and coauthors are never entirely clear regarding what they mean by the term "economic efficiency." One standard understanding of the term, however, holds that an arrangement is economically efficient if the total benefits it generates could not be produced at a lower cost. To say that an arrangement is economically efficient, on this understanding, is to make a claim about aggregate costs and benefits, and therefore requires some method of measuring and summing costs and benefits interpersonally. Furthermore, to say that the violation of labor laws is justified on grounds of economic efficiency would be to say that the aggregate benefits of such violations outweigh the aggregate costs. Such a claim, it's worth noting, is compatible with the violation of *harming* workers and other citizens of developing countries, as a class, so long as the gains to, say, the company or its consumers are large enough. In contrast, every serious academic defense of sweatshops has been based not on the generalized aggregate benefits that sweatshops produce but on the benefits that they produce *specifically for workers and citizens of the developing world*. This is true of Ian Maitland, Matt Zwolinski, Gordon Sollars, Fred Englander, and me.

[45] Arnold and Hartman, "Worker Rights," 690.

[46] The choice of "people" rather than "workers" is deliberate. Adhering to or violating labor regulations obviously affects the workers who are subject to those regulations. But to the extent that such regulations affect the cost of business for sweatshops, and thus affect the capacity of sweatshops to hire and expand, and ultimately the nature of economic growth in the host country, they affect the welfare not only of current sweatshop employees but of potential sweatshop employees, employees in other industries, the families of current and potential workers, and so on.

Part of the difference stems from empirical disagreements. I believe that there are some cases in which disregarding labor regulations would be better for workers than adhering to them. If, for instance, workers would prefer larger paychecks to a package of smaller paychecks and safer working conditions, then laws that mandate safer working conditions will harm workers to the extent that the costs of providing those safer working conditions are paid from funds that would have otherwise been used to compensate workers directly with wages. If adherence to minimum wage laws leads sweatshops to employ fewer workers in the poor country than they otherwise would have, then doing so will obviously set back the interests of those who will be unemployed as a result. The reason that sweatshop critics believe that adherence to labor laws is nevertheless morally obligatory is, in large part, because they do not believe that adhering to them will produce these harmful effects. But, as was argued in Chapter 3, their belief is based on serious misunderstandings of economic theory and data.

In this chapter, I argued that violating individual laws can be good for workers' welfare. Critics could respond that labor laws should be respected because "respect for the rule of law contributes to increased prosperity."[47] Thus, they may claim that even though an individual law might be harmful to workers, respecting even those laws benefits workers in the long run because of the increased prosperity from abiding by the rule of law.

However, the "rule of law" that brings economic prosperity is very different from simply respecting whatever laws happen to exist in a country. When economists find that growth comes from following the rule of law, they are writing about legal systems that protect private property rights, uphold contracts, and are applied universally, predictably, and clearly.[48] Most sweatshop-containing countries do not have such legal systems, and thus following their existing laws would not lead to prosperity.

The claim that sweatshops might be morally justified in violating the law in certain cases is hardly a radical philosophical position. If any conclusion can be gleaned from the massive philosophical literature on political authority, it is that justifying even a prima facie obligation to

---

[47] Arnold and Hartman make this argument, "Beyond Sweatshops," 220.

[48] See Fraser Institute, Economic Freedom, retrieved from www.freetheworld.org, for much of the research that has made use of the *Economic Freedom of the World* annual report showing the types of systems that produce prosperity are those that respect negative rights and do not have highly regulated labor markets.

obey the law is a tremendously difficult, and possibly hopeless, task. Traditional accounts of political authority, as Robert Paul Wolff has argued, seem to be incompatible with a respect for individual autonomy.[49] In short, as Leslie Green writes, "There are plausible objections to each of the dominant justifications for the duty to obey the law," to an even greater degree than is present for most philosophic issues.[50] And, of course, these problems plague the justification of a duty to obey even those laws that well-functioning democratic systems generate and that are neutral or even benign in their effect. How much more problematic, then, must be the justification of a duty to obey laws that are generated in an autocratic or unjust way, and which are harmful in their effects on the most vulnerable segments of the population?

CONCLUSION

Anti-sweatshop activists and scholars seem to think they have a trump card when they ask if defenders of sweatshops advocate breaking labor standards laws. Viederman writes that if you believe sweatshop jobs are good then,

Does that mean even an illegal job? ... ethical standards are the rule of law in almost every country in the world. Do pro-sweatshoppers think that legal standards shouldn't be implemented? Where that's the case, those in power can and do claim as much of the revenue pie as they can, cheating workers out of their wages, cutting corners on worker safety, and all manner of other tactics.[51]

Yes. Even an illegal job. Activists, such as Viederman, fail to understand the economics that determines wage levels and how wages relate to safety and other working conditions. Legal standards should not be implemented. When they are, they should be ignored. Contrary to Viederman's assertions, workers will be made better off as a result.

The issues of wage compensation and safety, comfort, and other benefits are intimately related. If activists push only to improve safety in factories, then either they are implicitly pushing for a reduction in monetary wages that workers have already demonstrated they prefer more than safety or they will unemploy workers by raising their total

---

[49] Robert Paul Wolff, *In Defense of Anarchism*, 3rd ed. (Berkeley: University of California Press, 1970).
[50] Leslie Green, *Legal Obligation and Authority*, October 1, 2010, retrieved from http://plato.stanford.edu/entries/legal-obligation/.
[51] Viederman, "Any Job Is a Good Job? Think Again."

compensation above their marginal productivity. Profit-seeking companies will make trade-offs on these margins when activists push for reforms. These trade-offs are binding constraints, not something activists can assume away. This is why economists do not separate the analysis of safety, health, comfort, and other in-kind benefits from wages. If any of these factors raise total compensation above worker productivity, the worker will be unemployed. Alternatively, if total compensation stays the same and reformers demand improved conditions, wages will decrease. Thus, activists should not push to mandate improved working conditions in poorer countries. When these countries impose their own labor laws dictating minimum wages as well as health, safety, and working conditions, those firms that ignore the local labor laws often improve the welfare of the workers. First World activists should cease general calls to obey local labor laws and should instead focus only on those violations, such as forced labor, that actually harm the workers.

Readers who understand the economic reasoning and evidence in this chapter might be left wondering if this evidence applies in cases of extreme safety failures. After all, this chapter started off by describing the Tarzeen factory fire. Greater safety regulation, even if it meant lower wages and a risk of losing their job, clearly would have been better than the actual outcome for the 112 workers who lost their lives in the fire. The next chapter will consider this question in greater detail by examining the largest sweatshop disaster in modern times – the Rana Plaza factory collapse in Bangladesh.

6

The Rana Plaza Disaster and Its Aftermath

On April 24, 2013, Husnara Akhtar and her husband, Abu Sufyan, sipped tea before work, just like on any other morning. Then they traveled to work together where they each worked in different garment factories in the Rana Plaza building in Dhaka, Bangladesh. Husnara worked in a factory on the seventh floor, while Abu worked on the fifth floor. When the Rana Plaza building collapsed at 9 a.m., April 24th became a day like no other. Husnara regained consciousness, only to find herself trapped between two dead bodies. Ten years later, she reflected that she "could hear people screaming and crying out for help. But I had taken in so much dust that every time I tried to open my mouth, no sound came out."[1] Husnara is among the 2,500 people who were injured but survived the collapse. Abu's body was found a week later, crushed by a concrete pillar. He is among the 1,129 workers who lost their lives in the factory's collapse. The Rana Plaza disaster is widely considered the worst accident in the history of the modern garment industry and one of the worst industrial accidents ever.

It's easy to learn of the Rana Plaza disaster and conclude that Bangladeshi workers would have been better off if the country had had stricter factory safety standards. Much of the logic in this book is premised on the fact that workers choose jobs that are their best (or least bad) alternative available to them. Clearly, for those who lost their lives

---

[1] This quote and the other details about Husnara and Abu are drawn from Sarah Butler and Thaslima Begum, "Abuses 'Still Rife': 10 Years on from Bangladesh's Rana Plaza Disaster," *The Guardian*, April 24, 2023, retrieved from www.theguardian.com/world/2023/apr/24/10-years-on-bangladesh-rana-plaza-disaster-safety-garment-workers-rights-pay.

in Rana Plaza, these jobs were not their best alternative. Even if stricter safety standards caused these jobs to disappear and the workers moved into lower-paying jobs, they would have been better off because they would still be alive. We know this now that the building collapsed. But no one knew that it was Rana Plaza, specifically, that was going to collapse, nor did they know that it would happen on April 24th. If they had, the disaster would have been averted even without regulation. The building was evacuated the day before, after cracks appeared on its exterior. However, the owner, Sohel Rana, said that the building was safe and workers should return the next day. He was eventually charged with murder and, while his trial still has not been completed, he remains in custody a decade later. He would have been better off if he had left the factory evacuated and would have had the incentive to do so – if he knew it was going to collapse. The problem is, no one knows which factories will have accidents and which won't. So, safety regulations apply to all factories, not just the unlucky ones that would otherwise eventually have a disaster. That means we must evaluate the impact that safety regulations would have on all workers, not just the ones who tragically lose their lives in a particular accident.

Bangladesh was the world's second largest textile producer (after China), employing roughly 4 million, mostly female, workers in more than 5,000 factories at the time of the Rana Plaza disaster.[2] As we saw in Chapter 4, the workers in firms that were reported as sweatshops earn significantly more than most people in Bangladesh. If safety mandates decrease job opportunities in the garment industry, the potentially large forgone earnings of displaced garment workers, and those they help with those earnings, need to be weighed against any lives saved by safety improvements.

The scale of the Rana Plaza disaster generated worldwide media attention. This attention led multinational firms, who sourced garments from Bangladesh, to become concerned about how future disasters could tarnish their brand image. It also led anti-sweatshop activists in NGOs to agitate for more safety regulation. The result was the creation of buyer-enforced nongovernmental safety standards and monitoring through agreements that included the cooperation of these anti-sweatshop NGOs, unions, and multinational brands sourcing from Bangladesh. The next section describes the history of regulation in Bangladesh's garment

---

[2] Juliane Reinecke and Jimmy Donaghey, "After Rana Plaza: Building Coalitional Power for Labour Rights between Unions and (Consumption-Based) Social Movement Organizations," *Organization* 22, No. 5 (2015), 720–740.

industry and how the reaction to the Rana Plaza disaster changed the regulations. Then the remainder of the chapter assesses how this change in regulation impacted the number of jobs and firms in the industry, to evaluate the impact on workers' welfare.

GARMENT INDUSTRY REGULATION
BEFORE AND AFTER RANA PLAZA

The garment industry was not heavily regulated prior to Rana Plaza. Bangladesh's relatively weak labor movement, strong representation among garment factory owners in parliament, and generally weak regulatory capacity led to a political equilibrium of essentially laissez-faire regulation of the garment industry. Writing at around the time of the Rana Plaza disaster, economists Faisal Ahmed, Anne Greenleaf, and Audrey Sacks describe the situation:

[T]he government's policy has been to facilitate the sector's growth via noninterference and a decentralized industrial policy. Indeed, unlike the policies of many East Asian governments, successive Bangladeshi governments have neither picked winners nor exclusively directed state subsidies to the RMG sector... Successive governments have pursued policies emphasizing privatization and export-led growth... Moreover, the state has decentralized and delegated responsibilities to private organizations, such as the various garments association. This consensus on liberal economic policies has occurred despite a political-economic environment that rewards political rent seeking and fosters a weak regulatory state.[3]

They further report that this equilibrium has been maintained "despite the cycling of governments every five years."[4] The Rana Plaza disaster finally broke that equilibrium. The long record of poor enforcement of building safety standards by the Bangladesh government led anti-sweatshop activists, international unions, and multinational brands sourcing garments from Bangladesh to cooperate to create buyer-enforced nongovernmental safety standards, for source factories in Bangladesh, in the wake of the Rana Plaza disaster. The Accord and the Alliance were two separate, though similar, agreements where major international buyers agreed to only source garments from factories that met the safety standards laid out in their agreements. Essentially, these agreements replaced government regulatory enforcement with private

---

[3] Ahmed, Greenleaf, and Sacks, "The Paradox of Export Growth in Areas of Weak Governance," 260.
[4] Ibid., 262.

enforcement consisting of a boycott of all Bangladeshi subcontractors who didn't meet the agreements' safety standards.

The Accord was created through cooperation between international anti-sweatshop activist organizations (Clean Clothes Campaign, Worker Rights Consortium, International Labor Rights Forum, Maquila Solidarity Network), global union federations (IndustriALL, UNI Global), and initially more than 190 (eventually more than 220) international brands and garment retailers from more than 20 countries across 4 continents.[5] While unions negotiated with brands, anti-sweatshop organizations created public relations campaigns to pressure brands to join the Accord. The Clean Clothes Campaign was instrumental in establishing a list of international brands sourcing from Rana Plaza firms.[6] Business professors Juliane Reinecke and Jimmy Donaghey explain that "social movement organisations benefitted from the freedom as 'outsiders' to agitate and 'name and shame' individual companies who refused to sign the Accord" and quote a UNI Global Union representative explaining that "once you have exhausted your area of negotiation, once you've got your point where it's just, you have to recognise as a union that you know, you just cannot get any further, the company is refusing to negotiate. That's when we very much need the campaign organisations because they are simply better than us in public campaigning."[7]

The largest garment buyer from Bangladesh, H&M, was the first brand to sign on to the Accord on May 15, 2013, a mere 21 days after the Rana Plaza disaster.[8] The brands signing on to the Accord agreed to source Bangladeshi exports from only those garment factories that allowed independent safety inspections by qualified engineers approved by the Accord; agreed to improve their factories to comply with building safety, fire, and electrical standards; maintained the employment of workers, while remediating any safety deficiencies; allowed workers to participate in occupational health and safety training; and allowed workers to make complaints to the Accord and refuse unsafe work without retaliation.[9] The inspections (and Accord operations generally)

---

[5] Reinecke and Donaghey, "After Rana Plaza," 725; Anne Trebilcock, "The Rana Plaza Disaster Seven Years On: Transnational Experiments and Perhaps a New Treaty?" *International Labour Review* 159, No. 4 (2020), 548.

[6] Pamina Koenig and Sandra Poncet, "The Effects of the Rana Plaza Collapse on the Sourcing Choices of French Importers," *Journal of International Economics* 137 (2022), 2.

[7] Reinecke and Donaghey, "After Rana Plaza," 732.

[8] Ibid., 731.

[9] Ibid., 725.

were financed by the signatory brands, who contributed on a sliding scale up to $500,000 each.[10] However, the cost of remodeling and updating factories to meet the building, fire, and electrical standards would be borne by the source factories in Bangladesh. To help incentivize source factories to invest in making such updates, the buyer signatories to the Accord agreed to keep purchasing volume constant for five years for source factories that live up to the standards of the agreement, while terminating contracts with source factories that failed safety inspections and then failed to remediate their deficiencies.[11] Scholars have classified the agreement as "previously unseen in the transnational supply chain,"[12] and "unprecedented,"[13] because the Accord is an agreement that can be enforced through binding arbitration in the legal systems of signatory brands' home countries.

The Alliance agreement, led by the Gap and Walmart, was created by 27 (later 29) North American brands and retailers to improve building and fire safety in their Bangladeshi source factories in July of 2013. Like the Accord, brands and retailers signing on to the Alliance made a five-year commitment to the agreement; used brand-financed inspections of garment factories that included specialized audits for structural, electric, and fire safety; brand-financed safety training; and shared with the Accord the same common set of inspection and safety standards.[14] The main difference between the Alliance and the Accord is that the Alliance followed a more traditional corporate social responsibility model, driven by brands and retailers, and did not commit companies to "maintain purchasing volumes or to legally binding arbitration."[15]

Bangladesh's government had signed numerous conventions on labor rights and safety prior to the Rana Plaza disaster, but the conventions were poorly implemented and enforced due to the lack of political power of laborers compared to factory owners and Bangladesh's lack of

---

[10] Jimmy Donaghey and Juliane Reinecke, "When Industrial Democracy Meets Corporate Social Responsibility – A Comparison of the Bangladesh Accord and Alliances as Responses to the Rana Plaza Disaster," *British Journal of Industrial Relations* 56, No. 1 (2018), 24.

[11] Reinecke and Donaghey, "After Rana Plaza," 725.

[12] Donaghey and Reinecke, "When Industrial Democracy Meets Corporate Social Responsibility," 24.

[13] Trebilcock, "The Rana Plaza Disaster Seven Years On," 547.

[14] Ibid., 552; Donaghey and Reinecke, "When Industrial Democracy Meets Corporate Social Responsibility," 23, 25–26.

[15] Donaghey and Reinecke, "When Industrial Democracy Meets Corporate Social Responsibility," 26.

regulatory capacity.[16] The creation of the Accord and the Alliance substituted multinational brand- and retailer-imposed safety requirements and enforcement on Bangladeshi garment factories, in place of government regulation and enforcement. The Accord was the larger of the two agreements and grew to cover more than 1,600 factories employing more than 2.5 million workers.[17] The Alliance covered an additional 587 factories,[18] as well as an estimated 537,214 workers.[19] Jointly, the safety requirements from the Accord and Alliance covered approximately 40 percent of Bangladesh's garment factories and 75 percent of its garment workers.

Unlike many official government regulations, the Accord and Alliance standards were enforced on source factories. The Accord reports that 156 of the 1,645 factories inspected received closure orders and a similar number were relocated by January 2020.[20] The Accord also resulted in at least 50 temporary evacuation orders.[21] Similarly, the Alliance suspended relations with 97 source factories and escalated remediation action against an additional 138 factories by late 2016.[22]

The Accord and Alliance appear to have had their intended effect on worker safety in Bangladesh. Professors Donaghey and Reinecke claim that "the best indication of the effectiveness of the Accord and Alliance is that, to date, there has been no other major industrial accident in Bangladeshi garment factories since Rana Plaza, despite serious safety issues being identified in almost all factories. Compared to the rate of accidents prior to Rana Plaza, this meant that many lives were saved."[23]

We next turn to examining some of the trade-offs created by the response to the Rana Plaza disaster by estimating the effect the response had on the number of firms and employment in Bangladesh's garment industry.

---

[16] Ahmed, Greenleaf, and Sacks, "The Paradox of Export Growth in Areas of Weak Governance," 267–268.

[17] Trebilcock, "The Rana Plaza Disaster Seven Years On," 550.

[18] Ibid., 552.

[19] Donaghey and Reinecke, "When Industrial Democracy Meets Corporate Social Responsibility," 32.

[20] Accord, "Quarterly Aggregate Report on Remediation Progress and Status of Workplace Programs at RMG Factories Covered by the Accord" (2020), retrieved from https://bangladesh.wpengine.com/wpcontent/uploads/2020/02/Accord_Quarterly_Aggregate_Report_January2020.pdf.

[21] Mark Anner, *Binding Power: The Sourcing Squeeze, Workers' Rights, and Building Safety in Bangladesh since Rana Plaza* (State College, PA: Penn State College of the Liberal Arts, Centre for Global Workers' Rights, 2018), 2.

[22] Donaghey and Reinecke, "When Industrial Democracy Meets Corporate Social Responsibility," 28.

[23] Ibid., 38.

QUANTIFYING UNINTENDED CONSEQUENCES
OF THE REACTION TO RANA PLAZA

Requiring investments in factory safety raises the cost of using low-skilled Bangladeshi laborers to produce garments. The economic theory discussed in Chapter 3 indicates that this should lead some firms to exit the market and that the overall garment industry will employ fewer workers in Bangladesh. Economic theory can indicate the direction of change, but empirical analysis is needed to estimate how many firms exit and how much smaller garment industry employment is because of the reactions to Rana Plaza.

Scientists conduct multiple experiments to estimate magnitudes in the natural sciences. Unfortunately for us social scientists (but fortunately for our would-be human subjects), we cannot conduct experiments on multiple identical Bangladeshes and give some Rana Plaza disasters and the regulations that follow and leave other Bangladeshes disaster-free and without the subsequent regulations, and then measure differences in the number of garment industry firms and employees. So, social scientists have created "quasi-experimental" methods. One such method, known as a synthetic control, is best suited to analyze the impact of the reaction to the Rana Plaza disaster.[24] I used this method to investigate the impact of the reaction to the Rana Plaza disaster in research coauthored with my colleague Kevin Grier and a Ph.D. candidate, who happens to be from Bangladesh, Towhid Mahmood. I give an intuitive description of what we did and our main results in this chapter. Readers interested in a more technical description, and all the various robustness checks on our results, should consult the original journal article.[25] Readers not inclined to torture themselves with that task can rest assured that what I report in what follows is consistent with everything in the more technical (and boring) study.

[24] The synthetic control method was developed by Alberto Abadie and Javier Gardeazabal, "The Economic Costs of Conflict: A Case Study of the Basque Country," *American Economic Review* 93, No. 1 (2003), 113–132, and expanded on in Alberto Abadie, Alexis Diamond, and Jens Hainmueller, "Synthetic Control Methods for Comparative Case Studies: Estimating the Effect of California's Tobacco Control Program," *Journal of the American Statistical Association* 105, No. 490 (2010), 493–505; Alberto Abadie, Alexis Diamond, and Jens Hainmueller, "Comparative Politics and the Synthetic Control Method," *American Journal of Political Science* 59, No. 2 (2015), 495–510. See these articles for more technical treatments of the method.

[25] Kevin Grier, Towhid Mahmood, and Benjamin Powell, "Anti-Sweatshop Activism and the Safety-Employment Tradeoff: Evidence from Bangladesh's Rana Plaza Disaster," *Journal of Economic Behavior and Organization* 208 (2023), 174–190, retrieved from https://doi.org/10.1016/j.jebo.2023.02.007.

The synthetic control method creates a counterfactual that can be used to measure what happened in Bangladesh against. To understand the intuition behind the synthetic control method, let's pause for a second and consider how we could empirically assess the economic growth of a capitalist versus a socialist economic system. One could compare the growth of the USSR to the United States, but there are many other important differences between the two countries that also impact their economic growth, thus making it hard to isolate the impact of just the difference caused by the capitalist system versus the socialist system. Instead, to better estimate the impact of economic systems, we would want to compare places that had similar initial levels of development, cultures, histories, and geographies and differed in only their economic system. The world gives us one such "natural experiment": North and South Korea. Unfortunately, for most interesting empirical questions there are no such similar natural experiments to consult. The synthetic control method creates a counterfactual that gives us a proxy for this type of natural experiment. In the case of the Rana Plaza disaster, the synthetic control creates a "Fake Bangladesh" that doesn't experience a Rana Plaza disaster so that we can evaluate how it differs in employment and firms from the real Bangladesh.

Fake Bangladesh is created from a weighted average of other countries that do the best job of tracking the real Bangladesh's performance on the outcomes we want to analyze (employment and firms) and are similar in other relevant economic indicators, right up until 2013. The relevant economic indicators, in this case, are per capita GDP, investment share of GDP, and population growth. The weighted average is constructed from a subset of countries that have important similarities to Bangladesh. So, Fake Bangladesh is constructed from a pool of donor countries that are similar to the real Bangladesh in either geography, level of development, the size of their garment export sector, or a history of having protested sweatshops. The art of the synthetic control method consists of picking reasonable potential donor countries and the relevant indicator variables. After that, the synthetic control algorithm creates a weighted average from a selection of these donor countries (giving some zero weight) that minimizes differences in the outcome variable (either garment firms or employment), in the period of analysis prior to the Rana Plaza disaster, and balances this control to look more like the real Bangladesh on the indicator variables. The synthetic control algorithm places greater weight on indicator variables that are more important for determining the outcome variable.

The synthetic control method requires two assumptions to hold for the method to identify the causal impact of the event under investigation. The first is that the effects we are measuring are due only to the treatment we are investigating and not to any subsequent additional treatments. The second, known as the stable unit treatment value assumption (SUTVA), is that only the country being analyzed is treated with the event under investigation. Both assumptions warrant further elaboration in the case of the Rana Plaza disaster.

It's important to clarify that the treatment in this case is the impact of the *overall reaction to the Rana Plaza disaster*. This reaction includes all actions taken by governments, multinational brands, and other buyers of Bangladeshi garments to avoid anti-sweatshop activism and its associated negative media coverage, and the potential consumer backlash against brands that might be associated with any subsequent disasters. As outlined earlier in the chapter, the creation of the Accord and the Alliance were two major reactions by brands to the Rana Plaza disaster. However, they were not the only reactions. Fears of future consumer backlash, driven by media coverage or anti-sweatshop activism, clearly led to brands forming the Accord and the Alliance, but these same fears may also lead brands to shift purchases away from Bangladesh and toward safer factories in more developed countries that have both higher-cost and higher-productivity workers.[26] The synthetic control measures the effect of all these reactions to the disaster but cannot distinguish between them. Since all these reactions happened during the immediate aftermath of the Rana Plaza collapse, we are left with a single treatment year and do not violate the single treatment assumption of the synthetic control method. It's just that, in this case, the single treatment "reaction" has multiple channels.

None of the donor pool countries in our sample experienced a factory disaster anything like the Rana Plaza disaster during the period under examination. Nor was anything like the Accord or Alliance created in any of the donor pool countries. Thus, in that sense, they do not violate

[26] Bangladesh's government also increased the minimum wage in the garment industry in 2013. However, it is unlikely that this change in the minimum wage is likely to be responsible for much of the difference between Fake Bangladesh and Bangladesh (in either the number of firms or employment) after the disaster, because Bangladesh also increased its minimum wage in 2006 and 2010. These earlier changes were both slightly larger in magnitude and occurred in the pre-treatment period. Thus, Fake Bangladesh was built to track a real Bangladesh that increases its minimum wage. Thought of another way, Fake Bangladesh implicitly attempts to control for changes in minimum wage policy of the magnitude enacted in 2013.

the SUTVA. However, it is possible that, because of the Rana Plaza disaster, brands came to believe that it was more likely than they had previously thought that they could experience a similar disaster in other poor garment-exporting countries. If brands shifted sourcing away from these poorer garment-exporting countries in general, as opposed to just from Bangladesh, then the SUTVA could be violated if these other countries received weight in constructing Fake Bangladesh. However, this has an important implication for the analysis. To the extent that the SUTVA is violated through this channel, it causes an underestimation of the overall reaction to the Rana Plaza disaster on subsequent garment industry employment and the number of firms in Bangladesh. Thus, the estimates reported in what follows are lower-bound estimates.

Conversely, if brands shifted supply chains to source garments from other donor pool countries to replace imports from Bangladesh, one could argue that this synthetic control overestimates employment or firm loss in Bangladesh by essentially double counting when we use the gains in these countries to compare against the losses in Bangladesh. However, this concern is somewhat mitigated by the fact that the only empirical study of importer behavior in response to the Rana Plaza disaster, that I am aware of, finds that French companies that decreased apparel imports from Bangladesh replaced them with imports from Turkey, Morocco, Portugal, and Poland while not significantly increasing imports from other important Asian suppliers.[27] As described in the remainder of the chapter, Asian countries constitute almost all of the weight in our synthetic models of Bangladesh and Turkey, Morocco, Portugal, and Poland do not receive any weight. Perhaps more importantly, as the subsequent figures will show, Fake Bangladesh, for both employment and firms, continues on its same trajectory post Rana Plaza. If brands had changed sourcing to the countries used to construct Fake Bangladesh, we would observe an increase, relative to the pre-2013 trend, in the growth of employment and firms in Fake Bangladesh that doesn't take place.[28]

To assess how garment industry employment was impacted by the reaction to the Rana Plaza disaster, Fake Bangladesh was constructed

---

[27] Koenig and Poncet, "The Effects of the Rana Plaza Collapse," 18.
[28] As an additional check, I also used data from the World Bank's World Integrated Trade Solutions to observe how the import share in each of the three largest importers of Bangladesh apparel changed from any country that receives a positive weight in our construction of synthetic Bangladesh and do not observe any significant changes post Rana Plaza.

TABLE 6.1 *Bangladesh employment predictor means*

Variables	Real	Fake
Population growth (year to year)	1.37	0.98
Per capita real GDP (log)	7.80	8.41
Investment share of GDP	0.23	0.27
Employment (in millions) (scaled) (2001)	0.40	0.37
Employment (in millions) (scaled) (2002)	0.45	0.43
Employment (in millions) (scaled) (2003)	0.45	0.47
Employment (in millions) (scaled) (2004)	0.50	0.51
Employment (in millions) (scaled) (2005)	0.50	0.50
Employment (in millions) (scaled) (2006)	0.50	0.55

using the three economic indicator variables and six lags of pre-disaster garment industry employment. The synthetic control algorithm created a Fake Bangladesh comprised of 92.5 percent Vietnam and 7.5 percent Kazakhstan.[29] Table 6.1 illustrates that synthetic Bangladesh resembles the real Bangladesh reasonably well on indicator and lagged outcome variables.

Figure 6.1 plots the garment industry's normalized employment in Bangladesh against its Fake Bangladesh. Employment in both real Bangladesh and Fake Bangladesh track each other well from 2001 up until the 2013 Rana Plaza disaster.[30] However, after the disaster, garment employment flattens out in Bangladesh, while employment predicted by Fake Bangladesh continues to grow at roughly the same rate.

Garment industry employment in Bangladesh is about 28.3 percent lower by 2017 than predicted by the Fake Bangladesh that does not experience the Rana Plaza disaster. The differences between real and Fake Bangladesh seen in this figure are statistically significant. The bars in Figure 6.2 plot the magnitude of the difference between garment industry employment in real and Fake Bangladesh and lists the associated *p*-value on top of each bar. The difference in garment industry employment between Bangladesh and Fake Bangladesh is significant at the 1 percent confidence level for every year since the Rana Plaza

[29] Since Vietnam receives such a large weight in constructing Fake Bangladesh, it is important to verify that there were not any major idiosyncratic shocks to Vietnam's garment industry that would cause Fake Bangladesh to deviate from real Bangladesh. There does not appear to be any such shock. Apparel industry employment growth in Vietnam was fairly similar pre and post Rana Plaza, averaging 10 percent per year from 2010 to 2013 and 7 percent from 2014 to 2017.

[30] For the more technically inclined, the root mean square percentage error (RMSPE) was 0.054.

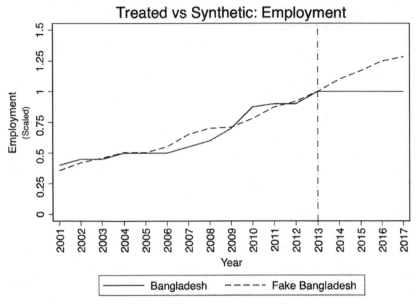

FIGURE 6.1 Garment industry employment

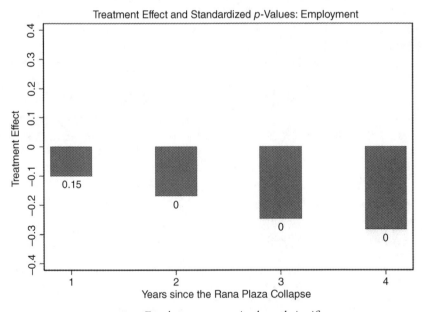

FIGURE 6.2 Employment magnitude and significance

disaster except for 2014. The magnitude of the difference in employment in these statistically significant years ranges between 16.9 percent
and 28.3 percent. This is strong evidence that the overall reaction to

TABLE 6.2 *Bangladesh firm predictor means*

Variables	Real	Fake
Population growth (year to year)	1.23	1.64
Per capita real GDP (log)	7.89	9.43
Investment share of GDP	0.24	0.30
Establishment (in thousands) (scaled) (2005)	0.73	0.75
Establishment (in thousands) (scaled) (2006)	0.75	0.78
Establishment (in thousands) (scaled) (2007)	0.80	0.77
Establishment (in thousands) (scaled) (2008)	0.85	0.83
Establishment (in thousands) (scaled) (2009)	0.88	0.87
Establishment (in thousands) (scaled) (2010)	0.90	0.92

the Rana Plaza disaster resulted in a large and statistically significant decrease in garment industry employment in Bangladesh.

This same method can be used to evaluate how the reaction to the Rana Plaza disaster impacted the number of firms in the garment industry. Again, the three economic indicator variables are used, and now six lags of the pre-disaster number of firms in the garment industry, rather than workers, are used to construct another Fake Bangladesh. This Fake Bangladesh is comprised of 30.5 percent Singapore, 28.8 percent India, 17.9 percent Armenia, 15.9 percent Mongolia, and 7 percent Indonesia. Table 6.2 illustrates that Fake Bangladesh again resembles the real Bangladesh reasonably well on indicator and lagged variables.

Figure 6.3 plots the number of garment industry firms in Bangladesh against Fake Bangladesh. The normalized number of garment industry firms in Bangladesh and its fake counterpart track each other well from 2005 up until the 2013 Rana Plaza disaster.[31] However, after the disaster the number of firms in Bangladesh's garment industry declines, while the number of firms in this industry continues to grow in Fake Bangladesh.

The number of firms in Bangladesh's garment industry is 33.3 percent lower by 2016 than that predicted by the Fake Bangladesh. The deviations between real and Fake Bangladesh are again statistically significant. The bars in Figure 6.4 plot the magnitude of the difference between the number of firms in the garment industry in real and Fake Bangladesh and lists the associated *p*-value on top of each bar. The difference in the number of firms in Bangladesh and its synthetic counterfactual is significant at the 1 percent or 10 percent confidence level

[31] Again, for the more technically inclined, with a RMSPE of 0.037.

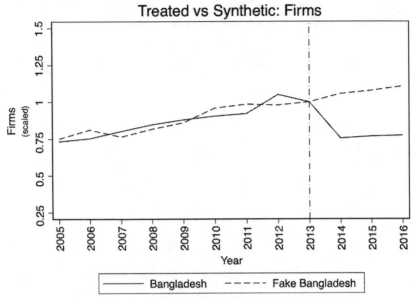

FIGURE 6.3 Garment industry firms

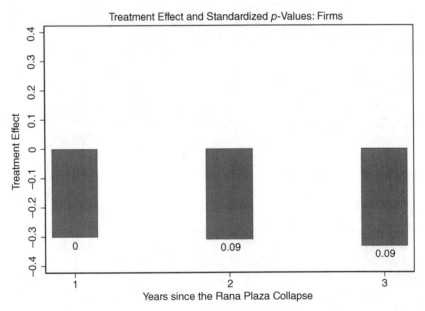

FIGURE 6.4 Firm magnitude and significance

for every year since the Rana Plaza disaster. The magnitude of the difference in these years ranges between 30.1 percent and 33.3 percent. This is strong evidence that the reaction to the Rana Plaza disaster resulted in large and statistically significant decreases in the number of firms in Bangladesh's garment industry.

These results are robust to an alternative synthetic control methodology that uses all pre-treatment outcome variables, while excluding the other indicator variables, to construct synthetic Bangladesh. Using either methodology, we find that the reaction of multinational firms to the Rana Plaza disaster led to large and statistically significant decreases in employment and the number of firms in Bangladesh's garment industry.

CONCLUSION

In the wake of the Rana Plaza disaster, numerous activist organizations and unions called for greater regulation and stronger safety standards to be imposed on Bangladesh's garment industry. The day after the disaster, Brad Adams, the Asia director of Human Rights Watch, stated, "It is time for companies to say that they will take no clothes from companies that do not meet minimum standards. Ignorance and cost can no longer be an excuse for some of the biggest companies in the world."[32] The Accord and the Alliance accomplished precisely what Adams demanded. Have the results been desirable?

The data analyzed in this chapter indicates a trade-off between increased safety and garment industry employment – precisely as economic theory described in Chapter 5 predicts. The overall reaction, including the boycott of noncompliant firms, led to nearly one-third fewer garment firms in Bangladesh in the years following the disaster. The exit of firms, coupled with higher labor costs for remaining firms, led to the existence of about 28 percent fewer Bangladeshi garment industry jobs. These lost jobs were a significant step up compared to alternatives for most of those workers. Chapter 4 indicated that the average pay of workers in Bangladeshi factories that were identified as a sweatshop in the international media during the decade of the Rana Plaza disaster provided a living standard of $5.81 per day (purchasing power adjusted). Meanwhile, nearly 87 percent of Bangladesh's population lived on less than $6.85 per day and more than 51 percent lived on less than $3.65 per day. The potentially large forgone earnings for more than a quarter of Bangladesh's garment workers need to be weighed against any potential safety improvements generated by the boycotts.

[32] Human Rights Watch, "Bangladesh: Tragedy Shows Urgency of Worker Protections," April 25, 2013, retrieved from www.hrw.org/news/2013/04/25/bangladesh-tragedy-shows-urgency-worker-protections.

Furthermore, the apparel industry has played an important role in Bangladesh's development. At the time of the disaster, the apparel industry comprised 13 percent of the country's GDP and accounted for 80 percent of its exports. Any slowdown of this process of development, which ultimately leads people out of poverty (see Chapters 9 and 10), caused by increased labor costs and boycotts must also count as a long-run cost. The apparel industry also helps to alleviate rural poverty, as 90 percent of garment workers come from rural households, and they remit about 25 percent of their earnings to those rural areas.[33] The industry is particularly important for disadvantaged women. The garment industry employs roughly 12 percent of women aged 15 to 30.[34] In addition to providing wages higher than what rural women could otherwise earn, these jobs also empower women in other ways. They helped to break down the stigma against women appearing in public alone, they help women delay marriage and pregnancy, which often come shortly after puberty in rural areas, and they allow women control over their earnings, which helps give women greater independence.[35] These constitute additional costs that must be weighed against safety improvements.

Even if the safety improvements generated by these boycotts prevented disasters that, in the aggregate, equal the scale of Rana Plaza, which seems unlikely, this means an evaluation of the reaction to the Rana Plaza disaster would need to weigh 1,129 lives saved (and 2,500 injuries prevented) against the harms caused to roughly 1.13 million people who are not employed in the garment industry but otherwise would have been. These harms include a substantially lower living standard, other nonpecuniary harms for women, and a slowdown in Bangladesh's development that is the main channel through which poverty is ultimately reduced. Economic reasoning can only establish trade-offs. But, in this case, it would not be hard for a reasonable person to judge these trade-offs in such a way as to deem the overall costs of the reactions to the Rana Plaza disaster to be greater than the benefits.

---

[33] Rita Afsar, "Sociological Implications of Female Labor Migration in Bangladesh," in *Globalization and Gender: Changing Patterns of Women's Employment in Bangladesh*, edited by Rehman Sobhan and Nasreen Khundker (Dhaka: Centre for Policy Dialogue and University Press Limited, 2001).

[34] Sajeda Amin, "Responding to Rana Plaza: A Made-in-Bangladesh Boycott Won't Help Girls," *The Guardian*, October 19, 2022, retrieved from www.theguardian .com/global-development-professionals-network/2014/apr/30/rana-plaza-boycott-bangladesh-garment-factory.

[35] Ibid.

7

Save the Children?

The thought of a young child working in a Third World sweatshop is repulsive to most people. And rightly so. Consider the case of Halima.[1] She's an 11-year-old girl who clips loose threads off of Hanes underwear in Bangladeshi factory. She works about eight hours a day, six days per week. She must process 150 pairs of underwear an hour. When she falls behind, supervisors shout at her or slap her. She's only allowed to go to the bathroom two or three times per day, and it doesn't have soap or toilet paper. At work, she feels "very tired and exhausted" and sometimes falls asleep standing up. She makes 53 cents a day for her efforts.

You might understand the logic of the preceding chapters and have revised your views on the desirability of sweatshops, but there is probably a lingering fear that, if we allowed the global market to determine employment without governmental regulation, we would end up with many children like Halima working in the factories. So, some laws must be needed to save the children. Right?

Anti-sweatshop groups almost universally condemn child labor. Provisions against child labor are part of the ILO's core labor standards. Yet, as repulsive as child labor is, all of the analysis in preceding chapters applies to children as well as adults. We should desire to see an end to child labor. But it must come through a process that generates better opportunities for them – not from legislative mandates that prevent children from taking the best option available to them.

---

[1] The National Labor Committee interviewed Halima in 2006. A video of the interview is available online: "Child Labor: 11 Year-Old Halima Sews Clothing for Hanes," retrieved from www.youtube.com/watch?v=pTIfY9SmJdA.

Children don't work because their parents are mean or stupid. They work because their families are desperately poor, and the meager addition to the family income children can contribute is often necessary for survival. Banning child labor through trade regulations or governmental prohibitions simply forces the children into less-desirable alternatives. When US activists started pressuring Bangladesh to eliminate child labor, the results were disastrous.

In 1993, US Senator Tom Harkin introduced the Child Labor Deterrence Act, which would have banned imports from countries employing children. In response, Bangladeshi garment companies fired approximately 50,000 children. According to the U.S. Department of Labor, "it is widely thought that most of them have found employment in other garment factories, in smaller, unregistered subcontracting garment workshops, or in other sectors."[2] That makes the introduction of the bill seem simply ineffective. The Department of Labor is sugarcoating it. Paul Krugman summarizes what happened more bluntly: "The direct result was that Bangladeshi textile factories stopped employing children. But did the children go back to school? Did they return to happy homes? Not according to Oxfam, which found that the displaced child workers ended up in even worse jobs, or on the streets – and that a significant number were forced into prostitution."[3] Much like adults, and sometimes with the advice of adults, children tend to choose the job that they believe is their best available option. Taking that option away doesn't eliminate the necessity of work. It forces them to take a less-desirable job. As repulsive as a child working in a sweatshop may be, it's not nearly as repulsive as a child forced into prostitution through the actions of unthinking Western activists.

The Bangladesh story is a dramatic one, but it's representative of many of the alternatives the children face.[4] This chapter examines the general alternatives available to children in countries where sweatshops are located and then explores ways that child labor can be eliminated without throwing children into worse alternatives.

---

[2] Bureau of International Labor Affairs, Bangladesh, retrieved from www.dol.gov/ilab/media/reports/iclp/sweat/bangladesh.htm.

[3] Paul Krugman, "Reckonings; Hearts and Heads," *New York Times*, April 22, 2001, 17. Similarly, the UNICEF report *The State of the World's Children* (1997), retrieved from www.unicef.org/sowc97/, 23, reports that many of these children turned to prostitution.

[4] For an excellent survey of the economics and composition of child labor, see Eric Edmonds and Nina Pavcnik, "Child Labor in the Global Economy," *Journal of Economic Perspectives* 19, No. 1 (Winter 2005), 199–220.

ALTERNATIVES AVAILABLE TO CHILDREN

Implicit in the condemnation of child labor in sweatshops is an assumption that these factories have taken advantage of children, who otherwise would have had better opportunities, such as attending school. But garment factories are not unique in their employment of children in these countries. In countries where sweatshops are located, child labor is often the norm, and most of the children work in less remunerative sectors with fewer opportunities for advancement than manufacturing, such as agriculture or domestic services. In 2004, the ILO copublished a series of similar national child labor studies.[5] Among the reports were studies in El Salvador, Costa Rica, and the Dominican Republic; in all of these countries, firms were accused of being sweatshops around the time of the studies. A look at these studies helps to put child sweatshop labor into the proper perspective.

The studies examined the work and school attendance of children aged 5–17 years old. Approximately 10 percent of these children worked in Costa Rica, 18 percent in the Dominican Republic, and 12 percent in El Salvador. Low rates of work among children aged 5–9 years old bias these numbers downward significantly. The average child worker's age was 14 in Costa Rica and El Salvador and 12 and a half in the Dominican Republic. Although most children went to school in these countries, a significant number did not. Seven percent of Dominican children, 15 percent of Costa Rican children, and 23 percent of El Salvadorian children did not attend school.

The manufacturing industry, where sweatshops are located, was not the dominant employer of children. In Costa Rica and El Salvador, agriculture was the main occupation of most working children, at 44 percent and 49 percent, respectively. This was followed by trade, hotels, and restaurants, which accounted for 27 percent in Costa Rica and 23 percent in El Salvador, whereas manufacturing employed only 9 percent and 16 percent of children, respectively. In the Dominican Republic, the service industry was the main employer of children (41 percent), followed by trade, agriculture, and lastly, manufacturing.

Forms of compensation varied, but in Costa Rica and El Salvador unpaid family work was the most common form of child labor. Salaried

---

[5] ILO, "Summary of the Results of the Child and Adolescent Labour Survey in Costa Rica," 2002; "Summary of the Results of the National Child Labour Survey in the Dominican Republic," 2000; "Summary of the Results of the Child Labour Survey in El Salvador," 2003. All retrieved from www.ilo.org/ipec/ChildlabourstatisticsSIMPOC/ Questionnairessurveysandreports/lang--en/index.htm.

compensation was more common in the Dominican Republic. Regardless of the form of compensation, or industry that the children worked in, their hours were significant. In Costa Rica and El Salvador, working children worked an average of 31 hours per week, and in the Dominican Republic they averaged 21 hours.

The ILO also examined a "child labor" population that consisted of children whose "involvement in economic activities violates national legislation and/or international agreements, because it is physically, mentally, socially, or morally harmful or detrimental to children, or because it somehow interferes with their schooling."[6] The ILO found that 65 percent of working children in Costa Rica, 80 percent in the Dominican Republic, and 50 percent in El Salvador are engaged in this sort of child labor. Manufacturing jobs weren't systematically more likely to be classified as this form of child labor than other sectors. In the Dominican Republic, agriculture had the largest percentage of its jobs classified as child labor, whereas manufacturing, services, and trade each had a similar proportion. In El Salvador, the trade sector had the highest percentage of jobs classified as child labor, whereas manufacturing had the lowest proportion. In Costa Rica, 68 percent of manufacturing jobs were classified as child labor, followed closely by agriculture at 67 percent and trade at 57 percent.

The picture these reports paint is that child labor is common in these countries. Most child labor is not in the manufacturing sector, and manufacturing jobs are not systematically more likely to be classified as harmful by the ILO. How well do these cases generalize?

The World Bank's *World Development Indicators* report statistics on child labor indicating the percentage of children aged 7–14 that were working in most countries.[7] A look at the subset of countries where sweatshops have been reported in the press, and where child labor data was also available, reveals that, like the above three examples, while most children aren't working, child labor is still common in most of these countries. Table 7.1 reports that rates of child labor range from a high of nearly 38 percent of children in Haiti to a low of 1.7 percent in India.

Educational statistics are also similar to the abovementioned case studies. In most countries where sweatshops locate, most children complete primary education. Thus, despite the presence of child employment,

[6] ILO, "Costa Rica Survey," 7.
[7] World Development Indicators Online, retrieved from https://databank.worldbank.org/source/world-development-indicators.

TABLE 7.1 *Percentage of children aged 7–14 in the labor force*

Bangladesh	5.0%
Cambodia	11.5%
El Salvador	7.4%
Haiti	37.8%
India	1.7%
Nicaragua*	25.9%
Pakistan	13.0%
Philippines	9.0%
Vietnam	12.0%

* *UNICEF data for children aged 5–17*

TABLE 7.2 *Child education (percentage of relevant age group)*

	Completes primary education	Enrolled in secondary education
Bangladesh		58.0%
Cambodia	89.5%	
China		
El Salvador	92.5%	64.2%
Haiti		
India		61.6%
Indonesia		75.4%
Mauritius	96.9%	84.6%
Myanmar		57.2%
Nicaragua		
Pakistan	57.8%	35.2%
Philippines		66.0%
Sri Lanka	95.9%	88.5%
Vietnam	99.2%	

it doesn't necessarily come at the expense of basic education. However, secondary education enrollment rates are significantly lower. In Pakistan, only 35 percent of children, of the appropriate age, are enrolled in secondary education. Table 7.2 summarizes the primary education completion and secondary education enrollment rates for the countries where sweatshops have been reported and data was available.[8]

[8] Some countries were excluded because data wasn't available; however, primary education rates for the Philippines, Indonesia, and Myanmar were excluded because they are clearly incorrect (exceeding 100 percent).

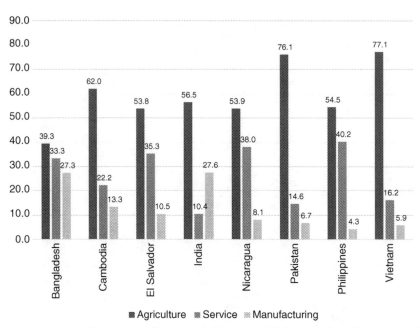

FIGURE 7.1 Percentage of economically active children employed by sector

Although they are more limited in coverage, the World Bank also collects data on the economic sectors in which children are employed. Figure 7.1 presents the distribution of employment of economically active children between the ages of 7 and 14 by sector in countries with reported sweatshops. As in our case studies from earlier in this chapter, the vast majority of employed children are not employed in manufacturing. More children were employed in agriculture than in any other sector in each country. The service sector was the second leading employer of children in each country except India. Bangladesh and India were the only two countries where more than a quarter of child laborers worked in manufacturing (at just over 27 percent each).

Protests against sweatshops that use child labor, or trade sanctions like the Child Labor Deterrence Act, implicitly assume that ending child labor in sweatshops, by taking away the option to work in a factory, will, on net, reduce child labor. Evidence on child labor in countries that have sweatshops indicates that they are wrong. It is not a few "bad apple" firms exploiting children in factories. Child labor is common. Moreover, sweatshops and manufacturing are not where most children work. Most work in agriculture or service sector jobs. These other sectors aren't necessarily safer, either. Child labor surveys show that 12 percent of children working in agriculture report injuries, compared with 9 percent for those who work in manufacturing.[9] If children lose their jobs in export manufacturing, the alternative for most is not time in school but another job in a lower-paying, lower-growth, lower-skill sector of the economy. Much like their adult counterparts, we don't help Third World children by taking options away from them. We help them only when their options are expanded. Chapter 11 will discuss some marginal differences activists could make in expanding their options, but the next section of this chapter explains the main way that child labor is eradicated.

ECONOMIC DEVELOPMENT AND CHILD LABOR

The thought of Third World children toiling in factories to produce garments for us in the developed world to wear is appalling, at least in part, because child labor is virtually nonexistent in the United States and the rest of the more developed world.[10] Sure, some kids have chores to do around the house, others might have a paper route, and high school aged "kids" might have a part-time job. But virtually nowhere in the developed world do kids toil long hours every week in a factory or on the family farm in a manner that prevents them from obtaining schooling.

This pleasant situation is taken for granted by many in wealthy countries. But historically it is not the norm. Children typically worked throughout human history, either long hours in agricultural employment or in factories once the industrial revolution emerged. The question is why kids don't work today. A tempting answer would be because the United States and other wealthy countries have laws against child labor. But it would be wrong.

Rich countries do have laws against child labor, but so do many poor countries. In Costa Rica, the legal working age is 15. But the ILO survey found 43 percent of working children were under the legal age. Massachusetts passed the first restriction on child labor in the United States in 1842. However, that law and other states' laws

---

[9] Kebebew Asshagrie, *Statistics on Working Children and Hazardous Child Labour in Brief* (Geneva: International Labor Office, 1997).

[10] The ILO estimates that 18 percent of children aged 5–14 are economically active worldwide. Of these, it estimates that 94 percent of them are in low-income countries, and only 2 percent are in what it classifies as developed countries. ILO, *Every Child Counts: New Global Estimates on Child Labour* (Geneva: ILO, 2002).

affected child labor very little.[11] By one estimate, more than 25 percent of males between the ages of 10 and 15 participated in the labor force in 1900.[12] Another study of both boys and girls in that age group estimated that more than 18 percent of them were employed in 1900.[13] Carolyn Moehling also found little evidence that minimum age laws for manufacturing implemented between 1880 and 1910 contributed to the decline in child labor.[14] Economists Claudia Goldin and Larry Katz examined the period between 1910 and 1939 and found that child labor laws and compulsory school attendance laws could explain at most 5 percent of the increase in high school enrollment.[15] The United States didn't enact a national law limiting child labor until the Fair Labor Standards Act was passed in 1938. By that time, the US average per capita income was more than $12,107 (in 2020 dollars), a level far above that of many of the countries with sweatshops today.

Furthermore, child labor was defined much more narrowly when today's wealthy countries first prohibited it. Massachusetts' law limited children who were under 12 years old to no more than 10 hours of work per day. This is hardly a restriction at all. Belgium (1886) and France (1847) prohibited only children under 12 from working. Germany (1891) set the minimum working age at 13.[16] England, which passed its first enforceable child labor law in 1833, really didn't have much of a restriction at all. The law merely set the minimum age for textile work at nine years old. When today's rich countries were poorer and developing, they simply did not put in place the type of restrictions on child labor that activists demand for Third World countries today. Binding legal restrictions came only after child labor had mostly disappeared anyway.

The main reason why children don't work in the United States and other wealthy countries is precisely *because* they are wealthy. Although

---

[11] The remainder of this paragraph and the next draws on research found in Joshua Hall and Peter Leeson, "Good for the Goose, Bad for the Gander: International Labor Standards and Comparative Development," *Journal of Labor Research* 28, No. 4 (2007), 658–676.

[12] Robert Whaples, "Child Labor in the United States," EH.Net Encyclopedia, edited by Robert Whaples, retrieved from http://eh.net/encyclopedia/article/whaples.childlabor.

[13] Samuel Lindsay, "Child Labor in the United States," *American Economic Association* 8 (February 1907), 256–259.

[14] Carolyn Moehling, "State Child Labor Laws and the Decline in Child Labor," *Explorations in Economic History* 36, No. 1 (1999), 72–105.

[15] Claudia Goldin and Larry Katz, "Mass Secondary Schooling and the State: The Role of State Compulsion and the High School Movement," NBER Working Paper No. 10075 (2003).

[16] France and Prussia both had earlier laws prohibiting child labor, but they were not enforceable. See Hall and Leeson, "Good for the Goose," 658–676.

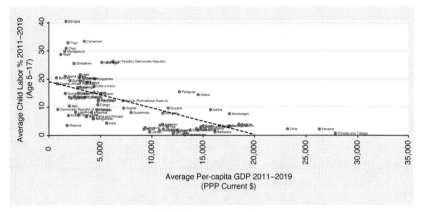

FIGURE 7.2 Child labor rates and per capita income

many parents may think a little part-time work helps to instill a good work ethic in their child, few desire to see their children work in risky jobs, or in jobs that would completely eliminate their playtime, or get in the way of their education and future development. The same is true of most Third World parents. Their problem is that they are poor and need their children's incomes to help feed and clothe the family.

The striking relationship between income and rates of child labor is illustrated in Figure 7.2 using data from UNICEF on the percentage of children working between the ages of 5 and 17 for 80, mostly poorer, countries.[17] Richer countries don't show up in the figure because they have essentially no child labor to report. As can be seen in the figure, child labor rates begin to approach zero as countries move past the $10,000 per capita income threshold. At incomes above that threshold, only 5 countries, out of the 28 with reported data, have child labor rates that exceed 5 percent.

It's only in the poorest countries where rates of child labor are significantly higher. Child labor rates average approximately 15 percent in countries with a per capita income of around $5,000. The average child labor rate rises to a little over 18 percent in countries with incomes below $3,000. Economists Eric Edmonds and Nina Pavcnick estimate that 73 percent of the variation of child labor rates can be explained by variation in GDP per capita.[18]

---

[17] Retrieved from https://data.unicef.org/resources/data_explorer/unicef_f/?ag=UNICEF&df=GLOBAL_DATAFLOW&ver=1.0&dq=.PT_CHLD_5-17_LBR_ECON.&startPeriod=2011&endPeriod=2019.

[18] Edmonds and Pavcnik, "Child Labor in the Global Economy," 210.

Of course, correlation isn't causation. But in the case of child labor and wealth, the most intuitive interpretation is that increased wealth leads to reduced child labor. After all, every country was once poor; in the countries that became rich, child labor disappeared. Few would contend that child labor disappeared in the United States or Great Britain prior to economic growth taking place – children populated their factories much like they do in the Third World today. A little introspection, or for that matter, our own moral indignation at Third World child labor, reveals that most of us desire for children, especially our own, not to work. Thus, as we become richer and can afford to allow children to have leisure and education, we choose to.

Scholars have debated these points, however. Some have claimed that child labor might impede the formation of human capital, reducing economic growth and thus trapping countries in poverty.[19] If child labor caused poverty, it would beg the question how most countries have virtually eliminated child labor. They all once used child labor. How did so many escape the trap? Furthermore, in even most of the poorest countries, fewer than 20 percent of children work. Why would the impediment to human capital formation of 20 percent of children prevent the other 80 percent of children from gaining human capital and causing economic development? Also, working isn't necessarily incompatible with school attendance. In 2000 and 2001, UNICEF surveyed 36 low-income countries on their use of child labor. They found that almost 74 percent of children aged 5–14 who worked also attended school.[20] And, as economists Eric Edmonds and Nina Pavcnik report, for those children who do sacrifice school for work, domestic work is at least as likely to crowd out schooling as manufacturing jobs.[21]

The overall cross-country empirical evidence in the economics literature suggests a strong link between the level of income and elimination of child labor.[22] So does the history of the many countries that have developed.[23] But some single-country, cross-sectional household

---

[19] For a couple of examples, see Kaushik Basu, "Child Labor: Cause, Consequence, and Cure, with Remarks on International Labor Standards," *Journal of Economic Literature* 37, No. 3 (1999), 1083–1119; and Christopher Heady, "The Effect of Child Labor on Learning Achievement," *World Development* 31 (2003), 385–398.

[20] Edmonds and Pavcnik, "Child Labor in the Global Economy," 205.

[21] Ibid., 204.

[22] For example, see Alan Krueger, "International Labor Standards and Trade," in *Annual World Bank Conference on Development Economics 1996*, edited by Michael Bruno and Boris Pleskovic (Washington, DC: The World Bank, 1997), 281–302.

[23] See Moehling, "State Child Labor Laws," 72–106.

survey research fails to find a strong link between a family's income and whether children work.[24] There are two interpretations for this. The first is that cultural norms may lead parents in some countries to not view child labor as a bad thing, and thus rising incomes won't reduce child labor. The other explanation is that higher incomes could result in more profitable opportunities for children to work and thus entice them away from school and leisure.

Both of these explanations are plausible, but another study points to a bigger problem. The single-country studies of income and child labor may not find a statistically significant relationship between the two because their empirical techniques are flawed. The studies looked for a general and uniform decrease in child labor as household income increased. However, a family that is below the poverty line may see its income increase but still need children to work because it remains below the poverty line. Similarly, wealthier families may not change the number of children working (if any) because they were already well above the poverty line. If changes in child labor are clustered around the poverty line, the statistical techniques of the household-level studies would likely fail to pick them up.[25]

Child labor studies that track family income over time almost universally find large declines in child labor when incomes increase.[26] Let's look at one of these studies in detail. An important study of child labor in Vietnam, a country where sweatshops were reported at the time, addresses the empirical shortcoming just discussed.[27] Between 1993 and 1997, Vietnam averaged 9 percent GDP growth, and child labor declined 30 percent. Economist Eric Edmonds used survey data that tracked individual households' expenditures and whether children aged 6–15 worked over a period of five years. Because he was tracking individual households over time, differences in rates of child labor as the economy grew can't be explained by differences in family preferences or cultural norms, as those are held constant.

[24] For a survey, see Drusilla Brown, Alan Deardorff, and Robert Stern, "Child Labor: Theory, Evidence and Policy," in *International Labor Standards: History, Theories and Policy*, edited by Kaushik Basu, Henrik Horn, Lisa Roman, and Judith Shapiro (Oxford: Basil Blackwell, 2003).

[25] In more technical terms, the studies were looking for a linear relationship between child labor and income, but there might be a strong nonlinear relationship between the two that these techniques would fail to discover if they were averaging child labor over data ranges in which child labor is and is not elastic. Instead, non-parametric techniques are needed.

[26] Edmonds and Pavcnik, "Child Labor in the Global Economy," 211.

[27] Eric Edmonds, "Does Child Labor Decline with Improving Economic Status?" *Journal of Human Resources* 40, No. 1 (2005), 77–99.

Importantly, he looked for changes in child labor as expenditures grew around poverty lines rather than for general changes. He specifically looked at how child labor changed when household expenditures moved from below what was necessary to supply a 2,100-calorie daily diet to above ($65 per year) and when expenditures moved above the official poverty line ($106 per year). In 1993, 25 percent of the population had expenditures below what it takes to satisfy a 2,100-calorie diet. That number had fallen to 8 percent by 1998. In 1993, 58 percent of the households were below the official poverty line, but by 1998 only 33 percent of households were below the 1993 line.

How did these changes correlate with child labor? For households whose expenditures rose but remained below what is necessary to sustain a 2,100-calorie diet, the answer is very little. After all, these families remained desperately poor and likely still needed their children to work. However, around the 2,100-calorie level, child labor begins to decline as expenditures rise. Then the decline in child labor accelerates as expenditures rise to the official poverty line. For the overall sample, Edmonds finds that child labor declines as expenditures increase, but the real action is around the poverty line. For households that emerged from poverty during the period, the increase in expenditure explains 80 percent of the decrease in child labor.[28]

This study of household-level data in Vietnam corrects for the statistical problems in other household-level research. The finding is consistent with the cross-country evidence that implies that when a country becomes wealthier child labor decreases. It also squares with common sense.

CONCLUSION

The thought of children laboring in sweatshops is even more repulsive than the thought of adults laboring in them. But that doesn't mean we can simply "think" with our hearts and not our heads. Adults who choose to work in sweatshops do so because they are poor and it is the best available alternative open to them. The same is true of children, who often come from even poorer families than the adults who work in sweatshops. The vast majority of children employed in countries with sweatshops work in lower-productivity sectors than manufacturing. However,

---

[28] Edmonds's results point to the importance of using nonlinear techniques. Although his method picked up 80 percent of the decline in child labor for groups emerging from poverty, linear techniques pick up only 51 percent of the decline.

people in wealthy countries eat few of the agricultural products grown by child laborers and consume few services provided by them. This means that passing trade sanctions or other laws targeting manufactured goods takes away the option of children working in sweatshops, generally throws children out of manufacturing jobs, and pushes them into these less remunerative and, in the case of agriculture, more dangerous sectors. In short, our prohibitions on consuming goods produced with child labor only limit children's options further, throwing them into these other industries, or the even worse alternatives, such as prostitution. Luckily, as families escape poverty, child labor declines. As countries become rich, child labor virtually disappears. The answer for how to cure child labor is the same as the answer for how to improve the lives of adult sweatshop workers. It lies in the process of economic development – a process in which sweatshops play an important role.

8

Is It Ethical to Buy Sweatshop Products?

The standard economic defense of sweatshops holds that sweatshop jobs should not be jeopardized because they are better than the other alternatives workers face. Is that enough to make it ethical for companies to offer jobs with such low pay and poor working conditions, and ethical for us to buy their products? Economist Ludwig von Mises made a moral claim that many economists who have defended sweatshops have implicitly endorsed when he defended the factory owners of the industrial revolution, writing,

It is deplorable that such [impoverished] conditions existed [outside the factories]. But if one wants to blame those responsible, one must not blame the factory owners who – driven by selfishness, of course, and not by "altruism" – did all they could to eradicate the evils. What had caused these evils was the economic order of the precapitalistic era.[1]

Is he right that firms are not blameworthy for taking advantage of the poverty caused by the prior economic order? The poverty that leads workers to choose sweatshops today is often caused by background injustices that aren't the direct fault of the firm. This raises many important ethical questions.

Are we unfairly exploiting sweatshop workers when we buy products made with their labor? Do we benefit a great deal, while they get only a pittance? Many people experience moral outrage when others buy products made in sweatshops, but that same moral outrage is seldom directed at those who don't give charitably to impoverished subsistence farmers throughout the world. Why? The subsistence farmers

[1] Ludwig von Mises, *Human Action*, 1949 (Auburn: Ludwig von Mises Institute, 1998), 615.

are often poorer and more in need of our help. By trading with sweat-shop workers, do we take on a moral responsibility to do something more for them than we have the moral responsibility to do for other poor people with whom we don't trade? If the lack of good alternatives is the result of grave injustices, are people who deal with sweatshop workers obligated to try to correct these injustices? These ethical concerns are important because they may lead you to feel "dirty" for buying sweatshop products, even if you believe the economic arguments in the preceding chapters.

IS IT WRONGFUL EXPLOITATION?

Several academics have argued that sweatshops are wrongfully exploitative.[2] Philosophers dispute what exactly it means to be exploited, and my purpose is not to try to resolve that dispute.[3] Most accounts, however, hold that wrongful exploitation consists of taking advantage of another person in a way that is either unfair or fails to manifest sufficient respect for that person's dignity. An interaction can be both voluntary and beneficial to both parties (relative to how they would have fared in the absence of any interaction) while still being wrongfully exploitative.

[2] See, for instance, Arnold and Bowie, "Sweatshops and Respect"; Robert Mayer, "Sweatshops, Exploitation, and Moral Responsibility," *Journal of Social Philosophy* 38, No. 4 (2007), 605–619; Chris Meyers, "Wrongful Beneficence: Exploitation and Third World Sweatshops," *Journal of Social Philosophy* 35, No. 3 (2004), 319–333; Jeremy C. Snyder, "Needs Exploitation," *Ethical Theory and Moral Practice*, 11, No. 4 (2008), 389–405; Jeremy C. Snyder, "Exploitation and Sweatshop Labor: Perspectives and Issues," *Business Ethics Quarterly* 20, No. 2 (2010), 187–213; and Iris Marion Young, "Responsibility and Global Justice: A Social Connection Model," *Social Philosophy and Policy* 23, No. 1 (2006), 102–130.

[3] Some of the most influential accounts include Robert E. Goodin, "Exploiting a Situation and Exploiting a Person," in *Modern Theories of Exploitation*, edited by Andrew Reeve (London: Sage, 1987), 166–200; Allen W. Wood, "Exploitation," *Social Philosophy and Policy* 12, No. 2 (1995), 136–158; Alan Wertheimer, *Exploitation* (Princeton: Princeton University Press, 1996); Ruth Sample, *Exploitation: What It Is and Why It's Wrong* (New York: Rowman and Littlefield, 2003); Robert Mayer, "What's Wrong with Exploitation?" *Journal of Applied Philosophy* 24, No. 2 (2007), 137–150; Mikhail Valdman, "Exploitation and Injustice," *Social Theory and Practice: An International and Interdisciplinary Journal of Social Philosophy* 34, No. 4 (2008), 551–572; and Mikhail Valdman, "A Theory of Wrongful Exploitation," *Philosophers' Imprint* 9, No. 6 (2009), 1–14. Wertheimer, *Exploitation*, available at: http://plato.stanford.edu/archives/fall2008/entries/exploitation/, January 12, 2010, provides an overview of most of the main philosophical accounts. Snyder, "Exploitation and Sweatshop Labor," provides another overview with specific focus on the application of such accounts to the issue of sweatshop labor.

Suppose, for example, that a boater offers to rescue a drowning man by selling him a spot on the boat for $10,000 and the drowning man accepts the offer. The deal is clearly beneficial to the boater – I assume he values the $10,000 much more highly than the time and effort he must sacrifice – and it is no less clearly beneficial to the drowning man. The drowning man surely values his life more highly than the $10,000 he had to give up to save it. If he did not, he would not have accepted the boater's offer. Still, most people (including me) would judge that the boater has acted wrongly in making his rescue contingent upon paying such an exorbitant sum. In doing so, the boater seems to be taking wrongful advantage of his monopoly on the means of rescue and failing to treat the drowning man with the respect he deserves.

Can sweatshop labor be analyzed in a similar way? Perhaps potential sweatshop workers are like people drowning in lakes and the multinational enterprises (MNEs) that ultimately finance their employment are like the boater. The potential workers are in a desperate situation, "drowning" in poverty, and perhaps unable to adequately provide for themselves and their families. MNEs have power in the form of wealth to rescue these individuals. But rather than providing that rescue out of common kindness or a sense of moral obligation, they make it contingent on an onerous payment. The MNE provides the worker with just enough money to make the employment offer attractive and demands in exchange that the worker toil for long hours in dangerous and unpleasant conditions. Such an offer might present the worker with a better alternative than anything else he has available. But so does the boater's offer and this does not make it any less unfair, demeaning, or objectionable.

There are good reasons for thinking that the standard cases of sweatshop labor – even those involving low wages and very bad working conditions – are not wrongfully exploitative. First, it is not clear that the distribution of burdens and benefits between sweatshop workers and MNEs is unfair, and hence that MNEs are taking unfair advantage of sweatshop workers. Part of the problem in credibly establishing the charge of unfairness stems from the immense difficulty in specifying a general principle of fair distribution, something no critic of sweatshops has yet managed to do. Even without such a principle, of course, critics of sweatshops might hold that the division is unfair in some obvious and intuitive way – perhaps because MNEs are clearly getting more than they ought to out of the transaction, or because workers are clearly getting less. But neither of the factual claims on which this "obvious and intuitive" account of unfairness rests is accurate. The rate of profit in MNEs that outsource is generally no higher than it is in other industries with a similar level of risk. The often-cited fact that a sweatshop worker who produces, say, a pair of Nike shoes is paid only one US dollar to make a pair of shoes, which sells for around $100, does not mean that Nike is walking away from the exchange with $99 and the worker with only $1.[4] Most of the $100 goes to paying for advertising, retailer markup, raw materials, transportation costs, and so on. The amount that actually accrues to Nike as profit is generally no greater as a percentage of their investment than the profits in any other competitive industry. Thus, MNEs are not earning unusually high profits off the backs of sweatshop workers. Nor is it obvious that sweatshop workers are receiving less than they ought to earn in wages. Such a claim might be credible if MNEs were, as some critics have charged, utilizing their monopsonistic power to pay workers less than the market rate for their labor. But as I argued in Chapter 3, there is no reason to think that workers' wages are not determined, by and large, by their productivity – just as the wages of non-sweatshop workers are.

Let's put dollars and cents aside for a moment and think about how trading with sweatshop workers impacts lives. The small amount of pay they receive often represents a large improvement in their ability to feed, clothe, and shelter their families. The slightly cheaper shirt for a consumer in the United States, or the little bit of extra profit the sweatshop employee generates for a corporation, makes a trivial difference in our lives. In fact, a T-shirt could capture this point nicely. It would have a sweatshop worker on the front with a caption that says, "She fed and clothed her family," and the back of the shirt would read, "and all I got is this lousy T-shirt." Thought of this way, it is the sweatshop workers who are getting the lion's share of the total benefits from their interaction with US firms. Unfortunately, we have no objective way to measure and compare these gains, but it is these gains that are really important – not just the dollars and cents we can measure.

The problem stems from the fact that economists have long recognized that there is no way to measure cardinal utility or welfare, or to make interpersonal comparisons of utility, as discussed in Chapter 3's appendix. Instead, economists typically measure wealth maximization in dollars. Wealth maximization maps to utility maximization only with the unrealistic assumption that a dollar generates an equal amount of

[4] This particular version of the claim is taken from Meyers, "Wrongful Beneficence," 331.

welfare (utility) no matter who gets it. This is particularly relevant for sweatshop workers who have little wealth relative to Western investors and consumers. There may be no way to measure it, but intuitively, in most cases, an extra dollar for a sweatshop worker generates more welfare for him than an extra dollar for a typical US investor or consumer. Thus, even if US citizens benefited more in dollar terms from trade with sweatshop workers, it is unlikely that they benefited more in terms of utility or welfare.

The charge of unfairness, and hence of exploitation, seems to derive some traction in the comparison drawn between sweatshops and the boat rescue case described earlier in the chapter. But on closer examination, these cases are dissimilar in ways that are morally significant. First, part of what drives our intuition in the rescue case is the belief that the boat owner will not be made significantly worse off by performing the rescue for free. However, as argued in earlier chapters, increases in sweatshop wages or improvements in employees' working conditions will come at a cost to someone – if not to the employer, then to potential workers. Moreover, the rescue in the example I provided is entirely fortuitous. The boat owner just happened to be there when the victim needed rescuing. Our intuitions might be different if the boat owner were there precisely because he anticipated that people might need rescuing, especially if his being there required significant investment of time and capital. With this contrast in mind, sweatshops look less like cases of fortuitous rescue and more like cases of professional rescuers, who acquire the skills and machinery to rescue people only because they expect to get paid. Absent the expected pay, there would be no rescue at all.

BACKGROUND INJUSTICE

Even if sweatshops are not guilty of providing their workers with less compensation than they should, it is still possible that workers' income is lower than it ought to be. The claim that MNEs do not exploit sweatshop workers is entirely compatible with the claim that sweatshop workers are suffering grievous injustice and, with it, the claim that the income of sweatshop workers is lower than it would otherwise be because of this injustice.

The explanation for this paradoxical claim lies in the fact that the labor agreements between sweatshops and their employees are a product of a wide variety of factors, many of which fall well outside the responsibility of multinational enterprises. The background political and economic institutions of the host country, for instance, shape and constrain the opportunities available to potential sweatshop workers. To the extent that those institutions erect barriers to entry to new businesses, deny workers the freedom to voluntarily organize collectively, fail to protect private property, and deny people economic freedom, workers' opportunities to advance their interests and the interests of their families will be severely limited.[5] Workers' opportunities are further restricted by injustices in the global economic order, including the unjust seizure of land and natural resources, by states and other entities, as well as the unjust restriction of free access to Western markets by various forms of protectionism.[6] The more limited their opportunities are as a result of these injustices, the more likely it is that an offer of sweatshop labor will be workers' most attractive option.

Sometimes MNEs themselves bear partial responsibility for the unjust background conditions against which labor agreements are formed. Because of the benefits that MNEs can bring to host countries, especially in the form of increased tax revenue, they are often well positioned to influence the behavior of the host country government. MNEs can make their economic investment in a country contingent upon the government's willingness to use its power to secure special benefits for the MNE – benefits that can come at the cost of the MNE's competitors as well as the country's workers and citizens. These benefits might consist of limitations on other firms entering, seizure of land, or bans on workers voluntarily bargaining collectively. To the extent that MNEs influence governments to act unjustly in a way that constrains workers' options, they do bear moral responsibility for the background conditions against which labor agreements are made. In this case, however, the real wrong of which MNEs are guilty is a form of joint coercion with the government, rather than exploitation per se. Going back to our boating rescue analogy, this joint coercion would be equivalent to torpedoing someone's boat so that it will sink and they will need to be rescued. The torpedoing is wrong independent of any price offered for rescue.

---

[5] I defend workers' freedom to organize collectively voluntarily, which is distinct from laws that allow labor unions to organize workers, where a subset of all workers has the legal right to collectively bargain for all workers, even when some workers and the employer would rather bargain individually. I support laws allowing collective bargaining but not laws requiring people who don't wish to collectively bargain to participate.

[6] For the story of many modern unjust land seizures see Fred Pearce, *The Land Grabbers: The New Fight over Who Owns the Earth* (Boston: Beacon Press, 2012).

More often, however, limiting background conditions are not the result of any injustice assignable to MNEs. Sometimes the main constraint on workers' options is a poverty that is due not to any positive evil but rather to the absence of the delicate combination of social, political, and institutional factors needed for the production of wealth and economic development. At times we forget that the natural standard of living throughout most of human history has been one of poverty. Until a society discovers and adopts that combination of factors, poverty with few options is the norm.

Often the background injustices are perpetrated by the workers' own governments. Consider what has happened in Indonesia. Ever since Jeff Ballinger's campaign against Nike in the early 1990s, Indonesia has been a target for anti-sweatshop activism. The sweatshop jobs in Indonesia attract workers because they are better than the available alternatives, but many of the alternatives to sweatshops have been unjustly destroyed by companies in cooperation with the Indonesian government. For instance, in the Riau province on the large island of Sumatra, the people held forest land in common and depended on the forests for their livelihood for centuries.[7] But nearly 50 years ago President Suharto said that customary land rights were not going to be respected and declared "the forestlands of his sprawling nation of a thousand islands to be 'state forest.' They were to be deployed in the name of national development."[8] Journalist Fred Pearce reports that in practice this "meant they would be handed out to anyone with the cash and the connections."[9] Frequently, that meant paper and plywood mill owners. Riau was 80 percent jungle in the late 1980s. By the 2010s, it was down to 30 percent. The local villagers are displaced as their land is seized and clear-cut. Mursyid Muhammad Ali, a village head, described the situation: "We have no means of living here now. People are leaving to get jobs elsewhere."[10] Sometimes, that "elsewhere" is in a sweatshop. But note, it's not the sweatshops causing the injustice. The property rights were violated by the Indonesian government and sold to lumber companies. The Indonesian government and the lumber companies are morally blameworthy for causing the injustice.

The governments of the countries where sweatshops are located systematically violate the economic freedoms and property rights of their

---

[7] Facts in this paragraph are from Pearce, *The Land Grabbers*, 165–168.
[8] Ibid., 167.
[9] Ibid.
[10] Ibid., 166.

TABLE 8.1 *Economic freedom scores, 2019*

	Score	Rank
Bangladesh	5.89	133
Cambodia	7.07	74
China	6.23	120
El Salvador	7.34	56
Haiti	6.51	102
India	6.68	93
Indonesia	7.1	72
Mauritius	8.15	12
Myanmar	5.6	145
Nicaragua	6.76	87
Pakistan	6	130
Philippines	7.2	65
Sri Lanka	6.64	94
Vietnam	6.15	125

Source: Economic Freedom of the World 2021 – Annual Report

citizens. Table 8.1 contains the economic freedom scores and rankings of the countries where sweatshops have been reported in the popular press.

The index ranks 165 countries based on scores between 1 and 10. The average country, with sweatshops reported in popular news sources, scores only 6.67 and would rank the 94th freest country in the world (dropping Mauritius from the sample causes the average to drop to 6.55 and the rank to fall to 102nd). For comparison, the United States scores 1.7 points higher and ranks 5th in the index, whereas Singapore and Hong Kong top the rankings with scores around 9. The governments in these sweatshop-using countries discourage business creation and investment by taxing away profits, regulating opportunities out of existence, tampering with their currencies, limiting the ability to trade with foreigners, and failing to protect property rights. The violation of these economic freedoms is one reason why these countries are poor and workers find sweatshops are their best option.

Some left-leaning libertarians are critical of a defense of sweatshops, such as the one outlined in this book, because the world is not a truly free market economy.[11] I fully recognize that we do not live in a free

---

[11] See, for example, Gary Chartier, "Sweatshops, Labor Rights, and Competitive Advantage," *Oregon Review of International Law* 10, No. 1 (2008), 149–188; Kevin Carson, "Vulgar Libertarianism," Mutualist Blog: Free Market Anti-Capitalism,

market economy that is devoid of current and prior injustices. Some countries, such as the United States, are relatively freer than others. Sweatshop countries, by and large, have many more injustices and a greater lack of freedom.

However, although there are prior injustices and governments fail to respect people's freedoms, as long as the labor agreements between workers and sweatshops are not plagued by any form of procedural wrongdoing, such as deception or coercion, and the sweatshops are not actively perpetuating the background injustices, it is difficult to see how the claim that sweatshops are taking unfair advantage of workers can be maintained. They are taking advantage, to be sure. But they are doing so by entering into an agreement with workers that is mutually beneficial, relative to their antecedent circumstances. Although sweatshop workers might reasonably wish that their antecedent circumstances were better, and hence that their bargaining power with sweatshops was stronger, it is far from obvious that they have any grounds for complaint against sweatshops in circumstances such as those that I have described here, as long as it is not the sweatshops themselves causing the unjust antecedent circumstance. Their complaint is against their own governments and those who have created injustices in their past that contribute to their current circumstances. I join them in protest of these injustices and explore how activism might address some of the injustices in Chapter 11.[12] But first we must examine whether companies have a moral duty to do more because of these injustices.

January 11, 2005, retrieved from http://mutualist.blogspot.com/2005/01/vulgar-libertarianism-watch-part-1.html; and Michael Kleen, "Sweatshops and Social Justice: Can Compassionate Libertarians Agree?" Center for a Stateless Society, November 17, 2011, retrieved from http://c4ss.org/content/8840.

[12] I'm not sure how to make this point clearer for philosophers who seem to willingly misconstrue the argument made in this book. For example, Michael Neu spends an entire chapter of his book criticizing my work on sweatshops that, while a bit scattershot and rambling, essentially amounts to the claim that, by defending sweatshops, I put in the background the injustices that should be in the foreground. I oppose the injustices, and activists should work to stop them. On that, we're on the same page. But Neu offers no argument for why workers would be treated more justly if we prohibited or otherwise interfered with their choice to sell their labor to sweatshops, while other injustices exist. His criticism of my work is that I focus too much on the immediate transaction between firms and sweatshop workers. Unfortunately, he errs in the other direction and offers no insight on how to improve on that immediate transaction. Nor does he seem to understand the longer-run process of development, and the role sweatshops play in that process, that will be covered in the next two chapters of this book. Michael Neu, *Just Liberal Violence* (London: Roman Littlefield, 2018).

DO WE ACQUIRE GREATER OBLIGATIONS TO HELP BY TRADING WITH SWEATSHOP WORKERS?

A complaint that sweatshops are wrongfully exploiting workers because of the background injustices could be grounded in the claim that sweatshops, or more plausibly the MNEs with which they contract, have some kind of moral obligation to rectify the injustice of the background conditions against which labor contracts are formed. Or, at least, to try to "correct" for this background injustice in some way, when forming labor agreements with workers – perhaps by entering into only agreements of the sort that would have been formed had background conditions not been unjust.[13] This way of understanding what a nonexploitative transaction requires seems to place an unduly heavy burden on those interacting with the victims of background injustice.[14] Why should MNEs bear special responsibility for rectifying injustices for which they were not responsible?[15]

Philosopher Alan Wertheimer suggested that what he calls the "interaction principle" underlies some objections to exploitation. The interaction principle holds that "one has special responsibilities to those with whom one interacts beneficially that one would not have if one had chosen not to interact with them."[16] Along these lines, philosopher Jeremy Snyder has argued that MNEs' special obligation has its origin in a Kantian duty of beneficence.[17] Part of what it means to respect other persons as ends in themselves, according to this line of reasoning, is to not merely refrain from interfering with their actions but to make some of their ends our own. This duty of beneficence has an imperfect form, meaning that individuals have "considerable leeway

---

[13] The suggestion of entering into only those agreements that would have emerged with just background conditions is impossible to operationalize. First World companies and workers suffer from many injustices as well as Third World workers. Absent a market process that reveals everyone's choices in the absence of injustices, there is no way to know what the actual market outcomes would be. This is one implication of the calculation and knowledge problems outlined by Ludwig von Mises, *Economic Calculation in the Socialist Commonwealth* (Auburn: Ludwig von Mises Institute, 1990) and Hayek "Use of Knowledge."

[14] Wertheimer, *Exploitation*, 234.

[15] The argument that follows is closely related to one made by Matt Zwolinski, "Structural Exploitation," *Social Philosophy and Policy* 29, No. 1 (Winter 2012), 154–179.

[16] Alan Wertheimer, "Matt Zwolinski's 'Choosing Sweatshops': A Commentary," Unpublished manuscript, presented at the Arizona Current Research Workshop in Tucson, January 2007 (2005).

[17] See Snyder, "Needs Exploitation," and "Exploitation and Sweatshop Labor," 187–213.

in determining when and where to direct their resources toward supporting" the autonomy of others.[18] But Snyder's key move, following
the interaction principle, is to argue that when we enter into certain
forms of special relationships with others, this general duty takes on a
"perfect, strict form."[19] MNEs that enter into relationships with particular sweatshop employees have a special obligation of beneficence
toward those employees. Because they are in a direct relationship with
other human beings in desperate need, they no longer have the leeway
they once had in determining how to discharge their duty of beneficence.
Rather, "they are required to cede as much of their benefit from the
interaction to their employees as is reasonably possible toward the end
of their employees achieving a decent minimum standard of living."[20]

But there is something puzzling about Snyder's position. As we have
seen, sweatshop labor generally represents a more attractive option
than any other option available to workers. By making such labor
opportunities available, MNEs confer considerable benefit upon their
workers. Why should the very act of providing such a benefit impose
upon MNEs a moral obligation to confer an even greater benefit? Why
does providing some help to workers in the developing world confer
an obligation to help more, especially when those who provide no help
are (by Snyder's account) guilty of no moral wrongdoing? This violates
a position known as the "non-worseness principle" that philosopher
Matt Zwolinski has frequently defended.[21] The non-worseness principle holds that it can't be morally worse for two people to interact than
to not interact at all if (1) both parties benefit from the interaction, (2)
both parties consent to the interaction, and (3) the interaction doesn't
have negative effects on others. For example, consider the following
two companies:

---

[18] Snyder, "Needs Exploitation," 396.
[19] Ibid., 390.
[20] Ibid., 396.
[21] See Zwolinski, "Sweatshops, Choice, and Exploitation," *Business Ethics Quarterly*
19, No. 4 (2007), 708–710; Matt Zwolinski, "The Ethics of Price Gouging," *Business
Ethics Quarterly* 18, No. 3 (2008), 357–360; Matt Zwolinski, "Price Gouging, Non-
Worseness, and Distributive Justice," *Business Ethics Quarterly* 19, No. 2 (2009),
295–306. Jeremy C. Snyder has responded in "Efficiency, Equality, and Price Gouging:
A Response to Zwolinski," *Business Ethics Quarterly* 19, No. 2 (2009), 303–306.
I don't find his response persuasive, but it is beyond this chapter to set out a full defense
of the non-worseness claim, though see Matt Zwolinski, "Exploitation and Neglect"
(San Diego: University of San Diego, Department of Philosophy, 2012, unpublished
working paper), for an attempt to do this.

Outsource Company: This company, based in the United States, out-sources production to a poorer country. The wages it pays are considerably higher than the wages paid elsewhere in that country, and workers' lives are greatly improved by the benefits those wages confer. Moreover, the company uses a portion of the profits it earns to fund various charitable causes in its home country. It does not, however, give to its sweatshop workers as much "as is reasonably possible."

Domestic Company: This company, based in the United States, does not outsource production at all. It does, however, use a portion of its profits to fund various charitable causes in its home country.

Let us stipulate that both companies give enough to charity to satisfy an imperfect duty of beneficence. Snyder's account nevertheless implies that Outsource Company is acting wrongly, whereas Domestic Company is not.[22] This implication would seem to hold even if workers in the poor country, in which Outsource Company hires workers, stand in greater need of aid than the beneficiaries of the charitable causes that both companies fund, because, according to Snyder, the perfect nature of Outsource Company's obligations toward its employees is not a function of their need but rather of their interaction with the company. This seems implausible.

Suppose Snyder's account is right that a company's entering into an employment relationship with a needy individual is sufficient to generate a strict, perfect duty of beneficence on the part of the company toward that employee.[23] Suppose compliance with such a duty would require the company to pay its employees at least $5 per hour. But let us suppose that the employer is only willing to provide its employees with $3 per hour. Would it be permissible, on Snyder's account, for the employer to make its offer of employment contingent upon its workers' willingness to waive their right to $5 per hour? Prior to entering into a relationship with employees, the employer has only an imperfect

---

[22] Alternatively, Snyder could hold that Outsource Company is guilty of exploitation, whereas Domestic Company is not, but that Domestic Company is guilty of some other and perhaps more serious form of moral offense. This would save Snyder's account from having to embrace the counterintuitive claim that Outsource Company is acting in a worse way than Domestic Company, but only at the price of reducing the moral significance of exploitation.

[23] Actually, Snyder does not quite hold that it is "sufficient." Several other conditions must be met for the employer to have this duty, but as they do not affect the present argument, these need not concern us here.

duty of beneficence. No prospective employee has any valid moral claim upon its assistance. Thus, the company would not be acting wrongly if it refused to hire or assist the prospective employee at all. But if it is permissible for the employer not to hire prospective workers, and if hiring prospective workers at $3 per hour is better for both the employer and the worker than not hiring the prospective workers at all, then how could doing so be wrong? If, on one hand, employees' claim to a wage of at least $5 per hour is waivable, then employers are not necessarily acting wrongly in providing their employees with $3 per hour. If, on the other hand, employees' claim to $5 per hour is not waivable, then Snyder's account is committed to holding that failing to benefit needy workers at all is better than benefiting them at a level that is (significantly) greater than zero but less than the morally required amount – even if workers themselves would strongly prefer, and would like to choose, the latter over the former. This seems implausible as well.

AUTONOMY, LIMITS OF CHOICE, AND GLOBAL LABOR JUSTICE

The arguments in this chapter, and throughout much of this book, rely on the importance of workers' choices in establishing what they believe improves their welfare. Philosophers Michael Kates and Joshua Preiss have argued that there are limitations about what we can learn from these choices that leave room for ethical anti-sweatshop regulation.[24] It's worth considering their arguments here.

Kates and Preiss both point out that all choices are made within the institutional status quo. Thus, those choices reveal what workers believe makes them better off only within that status quo. Perhaps their true autonomous preferences are different from what they can reveal by their choices within the existing status quo, which, as we have seen, is plagued by background injustices. This is obviously true, and irrelevant, in a superficial sense. If they were significantly richer, exercising their true autonomous preferences would not result in them working in sweatshops, just like readers of this book don't choose to work in sweatshops. But without a magic wand that transforms their wealth, I do not see

[24] Michael Kates, "The Ethic of Sweatshops and the Limits of Choice," *Business Ethics Quarterly* 25, No. 2 (2015), 191–212; Joshua Preiss, "Global Labor Justice and Limits of Economic Analysis," *Business Ethics Quarterly* 24, No. 1 (2014), 55–83; Joshua Preiss, "Freedom, Autonomy, and Harm in Global Supply Chains," *Journal of Business Ethics* 160, No. 4 (2019), 881–891.

how it is relevant. The point becomes relevant if there are legal changes that can be made to the status quo that would enable workers to make choices, based on their autonomous preferences, that they are currently unable to exercise.

In principle, such cases could be possible. Preiss, building on Mill, points out that without laws against theft and fraud it might be individually optimal to engage in these activities, and people's actions, in this environment, would reveal their preference for stealing and defrauding. However, if there were laws that prevented theft and fraud, options would become available that wouldn't have existed without these laws, and these options may allow people in the community to make choices that better realize their true autonomous preferences. In this case, I agree. The law is solving a collective action problem, where people might not individually all abide by an agreement not to rob or defraud. But the activities being prohibited are activities where one person gains at the expense of another. Sweatshop regulations outlaw "gains from trade" between the employer and the sweatshop worker. Does the above logic apply in that situation?

Michael Kates attempts to argue that sweatshop regulations solve this same sort of collective action problem for sweatshop workers. He models workers' choice between a 9-hour and 10-hour workday, where workers are paid the same regardless of the number of hours worked, as what economists call a "prisoners' dilemma game." He asserts that individual decision-making, where pay could vary based on number of hours worked, would result in all workers working 10 hours for the same pay, and that all rational workers would prefer to work a 9-hour day for the same pay. Thus, a sweatshop regulation limiting working days to 9 hours would allow workers to better exercise their true autonomous preference (and be better off). Unfortunately for Kates, he badly misconstrues the situation of sweatshop workers and misapplies basic economic game theory. First, he describes a labor market process where workers choose between 9 hours for a pay of X, and 10 hours for a pay of X + epsilon, and assumes all workers would choose 10 hours and the extra pay.[25] Then he incorrectly implicitly assumes that workers can only earn the extra pay, for the extra hour, if no other worker chooses to work the 10th hour. There is no reason to assume that. If worker pay is based on productivity, as argued in Chapter 3, and an extra hour of work is productive, then there is no reason why all workers choosing

[25] He offers no compelling reason why they would all choose more hours and more pay.

to work 10 hours wouldn't result in them all earning more than if they had worked only 9 hours. Prisoners' dilemma games depend on one person's choice impacting the payoff to the other party. Kates assumed a prisoner's dilemma game where there isn't one.

Kates considers a possibility, raised by a colleague, that worker autonomy would be better realized if workers who preferred 9 hours and less pay could choose that, and workers who preferred 10 hours and more pay could also choose that. But then Kates erroneously dismisses the possibility, because his misapplication of the prisoners' dilemma game to sweatshop employment precludes that outcome. However, when we observe real-world sweatshop labor markets, we observe exactly the outcome Kates assumes away. The wage data reported in Chapter 4 is derived from real-world cases. In general, sweatshop work hours are long, but there is still significant variation in those hours across individual reports, indicating that there is not a collective action problem, in the form of a prisoners' dilemma, forcing all workers into working the same number of hours for the same pay. Thus, contrary to Kates's assertion, competitive labor markets enable workers to choose employment with differing hours and earnings, that better match their autonomous preferences, than sweatshop hours regulations, which would outlaw some of those choices.

The great early 20th-century journalist and social critic H. L. Mencken, once wrote that "We are here and it is now. Further than that, all human knowledge is moonshine."[26] To paraphrase: Sweatshop workers are here. The existing status quo is now. Philosophical musings about the true autonomous preferences of sweatshop workers, if these workers existed in a different status quo, are moonshine. Philosophers need to describe achievable legal changes, that could be made to the status quo, that would allow the better exercise of autonomous preferences, if they are going to do more than peddle moonshine. This book has argued that most suggested legal changes by anti-sweatshop scholars and activists would make sweatshop workers worse off – rather than moving them closer to exercising their autonomous preferences.

In a pair of articles, Joshua Preiss argues that the defenses of sweatshops based on economic reasoning, such as the one made in this book, are not sufficient to determine the morality of sweatshop employment conditions and activism related to demands for improved conditions. Like Kates, he addresses worker autonomy but does so

---

[26] H. L. Mencken, *A Mencken Chrestomathy* (New York: Vintage Books, 1982), 618.

in the context of a broader Kantian argument. Preiss argues that the disparity of bargaining power between sweatshop workers and employers results in exploitative offers and subjects workers to on-the-job coercion. Preiss argues that,

> Extreme inequalities of bargaining power make individuals dependent upon a given offer, and compelled to accept coercive working conditions that accompany that offer. Such an individual serves more than himself and the common-wealth, and is reduced to serving another in order to live (Kant 1996: 295). He is not his own master. Insofar as this characterization applies to sweatshop relationships, they fail to respect the humanity of all parties to that relationship. For the Kantian, it is dependence, rather than the existence of absence of a particular offer, that renders an individual, such as a sweatshop worker, unfree or not autonomous.[27]

Sweatshop regulations can be morally justified in this framework, even if they harm worker welfare, because Kantian understandings of freedom are incompatible with the large inequalities in bargaining power that result in a failure to respect workers' humanity.

Additionally, Preiss argues that sweatshop regulation can be morally justified if it helps promote global labor justice, by impeding a "global race to the bottom."[28] Economist Dani Rodrick expresses this sentiment clearly when he wrote that international trade

> renders what is illegal (and illegitimate) in a national setting to suddenly be legal (and, in the eyes of many economists and technocrats, fully legitimate). A firm cannot import child workers and put them to work at home; but it is perfectly able to do so when it employs those child workers abroad (directly, or through a subcontractor). An economist looks at this, and sees gains from trade. For the labor advocate and social reformer, however, what is taking place is an undercutting of domestic labor standards. Effectively, domestic workers are told: if you want to compete with imports, you need to sacrifice your hard-earned labor rights.[29]

This type of reasoning leads Preiss to write favorably that, "in many cases, the goals of labor activism are not only to further wages and working conditions of union members" and that "much union activism has frequently been to raise the pay and better the working conditions of non-union workers."[30] A person might favor labor market regulations,

---

[27] Preiss, "Global Labor Justice," 71.
[28] Preiss, "Autonomy, and Harm in Global Supply Chains," 889.
[29] Dani Rodrik, "A Primer on Trade and Inequality," NBER Working Paper No. 29507 (2021), 6, retrieved from www.nber.org/papers/w29507.
[30] Preiss, "Autonomy, and Harm in Global Supply Chains," 883.

in poor countries, that conform to a particular vision of "global labor justice." However, as argued in Chapter 3, one can enforce that vision, which increases the welfare of relatively wealthy union workers in First World countries, at the expense of the welfare of the poor workers in countries where sweatshops locate.

Preiss believes that the morality of sweatshop relationships and activism should be evaluated using a pluralistic understanding of value. As such, "the virtues and vices of these relationships cannot be reduced to a single value or principle, whether it be welfare, justice, freedom, reciprocity, and so on... Opposition to sweatshops is rooted in a number of values and sentiments that shape an agent's moral appraisal of these relationships."[31] However, nowhere in Preiss's writing can I find exactly how he thinks these competing values should be traded off against each other when they conflict.

The economic reasoning used throughout this book indicates that there are significant trade-offs that will harm sweatshop worker welfare by imposing wage and working condition regulations that might advance some of the other ends philosophers like Preiss also care about. As the famous economist Thomas Sowell argued years ago, there are no solutions. There are only trade-offs.[32] Economic reasoning establishes the trade-offs. Many participants in the debate surrounding sweatshops advocate for policies in the name of improving sweatshop workers' welfare. That is the standard used to evaluate policies throughout this book.[33] The economic reasoning in this book indicates that the policies activists advocate will often fail to achieve their stated end. Philosophers, who value other ends other than worker welfare, such as a particular vision of global labor justice, the welfare of union workers in the First World, or interactions only occurring on acceptable Kantian grounds, might not care that these same regulations harm sweatshop worker welfare. For such people, economic analysis is irrelevant if they do not care about what is traded off to advance their own desired end.[34] Economic analysis remains relevant for philosophers, like Preiss, who have "pluralistic"

---

[31] Preiss, "Global Labor Justice," 59.
[32] Thomas Sowell, *A Conflict of Visions: Ideological Origins of Political Struggles* (New York: William Morrow & Co., 1987).
[33] This does not commit me, or others who argue that the activists' chosen means are incompatible with the end of promoting worker welfare, to embracing a general global prioritarian frame as Preiss erroneously claims in his 2019 paper.
[34] As management professor Gordon Sollars and economist Fred Englander put it, "to the extent that consumers and political actors value philosophical purity over not under-cutting opportunities that make poor people better off, Preiss is correct about the

ends, which include sweatshop worker welfare. But it should be incumbent on such philosophers to argue exactly how much harm to worker welfare they believe is desirable to promote their other competing ends.[35]

CONCLUSION

It is morally wrong to violate a person's rights. When it comes to using physical coercion or the threat of physical coercion to get sweatshop workers into a factory, all reasonable people in the sweatshop debate are on the same side. It is morally wrong and unethical to buy products made with coerced slave labor. It is also very rare. In the vast majority of sweatshops, workers aren't physically coerced into working – they choose to. Most of this book has argued that this choice by the workers has important consequentialist implications, but their choice also has moral significance. Respecting a worker's autonomy means respecting their choice to waive one of their rights when they deem it in their best interest. A person's right to their own body means a firm can't demand that they work for the firm. But a person can waive a portion of their rights, in order to work for a firm, when the firm makes them an offer they deem in their best interest. Negative rights are rights protecting individuals from having things done to them. Everyone in the sweatshop debate should agree that workers have negative rights and that they can waive them when it's in their best interest.

Some scholars have argued that, by interacting with sweatshop workers, firms (or consumers) acquire new positive duties that sweatshop workers have a right to. I have argued that if sweatshop workers start with no positive rights, and acquire positive rights only by interacting with a firm, it would seem to be better if a firm benefited a worker a little bit, but less than what their positive right entitled them to, rather than not at all. Furthermore, even if a positive right exists, the worker may waive it, just like a negative right. Thus, firms are not wrongfully exploiting workers, so it seems ethical to buy products of sweatshop labor.

irrelevance of the economic case in this one regard." Gordon Sollars and Fred Englander, "Sweatshops: Economic Analysis and Exploitation as Unfairness," *Journal of Business Ethics* 149, No. 1 (2018), 15–29, 22.

[35] I often get the feeling that philosophers who are critical of sweatshops wish to pretend that such trade-offs do not exist. This stems, in part, from philosophers continuing to cite debunked papers (see Chapter 3) in the business ethics literature that attempt to use economic reasoning to argue these trade-offs do not exist, without engaging the arguments by economists (including me) that debunked these earlier papers and explaining why they think the economists are wrong.

Yet people often feel "dirty" because they benefit from sweatshop labor, but they don't feel dirty because of the existence of Third World poverty. Part of the reason why is that we don't directly benefit from the labor of the poor subsistence farmer. Another part of the reason is cognitive. As Matt Zwolinski put it, "neglect might feel less wrong to us, because we are not cognizant of the value we are neglecting."[36]

But in his rendering, and mine, the fact that we benefit from sweatshop labor and are more cognizant of workers' plight doesn't change anything. As Zwolinski states,

If the persons we neglect are ... just as valuable as those with whom we are engaged, then it is hard to see how neglect could actually be less wrong. Similarly, if those we neglect are indeed as valuable as those with whom we are engaged, then it is also not clear how we come to acquire new obligations to persons just by virtue of being engaged with them. The value of the persons is the same whether we are engaged with them or not, and if the value is the same, so too should be our call to respect that value.[37]

Whether neglect of the plight of the poor is morally wrong is beyond the focus of this book. For my purposes, it is enough to argue that there is nothing special about sweatshop workers that entitles them to more than any other similarly poor person. In fact, the moral theories that put more weight on the welfare of the least advantaged people should be much more concerned about the rest of the poor in the Third World, because this book has shown that sweatshop workers are better off than most of them.[38]

Economic reasoning, as employed in this book, cannot by itself establish the morally correct position on sweatshop regulations. Economics, without philosophy, can promote immoral ends. However, philosophy, without economics, is just daydreaming. Economic reasoning allows us to assess the harm to sweatshop worker welfare that would be traded off in the pursuit of other philosophical values. I think that reasonable participants in debates surrounding sweatshops should judge these trade-offs as morally undesirable, all things considered. No philosopher has explicitly made an argument about how much worker welfare should be traded off in pursuit of other desirable philosophical values. Perhaps such an argument will be convincingly made in the future, but I doubt it. Until such an argument is made, as long as one cares about the welfare of sweatshop workers, it remains ethical to buy their products.

---

[36] Zwolinski, "Sweatshops, Choice, and Exploitation," 710.
[37] Ibid.
[38] John Rawls, *A Theory of Justice* (Cambridge, MA: Harvard University Press, 1971).

The fact that sweatshops are these workers' best available option, and that it is ethical to buy their products, isn't the end of the story. Even if the workers don't have a moral right to anything more from businesses or consumers, it doesn't mean that we don't wish that they could obtain a higher standard of living. With that in mind, for the next three chapters, let's explore how sweatshops have been eliminated in countries that are wealthy today, and what good activists might be able to do to help current sweatshop workers.

9

A History of Sweatshops, 1780–2019

Whenever I raise the point that it is immoral to shut us up in a close (*sic*) room twelve hours a day in the most monotonous and tedious of employment, I am told that we have come to the mills voluntarily and we can leave when we will. Voluntarily! … The whip which brings us to Lowell is necessity. We must have money; a father's debts are to be paid, an aged mother to be supported, a brother's ambition to be aided and so the factories are supplied. Is this to act from free will? Is this freedom? To my mind it is slavery.[1]

These were the words, in 1845, of Sarah Bagley, who worked in Lowell, Massachusetts, and became the vice president of the Lowell Union of Associationists, a utopian reform organization. But they could easily be the words of an anti-sweatshop activist describing Third World sweatshops today.

Sweatshops are not new. They first appeared in Great Britain in the late 18th century and persisted there until the early 20th century. In the United States, the first textile sweatshops appeared in the early 19th century in Rhode Island and Massachusetts. In fact, they flourished in the cities where I grew up and went to college. Lowell and Lawrence dominated the textile industry in the 19th century, and Haverhill, my hometown, still has the nickname "the shoe city," which it earned in the 19th and early 20th century, because of all the shoe factories located there. Virtually every wealthy country in the world had sweatshops at one point in their past. Sweatshops are an important stage in the process of economic development. As Jeffery Sachs, an economist and the director of the Earth Institute at Columbia University, put it, "sweatshops are the

---

[1] Quoted in Lowell Mills Museum, Lowell National Historical Park, Lowell, MA.

first rung on the ladder out of extreme poverty."[2] Let's examine what that rung was like in countries that are wealthy today.

SWEATSHOPS IN 19TH-CENTURY GREAT BRITAIN AND THE UNITED STATES

Working conditions have been harsh and standards of living low throughout most of human history. Farmers worked long hours for near-subsistence returns for much of recent human history. There is no doubt that chattel slavery imposed horrid working conditions and standards of living on innumerable people throughout history. But it wasn't until the industrial revolution that something resembling modern-day sweatshops emerged.

Prior to the industrial revolution, textile production was decentralized to the homes of many rural families or artisans, and output was limited to what could be produced on the spinning wheel and handloom. The invention of the flying shuttle increased the demand for yarn by boosting the production of each weaver in 1833. Yarn spinning was mechanized in 1767, with the invention of the spinning jenny, and water power was harnessed shortly thereafter. With these inventions, and later steam power, large-scale textile factories, that are similar to today's sweatshops, emerged.

The conditions in these early sweatshops were worse than those in many Third World sweatshops today. In some factories, workers toiled for 16 hours a day, 6 days per week. Attendance at traditional festival days was curtailed because factories would fine workers for absences. The working conditions were unhealthy and dangerous. Dust from textile fibers was inhaled in poorly ventilated rooms, and workers were maimed by fast-moving machinery.[3] Child labor was common. Factories employed orphan children, from London and other major cities, in exchange for providing them room and board.[4] As historian Peter Sterns summarized it,

---

[2] Jeffrey Sachs, *The End of Poverty: Economic Possibilities for Our Time* (New York: Penguin Press, 2005), 11.

[3] Peter Stearns, *The Industrial Revolution in World History*, 3rd ed. (Boulder: Westview Press, 2007), 35.

[4] An important distinction within child labor during Britain's industrial revolution is often overlooked. There were "free-labour" children, who lived with their families and freely chose to work, and there were "apprentice children," who were orphans and under the direct control of government officials. Many of the worst accounts of child labor during this time describe factories employing apprentice children, who were forced to work by

Extensive use of child and female labor was not in itself novel – families had always depended on work by all members to survive – but use of children and young women specifically because of the low wages they could be pressed to accept reflected the pressures of early industrial life and unquestionably constrained the nascent working class in the factories.[5]

It wasn't just the work in the factories that was dangerous. The cities themselves were unhealthy. Their swelling population and poor sanitation led to the spread of disease. Housing was cramped, poorly constructed, and sometimes expensive. On many margins, the quality of life in cities was lower than in the country. Yet workers flocked to the mills. The proportion of people in Great Britain living in cities with more than 5,000 people rose from 21 percent in 1750 to 28 percent in 1800, and then ballooned to 45 percent by 1850.[6] Meanwhile, the share of the labor force working in agriculture shrank from 35 percent in 1801 to 22 percent in 1851.[7] Why did people move to the cities in such numbers? Partly it was due to involuntary enclosure of agricultural lands but also, much like today's Third World sweatshop workers, they were attracted by the opportunity to earn higher wages than they could elsewhere. In fact, economist Ludwig von Mises defended the factory system of the industrial revolution in much the same manner as I have defended modern sweatshops, writing, "The factory owners did not have the power to compel anybody to take a factory job. They could only hire people who were ready to work for the wages offered to them. Low as these wage rates were, they were nonetheless more than these paupers could earn in any other field open to them."[8] He continued,

It is a distortion of facts to say that the factories carried off the housewives from the nurseries and the kitchens and the children from their play. These women had nothing to cook with and to feed their children. These children were destitute and starving. Their only refuge was the factory. It saved them, in the strict sense of the term, from death by starvation.[9]

Mises's argument is supported by historical evidence. Economist Joel Mokyr reports that workers earned a wage premium of 15–30 percent

---

the authority of the state. The first reform laws were targeted at the abuses of apprentice children who didn't have normal market mechanisms protecting them. See Lawrence Reed, "Child Labor and the British Industrial Revolution," *The Freeman* 41, No. 8 (1991).

[5] Stearns, *The Industrial Revolution*, 34.

[6] Joel Mokyr, *The Enlightened Economy: An Economic History of Britain 1700–1850* (New Haven: Yale University Press, 2009), 456.

[7] Ibid., 476.

[8] Mises, *Human Action*, 615.

[9] Ibid.

by working in the factories compared with other alternatives.[10] The transformation of Great Britain during this time was dramatic. As economist and historian Deirdre McCloskey describes it,

In the 80 years or so after 1780 the population of Britain nearly tripled, the towns of Liverpool and Manchester became gigantic cities, the average income of the population more than doubled, the share of farming fell from just under half to just under one-fifth of the nation's output, and the making of textiles and iron moved into steam-driven factories.[11]

The increased income translated into meaningful improvements in the standard of living. McCloskey reports that "the amounts of bread, beer, trousers, shoes, trips to London, warmth in winter, and protection against conquest increased from 11 (pounds) per head in 1780 to 28 in 1860... Because he produced two-and-a-half times more than his great-grandfather produced in 1780, the average person in 1860 could buy two-and-a-half times more goods and services."[12] Similarly, Peter Lindert and Jeffrey Williamson find impressive gains in the standard of living between 1781 and 1851. They find that farm labor's standard of living went up more than 60 percent, blue-collar workers' standard increased more than 86 percent, and overall workers' standards increased more than 140 percent. Along with this increase in the standard of living came a decrease in the share of women and children working beginning sometime between 1815 and 1820. As Lindert and Williamson summarize, "The hardships faced by workers at the end of the Industrial Revolution cannot have been nearly as great as those of their grandparents."[13]

By 1851, Great Britain's per capita income stood at about $2,800.[14] This was 65 percent higher than that in Germany and 30 percent higher than that in the United States.[15] Some historians debate whether the industrial revolution improved the standard of living much before 1820. That analysis is complicated by an expensive foreign war and other

---

[10] Mokyr, *The Enlightened Economy*, 457.

[11] Deirdre McCloskey, "The Industrial Revolution 1780–1860: A Survey," in *The Economics of the Industrial Revolution*, edited by Joel Mokyr (Totowa, NJ: Rowman and Allanheld, 1985), 53.

[12] Ibid., 56.

[13] Peter Lindert and Jeffrey Williamson, "English Workers' Living Standards during the Industrial Revolution: A New Look," in *The Economics of the Industrial Revolution*, edited by Joel Mokyr (Totowa, NJ: Rowman and Allanheld, 1985).

[14] Income figures are updated for inflation to 2020 US dollars from Maddison's income data, which was in constant 1990 International Keary-Khamis dollars. Angus Maddison, retrieved from www.rug.nl/ggdc/historicaldevelopment/maddison/original-maddison.

[15] Mokyr, *The Enlightened Economy*, 476.

unfavorable external circumstances. At a minimum, historians agree that the early industrial revolution prevented the standard of living from falling when facing these circumstances, plus an enormous increase in the population, which traditionally would have been expected to drag down living standards. But there is little doubt that there was a meaningful improvement in people's living standards during the first 70 years of the industrial revolution. Furthermore, all but the most willfully blind can recognize that living standards improved greatly for the generations born within the century following 1850.

The industrial revolution began in Great Britain, but the United States was one of the earlier places it spread to. When textile production was mechanized in Great Britain, all of the technology had to be created, and new capital had to be accumulated that could embody that technology. The United States was in a position more like many Third World countries today. It could import technology and capital from abroad to jump-start its industrial revolution. The British were extremely secretive and protective of their technology. But eventually Samuel Slater, who had worked his way up from apprentice to overseer in a British factory, immigrated to America with the plans for an Arkwright water frame memorized. In 1790, he set up the first cotton spinning mill in the United States in Rhode Island. At first, textile factories in the United States were limited to carding and spinning. Then, Francis Cabot Lowell introduced a workable power loom, and all stages of textile production were integrated into a single factory. He and his associates opened a factory in Waltham, Massachusetts, in 1814 and went on to found factories in Lowell, Lawrence, and throughout New England.

The United States later, particularly in the latter half of the 19th century and on, contributed many of its own technological breakthroughs, but for much of the 19th century, it remained dependent on foreign technological advances. At first, US businesses imitated technology mostly from Britain and France; later, in industries such as chemicals, they imitated the Germans and Swedish.[16] The United States also embraced the investment of foreign capital. Peter Stearns reports that "the United States also relied unusually heavily on foreign capital. The nation was rich in resources but lacked the funds to develop them as rapidly as industrialization required. Huge investments from Europe, in particular Great Britain, fueled U.S. industry throughout the nineteenth century."[17]

[16] Stearns, *The Industrial Revolution*, 62.
[17] Ibid., 66.

This infusion of foreign capital and technology allowed the United States to proceed through its industrial revolution more rapidly than Great Britain. In 1820, before the United States had started its industrial revolution, its per capita income was just more than $2,300 – approximately the British income level in 1700. But by 1903, roughly 75 years into its industrial revolution, the United States had caught up to Britain's per capita income.[18]

The infusion of foreign capital and technology did not allow the United States to skip the stage of sweatshop development, however. Early textile factories were similar to those in Great Britain at that time, and the Third World today. Hours were long. In 1845, more than 2,000 Lowell textile workers unsuccessfully petitioned the state legislature for a 10-hour workday. Their petition described some of their working conditions:

We the undersigned peaceable, industrious and hard working men and women of Lowell, in view of our condition – the evils already come upon us, by toiling from 13 to 14 hours per day, confined in unhealthy apartments, exposed to poisonous contagion of air, vegetable, animal and mineral properties, debarred from proper physical exercise, mental discipline, and mastication cruelly limited, and thereby hastening us on through pain disease and privation, down to a premature grave, pray the legislature to institute a ten hour working day in all of the factories of the state.[19]

I visited the National Historic Park at the Lowell Mills while writing this chapter. The descriptions of the work environment in the museum there could be a description of many of the Third World sweatshops today:

Weave rooms were hazardous work environments. Life threatening accidents and long term health disabilities were common byproducts of employment in the textile mills. Cotton dust caused lung and respiratory diseases. The noise was deafening and impaired hearing. The lighting was poor, the hours long, the work tedious, and the machinery and belting dangerous.

In the weave room, both heat and humidity are kept high to prevent the yarn from breaking. Workers, who were paid by the piece, were often willing to endure the humidity because it increased both productivity and their pay checks. Nevertheless, work in this environment was eventually debilitating.

Compared to agricultural life, a worker's day was highly regimented and hectic. As one woman described it in a trade newspaper in 1841, "I object to the constant hurry of everything. We cannot have time to

---

[18] Income figures are updated for inflation to 2020 US dollars from Maddison's income data, which was in constant 1990 International Keary-Khamis dollars. Angus Maddison, retrieved from www.rug.nl/ggdc/historicaldevelopment/maddison/original-maddison.

[19] Published in *Voice of Industry*, January 15, 1845.

eat, drink, or sleep; we have only thirty minutes, or at most three quarters of an hour, allowed us, to go from our work, partake of our food, and return to the noisy clatter of machinery."[20]

Yet, despite these conditions, workers flocked to the mills. At first, in the cities north of Boston, it was mainly rural women and girls who left the farm to populate the early textile mills.[21] During the 1830s in Lowell, a woman could earn $12 to $14 a month, and after paying $5 for room and board in a company boarding house would have the rest left over for clothing, leisure, and savings. It wasn't uncommon for women to return home to the farm after a year with $25 to $50 in a bank account. This is far more money than they could have earned on the farm and often more disposable cash than their fathers had.[22] There was another benefit for the women as well. For many, it was the first time they had any independence from their fathers. For the first time, they earned their own money, lived on their own, and could choose their leisure activities without male interference.[23] The mill cities availed the young women with many more amenities, from libraries, to public lectures, to wider consumer goods options, than they had had in their rural lives. The story of a young female factory worker in early 19th-century America is not unlike stories described now in China in which young rural women move to the factories, for both better pay and greater independence, despite tough working conditions.

Eventually, as women demanded greater pay and more competitors in other regions entered the textile market, immigrants came to be the main textile workers in the United States. Still, much like in Great Britain, living standards improved over time. In 1820, before the industrial revolution, per capita income in the United States stood at just under $2,400. By 1850, it had grown by 50 percent to more than $3,500, and then it more than doubled by 1900 to more than $7,800.[24] Along with the rise in incomes came improvements in working conditions and greater consumption. By 1900, 10-hour workdays were becoming more common, and weekends were beginning to include

---

[20] *The Lowell Offering*, 1841.

[21] The factory system in these cities was known as the "Waltham System." South of Boston, factories employed the "Rhode Island System," which tended to hire entire families.

[22] National Park Service, "Lowell: The Story of an Industrial City," *Official National Park Handbook*, Handbook 140, Division of Publications National Park Service (Washington, DC: U.S. Department of the Interior, 1992), 40.

[23] See Jeff Levinson, ed., *Mill Girls of Lowell* (Boston: History Compass).

[24] Income figures are updated for inflation to 2020 US dollars from Maddison's income data, which was in constant 1990 International Keary-Khamis dollars.

Saturdays or at least Saturday afternoons off.[25] New forms of leisure also expanded and were related to advances in industry:

> Much of the new leisure also depended on industrial technology, from the tram lines that took the urban masses to large concrete and metal stadiums, to the vulcanized rubber balls that were mass-produced from the 1840s onward. Clearly a revolution in leisure was underway, but it came a bit later than the industrial revolution itself... By the late nineteenth century, however, consumerism could be more widely indulged throughout the West. New products like bicycles – an 1880s fad – and the automobile represented more expensive consumer items than had ever before been sold widely.[26]

In both Great Britain and the United States, from 1900 on, incomes continued to rise, hours were reduced, and working conditions improved. By midway through the 20th century, anything that could be meaningfully labeled a sweatshop for textile or apparel production ceased to operate on any widespread basis. In Great Britain, depending on when one dates the start of the industrial revolution, and how stringent wage and working condition standards one requires for a factory to be a sweatshop, the process of development involving sweatshops lasted from 130 to 160 years. In the United States, the process was faster, taking around 100 years. When we look at countries that have developed more recently, we see an even faster process of development.

POST–WORLD WAR II EAST ASIAN SWEATSHOP DEVELOPMENT SUCCESSES

If, when you think about South Korea, Taiwan, Hong Kong, or Singapore, you think of a wealthy First World country, you are right. They are. Taiwan has a per capita income levels on par with the 1990s United States, Korea and Hong Kong are on par with US income in the 2000s, and Singapore is roughly on par with current US income levels. But that wasn't always the case. Just 70 years ago, Hong Kong and Singapore had per capita income levels around $4,400, and Taiwan's and South Korea's levels were a little under $1,800 per capita. At that time, US income levels were around $19,000 per capita.[27] In 1950, these four East Asian countries were at roughly pre–industrial revolution income levels, and like the United States and Great Britain more than a century

---

[25] Stearns, *The Industrial Revolution*, 175–176.
[26] Ibid., 176.
[27] Income figures are updated for inflation to 2020 US dollars from Maddison's income data, which was in constant 1990 International Keary-Khamis dollars.

earlier, they went through a sweatshop stage of economic development. But, in these East Asian countries, the process of moving from a preindustrial standard of living, through a sweatshop stage of development, to a wealthy First World country took less than two generations rather than the more than 100 years in Great Britain and the United States.

Although the mix of industries involved in the development of each of these economies differed, a commonality ran through them. All these countries took advantage of their relatively cheap labor to produce textiles and often inexpensive consumer plastics for export. These factories often had long hours and poor working conditions, much the same as Third World sweatshops today.

Peter Stearns briefly summarizes some of the growth in these countries:

Taiwanese manufacturing sold widely around the world. Inexpensive consumer items, including plastic products and textiles, became a Taiwanese hallmark... Korea was competing successfully in cheap consumer goods, like plastics ... the same held true in textiles... Oil refineries and textiles and electronics factories joined shipbuilding as major sectors [in Singapore]... Export production in industry, particularly in textiles, combined high-speed technology with low wages and long hours for the labor force to yield highly competitive results.[28]

The textile exports from these countries eliminated almost one-third of textile jobs in wealthier and more expensive Japan.[29] In fact, Japan focused on high-tech production and came to rely on these countries for less expensive factory goods that were once key exports when Japan had its industrial surge.

Of course, cheap sweatshop production wasn't the only industry in these countries. But it was an important part of their recipe for development. "Although textiles and clothing formed 39 percent of Hong Kong's exports by the 1980s, other sectors, including heavy industry, had developed impressively as well. As in other Pacific Rim industrial nations, a large and prosperous middle class developed."[30] Eventually, as incomes rose, the sweatshops began to disappear in these countries, just like they did in the United States. These nations began shifting to higher-productivity sectors, while their textile factories saw stiffer competition from other nations with lower standards of living. The sweatshops moved from these East Asian tigers to many of the places where we see them today. Sweatshops were a necessary stage in their process of development, but one that they moved beyond, and did so more quickly than Great Britain and the United States.

[28] Stearns, *The Industrial Revolution*, 223, 225.
[29] Ibid., 223.
[30] Ibid., 226.

WHAT ROLE DO NATIONAL LABOR LAWS PLAY?

Sweatshops are eliminated mainly through the process of industrialization that raises a country's income. The increased income comes from increased worker productivity. That raises the upper bound of compensation. The increased productivity isn't just in one firm but in many firms and industries, and therefore workers' next best alternatives improve, raising the lower bound of compensation. Thus, as the economy grows, the competitive process pushes wages up. Because health, safety, leisure, and so on, are normal goods, workers demand more of their compensation on these margins as their total compensation increases. The result is the eventual disappearance of sweatshops. An obvious point that critics should raise concerns the adoption of labor laws. Didn't the minimum wages, laws against child labor, maximum work hour laws, and health and safety standards laws play a role in eliminating sweatshops? If they did historically in the United States and Great Britain, shouldn't other developing countries adopt them now?

The short answer is that the laws played very little role in ending sweatshop conditions. For the most part, the laws were adopted once the United States had already reached a level of development that had mostly eliminated the conditions the laws made illegal. As explained in the previous chapter, Great Britain's first restrictions on child labor applied only to children under 9 years old, and Massachusetts' child labor law, the first in the United States, only limited the workday to 10 hours for children under 12. The United States didn't pass meaningful national legislation against child labor until 1938, when its per capita income was more than $12,100 (in 2020 dollars). Economist Price Fishback explains the process that led to the adoption of the child labor laws:

Child labor laws appear to exemplify existing social trends coinciding with or preceding legislation. Between 1880 and 1920, the labor market participation rates of children fell nearly sixfold, while a well-organized social movement pressured state legislatures to enact limits on child employment. Studies of this period suggest that relatively little of the decline in child participation rates can be attributed to the introduction of child labor legislation... As their demand for child labor fell, the employers who had already eliminated it reduced their opposition to child labor laws. In fact, they may have actively supported the legislation to force recalcitrant employers to follow in their footsteps.[31]

[31] Price Fishback, "The Progressive Era," in *Government and the American Economy: A New History* (Chicago: University of Chicago Press, 2007), 307–308.

The process of limiting working hours for women was similar:

State laws limiting the number of working hours for women may also have passed after many employers had substantially reduced hours for women. Recent studies have found that the laws had relatively little effect... The legislation acted mainly to limit hours for a small number of women who had not yet succeeded in negotiating reduction in hours.[32]

Similarly, as explained in Chapter 3, the first federal US minimum wage wasn't introduced until 1938, and it set the minimum at 25 cents per hour – when average productivity was already 62.7 cents. The first state minimum wage law wasn't passed until 1912 in Massachusetts, and it applied only to women and children. Other national labor legislation didn't come until the United States was even more developed. Maximum work hour legislation was introduced in 1940, occupational health and safety wasn't passed until 1970, and maternity leave wasn't introduced until 1993.

The same pattern is true of workplace safety regulation. Fishback finds that "most [safety] regulations appear to have codified existing practices in the relevant industry."[33] When safety laws were passed that exceeded industry standards, they often weren't enforced. Potentially dangerous mines were inspected, at most, only once or twice a year, and factory inspections were even more limited. "Spending on factory inspection may have been less effective than spending on mine inspection. The number of factories per inspector was huge, making it impossible for inspectors to visit all workplaces within a year."[34] The anti-sweatshop movement often points to the famous 1911 Triangle Shirtwaist Factory fire as evidence of the need for regulation. Yet Fishback finds that the deaths in that fire "could be attributed in part to violations of building and factory codes that had gone unpunished. Soon after New York State tightened the laws, however, New York newspapers were still describing the inadequacies of enforcement, and statistical studies show no effect of state factory inspection budgets on accident rates."[35] In short, when laws mandated greater safety than industry practice, they were often ignored, much as they are in Third World sweatshops today. Safety improved instead in response to economic growth.

This is not to say that none of these laws had any effect. There are always occasional firms that lag behind, or some low-skilled workers

[32] Ibid., 308.
[33] Ibid., 310–311.
[34] Ibid., 311.
[35] Ibid.

who are affected. As Chapters 3 and 5 explain, unemployment for the least skilled is the main effect of these types of laws. The point is that the United States didn't adopt these labor laws until most workers' compensation and productivity already exceeded what the law mandates.[36] Thus, the United States didn't experience major disruptions in its process of development because of the laws. When the laws did set a standard above the norm, such as the first minimum wage in Puerto Rico, the result was a disaster.

All too often people see the strict labor laws in the United States and assume that they must be the cause of the good standards, rather than the codification of what had already happened. Ludwig von Mises explained, "The nineteenth century's labor legislation by and large achieved nothing more than to provide a legal ratification for changes which the interplay of market factors had brought about previously."[37] If the United States had today's labor laws in the mid 19th century, the result would have been massive unemployment and a halt to the development process. An excellent study by economists Joshua Hall and Peter Leeson, amusingly titled "Good for the Goose, Bad for the Gander," makes this point for sweatshop countries today.[38] If they were to adopt and enforce US-style labor laws, it would cut their process of development short. Hall and Leeson document the level of development the United States had achieved when it adopted each of its major labor laws and compare it to the level of development in countries that use sweatshops intensively today.[39] They calculated the average income in each of the sweatshop countries and then extrapolated from their recent rates of economic growth how many years it will take them to reach the level of development the United States had achieved when it adopted each of its major labor standards. Countries where sweatshops locate have per capita incomes far below those the United States had when it adopted

---

[36] Matthias Busse shows that higher per capita income, increased openness to trade, and enhanced human capital are all positively associated with the level of core labor standards a country adopts and that income is the most important factor in explaining differences in forced and child labor as well as unionization rights. See Matthias Busse, "On the Determinants of Core Labor Standards: The Case of Developing Countries," *Economics Letters* 83 (May 2004), 211–217.

[37] Mises, *Human Action*, 612.

[38] Hall and Leeson, "Good for the Goose." Incidentally, although their title is amusing, it would be more accurate, if less pithy, if it were "Mostly Indifferent for the Goose: Bad for the Gander."

[39] Their list of sweatshop-intensive countries included Bangladesh, Brazil, China, Costa Rica, Dominican Republic, El Salvador, Haiti, Honduras, India, Indonesia, Nicaragua, Peru, and Vietnam.

the type of labor standards many people want Third World countries to enforce today. Given their recent rates of economic growth, most of these countries are many years away from reaching a level of development at which adopting such standards wouldn't risk undermining the development process. Although that message may seem depressing, it need not be. Although the process of growth that ended sweatshops in Great Britain and the United States took more than 100 years, the process need not take that long anymore, as a quick look at some East Asian success stories revealed. Next, we examine how the process is playing out in countries with sweatshops in the 21st century.

21ST-CENTURY SWEATSHOPS

The list of countries and wages paid in Chapter 4 was compiled from news stories reporting on sweatshops in the decade of the 2010s. The first edition of this book followed the same methodology used in Chapter 4 but examined news stories reporting on sweatshops between 1995 and 2010. Now, more than a decade after the first edition of the book was published, we can use the list of 18 countries, that had sweatshops reported between 1995 and 2010, to examine how they have developed over the first two decades of this century. All data reported in this section is adjusted to account for inflation and purchasing power differences across countries (PPP), allowing us to make "apples to apples" comparisons in differences in real living standards.

Table 9.1 reports the growth in real GDP per capita in each of the countries for the first two decades of the 21st century and their average income level in 2019, before the onset of the COVID-19 pandemic. All the countries that had sweatshops reported experienced significant increases in GDP per capita, both during the time when the sweatshops were reported and during the subsequent decade. The 18 countries where sweatshops were reported grew, on average, nearly 80 percent in the first decade of the 21st century and a little over 60 percent in the second decade. Their average income rose to a little over $11,000 per capita.

There is, of course, significant variation in the growth rates between these countries. Short-run growth rates fluctuate for many reasons. Some countries show higher rates of growth in the first decade and some in the second. But long-run development, as indicated by growth in average incomes over 20 years, is evident in all these countries.

Long-run development, associated with increases in a country's overall productivity, has been the main driver of poverty reduction since the dawn of the industrial revolution. Not surprisingly, the economic

TABLE 9.1 *Economic growth in 21st-century sweatshop countries*

	2000–2009	2010–2019	GDP/capita 2019
Bangladesh	74.8%	96.1%	$5,699
Brazil	47.0%	7.4%	$15,308
Cambodia	112.4%	92.4%	$4,654
China	184.7%	80.0%	$16,655
Costa Rica	55.2%	77.5%	$22,608
Dominican Republic	56.2%	67.4%	$18,942
El Salvador	36.5%	51.6%	$9,398
Haiti	28.5%	20.9%	$3,244
Honduras	41.5%	57.3%	$5,852
India	86.5%	63.6%	$6,898
Indonesia	69.6%	46.6%	$12,361
Lao PDR	94.6%	116.3%	$8,173
Mauritius	65.2%	55.1%	$24,681
Myanmar	219.9%	63.6%	$5,436
South Africa	52.0%	13.0%	$14,438
Thailand	65.1%	44.4%	$18,760
Vietnam	98.2%	98.2%	$10,687
18 Country Avg	79.2%	60.8%	$11,634

Source: World Development Indicators (GDP in PPP)

development in these countries with sweatshops has also led to major reductions in abject poverty. Figure 9.1 reports the percentage of each country's population living below the World Bank's lowest poverty threshold, $2.15 per day, at the turn of the century, a decade later, and finally in 2019.[40]

Nearly 25 percent of the populations of these countries, on average, lived below the $2.15 threshold at the start of the century. That average fell to under 11 percent by 2010 and to under 5 percent by 2019. Abject poverty below this standard, which was pervasive in China and Vietnam at the start of the century, was virtually eliminated. While a significant number of people remain below this standard in Bangladesh, India, and Indonesia (between 4.4 and 13.5 percent), the numbers decreased significantly from averages between 33 and 44 percent two decades prior.

---

[40] When data was unavailable for the precise year, the data from the nearest available year was substituted, except for Lao PDR in 2000 and 2010, because nearby years were not available. Instead data from a few years before, and a few years after, each date was used to construct an average. Excluded countries did not have enough data available to construct reasonable estimates at these dates.

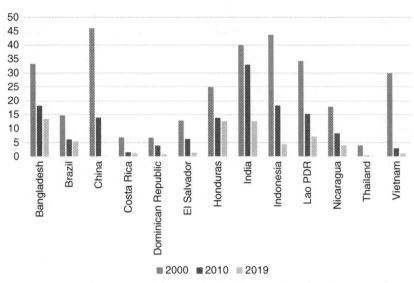

FIGURE 9.1 Percentage of the population living on less than $2.15 per day

Although people escaping the grinding poverty of living on less than $2.15 per day is vitally important, everyone concerned about sweatshops desires to see workers' living standards rise significantly higher than that. The World Bank also reports the percentage of each country's population living on less than $3.65 and $6.85 per day. Figures 9.2 and 9.3 report these numbers for countries with available data and indicate substantial reductions in poverty rates at these higher thresholds.

At the turn of the century, nearly half of the populations of countries with reported sweatshops lived on less than $3.65 per day. That number fell to under 30 percent by 2010 and to under 18 percent by 2019. Although the number of people living on less than $6.85 remains high across these countries, at a little more than 40 percent, the number is down significantly. The number of people living on less than $6.85 in these countries averaged more than 72 percent in 2000.

We can also see how child labor has decreased in these countries. Unfortunately, the World Development Indicators changed their definition of child labor since the first edition of *Out of Poverty* was published. The data in the first edition reported child labor rates for 10-to-14-year-olds. The current data, used in Chapter 7, reports child labor rates for 7-to-14-year-olds. Thus, direct comparisons will tend to understate the reduction in child labor that has occurred. Despite that, for the eight countries with data available in both periods, the average child labor

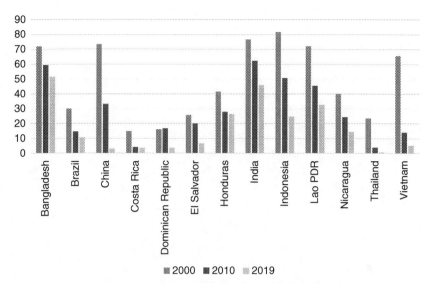

FIGURE 9.2 Percentage of the population living on less than $3.65 per day

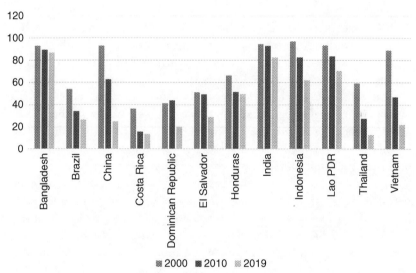

FIGURE 9.3 Percentage of the population living on less than $6.85 per day

rate decreased from 12.8 percent in the earlier period to 9.3 percent in the more recent decade.[41] However, that average decrease is misleading because Haiti, which went into an unrelated crisis, experienced a major

[41] The eight countries are Bangladesh, Brazil, Costa Rica, Dominican Republic, El Salvador, Haiti, Honduras, and India.

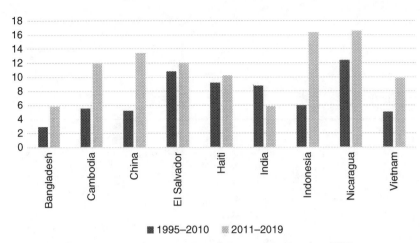

FIGURE 9.4 Average sweatshop earnings per day (PPP)

increase in child labor. Child labor rates decrease from 11.6 percent in the earlier period to 5.2 percent in the more recent decade when Haiti is excluded. The decrease in child labor in these countries is consistent with the arguments from Chapter 7 – the process of development that leads to poverty reductions naturally reduces rates of child labor.

We can also use the data from the first edition of this book to observe how wages in what is deemed a sweatshop have changed over this time. Perhaps tellingly, only half of the countries that had sweatshops reported in them in the earlier period also had sweatshops reported in them in the more recent decade. Figure 9.4 compares the average sweatshop wage reported during 1995 to 2010 to those reported in 2011 to 2019 for the nine countries that had sweatshops reported in both periods.[42]

In all countries, except India, reported sweatshop wages were higher between 2011 and 2019 than they were between 1995 and 2010. Reported sweatshop wages increased an average of 74 percent from the first period to the second in these nine countries. Reported sweatshop wages roughly doubled in Bangladesh, Cambodia, China, and Vietnam and nearly tripled in Indonesia. It seems that the standard of what is deemed a "sweatshop" worthy of reporting has risen roughly proportionately to the economic development of these countries.

The process of economic development has led average incomes to increase, poverty rates to decrease, child labor rates to decrease, and reported sweatshop wages to rise in the countries that had sweatshops

---

[42] Following the same methodology and assumptions used in Chapter 4.

reported in them between 1995 and 2010. The same process that played out in Great Britain, the United States, and the Asian tigers is beginning to play out in these countries today.

CONCLUSION

Anti-sweatshop activist Dan Viederman claims that "there are centuries of proof that jobs that are created without respect to ethical or legal standards do not make workers or societies more prosperous. December's factory fire in Bangladesh, where 20 people died, proves the point dramatically."[43] Of course, that fire no more proves that jobs in sweatshops don't make societies more prosperous than a house fire proves that housing doesn't generally provide superior shelter to dwelling in caves. More importantly, the brief review of the history of sweatshops in this chapter shows how wrong he is about jobs created without respect to ethical and legal standards. Factories with poor working conditions existed long before substantial legal standards, these jobs made these countries more prosperous, and that prosperity, rather than legal standards, led to improved wages and working conditions. We can see this same evolution playing out in countries that have sweatshops in the 21st century. This lesson is vitally important to understand if activists want to improve the lives of sweatshop workers today.

We need to understand how the process of development works, the role sweatshops play in that process, and what commonality the East Asian tigers, the United States, and Great Britain had that allowed them to develop while many nations have remained poor.

---

[43] Viederman, "Any Job Is a Good Job? Think Again."

IO

The Process of Economic Development

The process of economic development has been the greatest poverty cure in human history. Over the past 200 years, this process has eradicated countless sweatshops and replaced them with better jobs. Understanding this process is crucial for those who want to improve the lives of today's sweatshop workers.

People living in First World countries today often seem to forget that their living standards are the exception, not the norm, in our history. Most of human existence has been mired in poverty, with prospects for a short life, and famine a constant threat. Great Britain and the United States were among the first countries to break out of that dismal cycle. Fortunately, many other countries have joined them today.

To achieve and maintain a high standard of living, a country's workers need to have a high level of productivity. In other words, they need to get a lot of valuable output for every hour they work. The proximate causes of high productivity are physical capital, human capital, and technology. Sweatshops play a role in increasing all three of these.

Understanding human capital's role in development is the most straightforward. When workers have greater skills, they can get more output out of a given level of inputs. These greater skills can come from formal education, but they also can come from experience and on-the-job training. On-the-job learning can be important for developing greater human capital, particularly in low-skilled occupations. Think of the opportunities facing many Third World workers. For many, learning how to stitch quickly can be more valuable than learning the higher-level math, or even basic English, that they might learn in formal education. In any event, both formal education and on-the-job learning are ways to build human capital. Which builds more human capital depends on the endowment of the particular person and the opportunities available to them at the time.

Physical capital is vitally important to having a high standard of living. The most brilliant man in the world would quickly starve if he didn't have any tools to work with. But capital goods, such as tools, machinery, factories, buildings, and the computer I typed this chapter on, all must be created. Capital is created when people forgo some current consumption to use scarce resources to create the capital that will later produce even more consumption goods. Capital comes from savings. This is one reason the industrial revolution took so long to produce higher standards of living in Great Britain. Current consumption had to be forgone and capital slowly accumulated. As productivity and profits rose, there was a greater ability to save and create even more capital. As Peter Stearns put it, "Rising output boosted industrial profits, which provided additional capital for still further changes, and began to permit some definite if modest improvements in the standard of living of most workers."[1] Ludwig von Mises summarizes the crucial role prior capital accumulation plays in our standard of living by writing, "the heritage of the past embodied in our supply of capital goods is our wealth and the foremost means of further advancement in well-being."[2]

The East Asian success stories had a distinct advantage over Great Britain when they developed. Their capital formation could happen much faster because they could draw on savings from wealthy countries in addition to their own savings. When foreign firms made investments in those countries, they created many of the buildings and machines that the citizens of Hong Kong, Singapore, Taiwan, and South Korea would work with. The same is true in poor countries today. When multinational companies open sweatshops in Third World countries, they are using the savings in First World countries to create capital in Third World countries. Over time, the accumulation of capital in these countries leads to increased productivity and higher standards of living.

Although capital accumulation is crucial for economic development, it alone cannot explain high standards of living. A larger and larger capital stock will take larger and larger amounts of savings to maintain it. To maximize living standards, you also must get more production out of any given amount of capital. When it comes to the industrial revolution, McCloskey summarizes the point nicely:

[1] Stearns, *The Industrial Revolution*, 37.
[2] Mises, *Human Action*, 510.

Had the machines and men of 1860 embodied the same knowledge of how to spin cotton or move cargo that they had in 1780, the larger number of spindles and ships would have barely offset the fixity of land... The larger quantities of capital did make some difference... But the larger part of the difference between this dismal possibility and the 28 pounds per head actually achieved by 1860 was attributable to better technology.[3]

Better technology allows people to obtain more output from both their labor and capital inputs. In Great Britain, much of this technology needed to be invented for capital goods to embody it. But as we saw in Chapter 9, when the United States began to industrialize, it copied much of the technology that was already created in Great Britain. Furthermore, the United States benefited from foreign investment that brought new technologies with it. The same process is happening in Third World countries today.

Sweatshops don't just provide a better job than the lousy other options in these countries. Sweatshops themselves are part of the very process of development that will lead to their own elimination.[4] When foreigners make investments in Third World sweatshops, they bring in capital and new technologies, as well as give workers an opportunity to build human capital. All three of these things contribute to making workers more productive, which ultimately raises their wages and leads to improved jobs.

Although accumulating capital, improving technology, and creating a more skilled workforce are necessary for achieving a high standard of living, they are not sufficient. It's not simply "capital" that needs to be accumulated. Capital is heterogeneous, that is, an office building and a sewing machine are both capital, but they serve different purposes, so the right capital needs to be accumulated.[5] The right capital is the capital that best complements the existing capital and labor to produce the greatest value for society. To find out what capital is best, we need the market's competitive process to operate.

Prices convey information about relative scarcity. Prices of consumer goods indicate how much value people place on different items.

---

[3] McCloskey, "The Industrial Revolution 1780–1860: A Survey," 57.

[4] For more on the process of development, including several recent case studies of some of the biggest successes and failures in development, see Benjamin Powell, ed., *Making Poor Nations Rich: Entrepreneurship and the Process of Development* (Palo Alto: Stanford University Press, 2008).

[5] For more on the important implications of capital heterogeneity for economic theory, see Benjamin Powell, "Some Implications of Capital Heterogeneity," in *Handbook on Contemporary Austrian Economics*, edited by Peter Boettke (Cheltenham: Edward Elgar, 2010).

Entrepreneurs then bid on inputs, including capital goods, to make those consumer goods. The ability to buy all the necessary inputs and still sell the consumer goods for a profit is a signal that entrepreneurs have created value for society by transforming valuable inputs into a more valuable output. Losses are a signal that entrepreneurs are destroying value by taking scarce resources that could have been used to produce something else and turning those resources into less valuable final consumer goods. The market's profit and loss system provides feedback on which businesses and industries should expand and which should contract.

Capital goods get their value from the final consumer goods they create. But any given capital good can play a role in producing more than one consumer good. Thus, the alternative uses of the capital good need to be weighed against each other. This is what happens when entrepreneurs bid against each other for capital goods. Each entrepreneur assesses how much value he expects he can create by using the capital good, and that informs how much he is willing to bid for it. Those entrepreneurs who think they can create the greatest value outbid those who don't think they can create as much. This process helps allocate a given capital stock most efficiently. The array of capital goods prices also tells us how valuable different capital goods are. These prices signal other entrepreneurs that they can profit by creating more of the most valuable capital.

Market prices play the key role in transmitting the relevant information necessary for development to occur. First, they signal consumers' desires for consumption goods. Then, they signal the relative scarcity of capital goods in alternative uses, through the bidding of entrepreneurs. Finally, the capital goods prices signal what new capital should be created. Prices convey the information, and because entrepreneurs have property rights in their profits and losses, they have an incentive to only use capital goods where they can create the greatest value.

Absent this competitive process, no one knows which capital should be created to best promote economic development. There is simply no way to harness the subjective expectations and valuations of all the market participants without giving them the autonomy to act on their own. There has been no shortage of failed attempts to simply stuff "capital" into poorer countries to help them develop. Foreign aid for investment in capital through the financing gap model was the World Bank's largest development program for more than 60 years, and it was a failure. One reason it failed is because it lacks the price system that harnesses economic calculation to determine what capital should be created.[6] Aid for investment, or national economic planning that attempts to guide the structure of industry, suffers from the same economic calculation problem that, as economist Ludwig von Mises correctly determined, socialist economies cannot solve.[7] Absent a market process to decide which capital goods should be created, and how they should be allocated, there is no relative scarcity indicator to guide decision-making.

Although entrepreneurs are crucial for making the system work, they do not do so out of any conscious effort to promote economic efficiency or development. They are simply greedy profit seekers. Whenever the price system conveys the information that they can make a profit, they will seize the opportunity. That means when the price system conveys the wrong information, entrepreneurs could hinder development by making profits.

Economist William Baumol pointed out that entrepreneurship can be productive, unproductive, or destructive.[8] The process of socially productive entrepreneurship is that described earlier in this chapter. Socially unproductive entrepreneurship occurs when an entrepreneur profits without on net creating or taking any value from society. Socially destructive entrepreneurship occurs when an entrepreneur profits by making society poorer, for example when an entrepreneur successfully lobbies the government for a tariff barrier.

Because entrepreneurs are simply seeking profits and are largely indifferent to whether those profits are socially beneficial or not, it is crucial for economic development that the institutional environment promotes productive entrepreneurship, while limiting opportunities for unproductive and destructive entrepreneurship as much as possible. Well enforced private property rights and a large measure of economic freedom provide just such an institutional environment.

ECONOMIC FREEDOM: THE ENVIRONMENT
FOR PRODUCTIVE ENTREPRENEURSHIP

To best promote development, market prices must accurately convey information about the relative scarcity of goods. This requires people to

[6] Aid for investment and other aid programs also failed because they did not get the incentives right. On the role of incentives in these programs, see William Easterly, *The Elusive Quest for Growth* (Cambridge, MA: MIT Press, 2002).
[7] See Ludwig von Mises, *Economic Calculation in the Socialist Commonwealth* (Auburn: Ludwig von Mises Institute, 1990).
[8] William Baumol, "Entrepreneurship: Productive, Unproductive, and Destructive," *Journal of Political Economy* 98, No. 5 (1990), 892–921.

have strong property rights and the ability to freely exchange them on whatever terms to which they voluntarily agree. Anything that impedes voluntary exchanges also impedes the price system's ability to convey the information necessary for economic calculation. Without private property, exchange isn't possible. Inflation distorts the monetary system's ability to convey accurate prices. Taxes drive a wedge between people who would otherwise find gains from trade, and thus their valuations do not impact prices. Regulations that prohibit trades, or control prices, distort the system. Economic freedom is harmed whenever governments interfere on these margins.

Although we understand what economic freedom entails, it is not easily objectively quantifiable. Economists began trying to measure economic freedom in the 1990s. The *Economic Freedom of the World* report, now coauthored by James Gwartney, Robert Lawson, and Ryan Murphy, is the most widely used scholarly index that attempts to measure economic freedom across countries.[9] They measure economic freedom across five areas: the size of government, legal structure and property rights, freedom to trade internationally, sound money, and regulation of labor, credit, and business. A massive scholarly literature has developed using this index over the past 30 years.

The main finding in this literature is that economic freedom is beneficial for almost every measurable margin we care about in economic development. Economic freedom is associated with higher levels of per capita income, higher rates of economic growth, higher levels of entrepreneurial activity, higher rates of domestic investment, larger amounts of foreign investment, greater productivity of investment, longer life expectancies, lower poverty rates, better access to safe water, and lower infant mortality, among other things. Economists Josh Hall and Robert Lawson surveyed scholarly empirical studies on the relationship between economic freedom and "good" economic outcomes about a decade ago.[10] They found that, in 402 papers using the index, economic freedom is associated with "good" economic outcomes (growth, income, less poverty, etc.) in more than two-thirds of the studies, while economic freedom is associated with "bad" outcomes (such as inequality) in less than 4 percent of the studies. More recently, Lawson, along with economists Vincent Miozzi and Meg Tuszynski, conducted

[9] James Gwartney, Robert Lawson, and Ryan Murphy, *Economic Freedom of the World: 2022 Annual Report* (Vancouver: The Fraser Institute, 2023).

[10] Joshua Hall and Robert Lawson, "Economic Freedom of the World: An Accounting of the Literature," *Contemporary Economic Policy* 32, No. 1 (2014), 1–19.

a quantitative survey of the magnitude of the relationship between economic freedom and income, growth, investment, and inequality.[11] They compiled 696 estimates of the impact of economic freedom on economic growth, 386 estimates of its effect on income, 370 estimates of its effect on investment, and 759 estimates of its effect on inequality, from other scholarly studies. They find that "the published estimates support the view that economic freedom is positively related to growth, income, and investment. The level of economic freedom appears to be simply unrelated to inequality, though changes in economic freedom do seem to correlate with higher inequality." The size of the relationship between economic freedom on growth and income is the largest in magnitude. They find that across all these studies a one standard deviation increase in economic freedom is associated, on average, with about a half of a standard deviation in both growth and income.

Although a lot of sophisticated empirical work has been done examining the relationship between economic freedom and development, here we can present three simpler figures that illustrate the basic relationships, which are consistent with the general thrust of the findings in the scholarly literature.[12] Figure 10.1 presents the basic relationship between economic freedom and per capita income by dividing countries into quartiles based on how highly they rank in economic freedom. Per capita incomes average nearly $50,000 dollars in the 25 percent of countries with the highest economic freedom, while they average barely more than $6,000 in the quarter of countries with the lowest economic freedom.

Figure 10.2 illustrates that the gains in income associated with economic freedom don't just accrue to the wealthy but that they translate into increased income for the poorest members of society too. The poorest 10 percent of the population in the most economically free countries earn more than $14,000 per year, while the poorest 10 percent in the least economically free countries earn less than $1,800 per year. The poorest 10 percent of the population in the freest countries even earn more than the average person earns in countries in the bottom two quartiles of the economic freedom rankings.

[11] Robert Lawson, Vincent Miozzi, and Meg Tuszynski, "Economic Freedom and Growth, Income, Investment, and Inequality: A Quantitative Summary of the Literature," *Southern Economic Journal* (in press).
[12] All data is reported in 2017 dollars adjusted for purchasing power differences across countries (PPP) and comes from the *Economic Freedom of the World: 2023 Annual Report* and World Development Indicators online database.

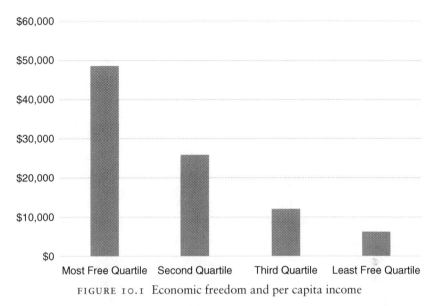

FIGURE 10.1 Economic freedom and per capita income

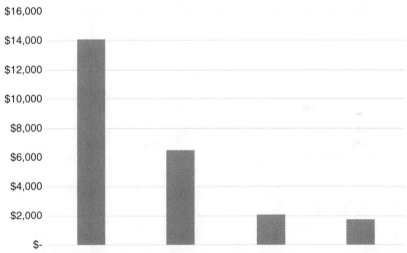

FIGURE 10.2 Economic freedom and earnings of the poorest 10 percent of the population

These higher incomes, for the poorest 10 percent of the population, translate into significantly lower poverty rates in more economically free countries. Figure 10.3 illustrates how poverty rates vary by economic freedom quartile. Poverty rates are substantially lower in countries with greater economic freedom at each of the standard poverty thresholds.

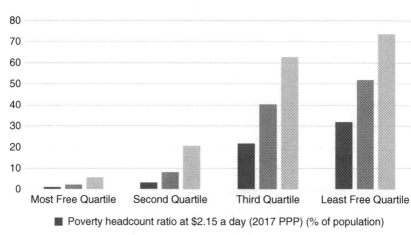

FIGURE 10.3 Economic freedom and poverty rates

Not only do levels of economic freedom matter but changes in free-dom matter too. Countries that improve in economic freedom, regard-less of their initial level, tend to grow faster than other countries. An old economics joke serves as a good metaphor for understanding why. Two economists are walking down the sidewalk, and the junior economist says, "Look, there's a $100 bill laying on the sidewalk." The senior economist scoffs, "No. There can't be because it would have already been picked up." So, the joke's not that funny, but it can serve a purpose here. In a normal economy, as profit opportunities pop up, entrepreneurs quickly seize them so that they are not left sitting there unexploited for others to take advantage of. Normal economic growth consists of the constant seizing of these opportunities as an economy chugs along. When economic freedom is suppressed, opportunities that should be profitably seized aren't, because laws or regulations prevent it. It's as if a metal grate suspends people above the sidewalk, so that they can't reach down and grab the $100 bills. When eco-nomic freedom increases, it's like lowering the metal grate: Suddenly a whole bunch of big bills are within reach. Similarly, when economic freedom increases, lots of profit opportunities suddenly become avail-able. Entrepreneurs seize them, and as a result, growth takes off.[13]

---

[13] Returns on investments are higher in countries with increasing economic freedom as well. See, Marshall Stocker, "The Price of Freedom: A Fama-French Freedom Factor," *Emerging Markets Review* 26 (2016), 1–19.

A lot of research has shown that improvements in freedom matter as much as, or more than, the absolute levels for rapid growth.

Economic theory, as described in this chapter, gives us strong reason to believe that economic freedom *causes* greater developmental success. But the empirical techniques used in most of the studies surveyed earlier in this chapter cannot rule out endogeneity, or some degree of reverse causality, impacting the magnitude of the empirical estimates. To address such concerns, a more recent study, by economists Kevin Grier and Robin Grier, uses matching methods to better estimate the magnitude of the *causal* relationship between changes in economic freedom and growth.[14] They identify 49 countries, out of a dataset of 141 countries, that had a large jump in economic freedom during a 5-year period and then sustained that jump over a 5-to-10-year period, between 1970 and 2015.[15] They find that jumps in economic freedom, that are sustained in subsequent periods, cause large and statistically significant increases in economic growth. Specifically, they find that countries that experience a jump in economic freedom experience growth that is 2.07 to 2.87 percentage points higher than could be expected over a 5-year period, and growth that is 1.03 to 1.93 percentage points higher over a 10-year period. To put this into concrete terms, for a poor country, with an initial income level of $6,000 per capita and a 2 percent rate of economic growth, a jump in economic freedom would lead them to be 13 percent richer ($857 more per capita) than otherwise after 5 years, and 16 percent richer ($1,182 per capita) than could otherwise be expected after 10 years.

The research on the effects of economic freedom is consistent with the narrative in this book about sweatshops and the process of development.[16] The industrial revolution began and flourished in Great Britain.

---

[14] Kevin Grier and Robin Grier, "The Washington Consensus Works: Causal Effects of Reform, 1970–2015," *Journal of Comparative Economics* 49, No. 1 (2021), 59–72. Technically, they use both matching methods, to better identify counterfactuals, and then also use first differences of the outcome variable, to remove the effect of time-invariant factors.

[15] They define a "large" jump as an increase of 1.0 points or more on the 10-point scale, though their results are robust to using alternative thresholds of "large."

[16] Unfortunately, some philosophers and political theorists who write about sweatshops appear to be unaware of the literature on the relationship between economic freedom and development and ignorant of how the competitive market process has been the main driver in poverty reduction over the last 200 years. The conclusion of philosopher Michael Neu's chapter on sweatshops is a prime example. He asserts that in my work I (with Matt Zwolinski) "categorically refuse to think beyond the narrow parameters of the immediate transaction" and don't realize that to get a just world "it is clear that

During this time, Great Britain was eliminating its mercantilist restrictions and respecting individual liberty and economic freedom. It had both a high level of economic freedom and, although it was not formally measured, economic freedom clearly was increasing. In her history of the industrial revolution, Deirdre McCloskey makes the case that liberty combined with dignity granted by society to entrepreneurs was responsible for launching the first industrial revolution.[17] The United States also had strong respect for individual liberty and property rights during its transformation.

Some would mistakenly conclude that the East Asian success stories of Hong Kong, Singapore, Taiwan, and South Korea are counterexamples, because some of them, particularly Taiwan and South Korea, engaged in industrial planning. Although some industrial planning did occur, these countries were overwhelmingly market-oriented.[18] The Economic Freedom index ranks countries back to 1970. In 1970, Hong Kong was ranked the most economically free country in the world, Singapore was the 7th, Taiwan 16th, and South Korea 31st (in the top 20 percent). Since that time, Hong Kong and Singapore have come to dominate the top two spots on the Economic Freedom index.

The countries where sweatshops are located today are not bastions of economic freedom. That's part of the reason why they are relatively poor and sweatshops are the best alternative for many workers. However, we

such a world can be constructed only politically, on the basis of sound moral analysis, and not by leaving the market to itself" and that "To think that there is no need for such action, but that we can display our lack of indifference to people desperately trying to survive by simply going shopping, might be one of the most deluded, deluding, and harmful ideas of our times" (Neu, *Just Liberal Violence*, 47–48). He cites passages from the first edition of *Out of Poverty* without explaining why my account of development is wrong or offering alternative systematic empirical evidence. Instead, he just asserts that this account is "patently absurd" (Neu, *Just Liberal Violence*, 47) and then illustrates his lack of understanding of the process in the following passages. Philosophical musings that aren't grounded in hardheaded economic analysis are just irresponsible daydreaming. If policymakers take them seriously, they are dangerous daydreams for the fate of the world's poor.

[17] Deirdre McCloskey, *Bourgeois Dignity: Why Economics Can't Explain the Modern World* (Chicago: University of Chicago Press, 2010).

[18] The industrial planning that did occur actually impeded development. See Benjamin Powell, "State Development Planning: Did It Create an East Asian Miracle?" *Review of Austrian Economics* 18, No. 3/4 (2005), for an account of how planning did not promote development but economic freedom did. Also see Bryan Cheang, *Economic Liberalism and the Developmental State: Hong Kong and Singapore's Post-war Development* (London: Palgrave Macmillan, 2023), for an account that also argues proponents of developmental planning overstate their case but also pushes back against how liberal Hong Kong and Singapore were at the time.

TABLE 10.1 *Sweatshop countries' 2019 economic freedom*

	Rank	Score	% change 1995–2019
Bangladesh	133	5.89	15.9%
Brazil	88	6.73	50.9%
Cambodia	74	7.07	
China	120	6.23	29.8%
Costa Rica	42	7.66	–3.4%
Dominican Republic	51	7.46	29.7%
El Salvador	56	7.34	–0.1%
Haiti	102	6.51	20.6%
Honduras	68	7.13	18.4%
India	93	6.68	19.3%
Indonesia	72	7.1	16.2%
Lao PDR	106	6.41	
Mauritius	12	8.15	8.7%
Nicaragua	87	6.76	16.4%
South Africa	92	6.69	–2.0%
Thailand	79	6.99	–3.9%
Vietnam	125	6.15	

can return to the countries where sweatshops were reported between 1995 and 2010 to see if progress is being made in improving economic freedom that will help speed the process of development. Table 10.1 reports the 2019 economic freedom score, where that score ranks out of 165 countries, and the percentage change in the economic freedom score since 1995 for the countries with data available.

Economic freedom scores averaged 6.88 across the 17 countries where sweatshops were reported in the earlier period. That average would result in a ranking of 82nd, just above the median, on the border between the 2nd and 3rd quintiles of countries. However, this is a substantial improvement from 1995, when sweatshops began to be reported in these countries. These countries improved their economic freedom scores by an average of 15.5 percent between 1995 and 2019. That improvement is understated because Cambodia, Lao PDR, and Vietnam, which have economic freedom scores today, didn't have economic freedom scores in 1995, due to lack of available data to rate them. Casual observation indicates that lack of available reliable data is likely correlated with very low levels of economic freedom (e.g., North Korea, Cuba, and South Sudan remain unranked today). Thus, though unmeasured, it is likely that those countries also substantially improved their economic freedom over these two and a half decades.

It is particularly encouraging that the two most populus countries, China and India, both made large improvements in economic freedom. China's economic freedom score has improved by nearly 30 percent during the period analyzed, but it is up by more than 50 percent since the time its reform process began shortly before 1980. However, this understates China's liberalization because much of the reform has taken place on the local level and doesn't make it into the national data used to construct the Economic Freedom index. Unfortunately, China's liberalization process seems to have stalled under President Xi Jinping. Economic freedom scores have remained essentially unchanged since he came to power in 2012. India's economic freedom scores increased approximately 19 percent during the period analyzed, but its reform process had begun a few years earlier in 1991. India's economic freedom score has improved by more than 25 percent since 1990. In both cases, the countries still have relatively low levels of freedom, but each illustrates how rapid growth can be achieved with improvements in freedom.

The overall picture is encouraging when we look at how countries with sweatshops reported in the late 1990s and 2000s have evolved. The previous chapter documented that all of them have experienced significant development that has resulted in poverty reduction. As a group, they are not at the "bottom of the barrel" when it comes to economic freedom, averaging just above the median country in the index, and particularly encouragingly, most of them are improving their levels of economic freedom and some of them are improving these levels quite substantially.

RACE TO THE BOTTOM?

Two hundred years ago, sweatshops existed in Great Britain, and they appeared soon after in the United States. As those countries grew richer, the sweatshops disappeared. Some of the textile jobs improved their wages and working conditions. Others saw their labor get bid away and the factories moved overseas to use cheaper, more abundant labor. The same process occurred more rapidly in Hong Kong, Singapore, Taiwan, and South Korea. Now the sweatshops locate in India, China, Indonesia, Central America, and elsewhere. As these countries grow wealthier, we are likely to witness the sweatshops moving again.

Some people mistakenly view this as a race to the bottom.[19] It's really a race to the top. Each of these countries was poor before it had

---

[19] For an example, see Preiss, "Autonomy, and Harm in Global Supply Chains," 889.

sweatshops. Sweatshops came as part of the process of development. As that process played out, the countries became wealthier because the workers became more productive. With that increased productivity came increased pay and workers who were better suited for doing tasks other than low-skilled textile work. As a result, the workers were bid away from working in textiles. In some cases, they were replaced with machines that made the remaining employees more productive and better paid. In other cases, they were replaced by workers in poorer foreign countries, where laborers had fewer valuable alternatives.

The poorest countries in the world today, those in the 3rd and 4th quartiles of economic freedom, are mostly without sweatshops. Sweatshops appearing in these countries would represent a step up the ladder of economic development for workers. Sweatshops will continue to relocate as the process of development plays out in these countries too. But what about the last country to get sweatshops? When there is nowhere with cheaper labor for factories to move to, what happens next?

No country or group of countries is doomed to sweatshop standards of living just because they are the last to develop. The same process of development that occurred everywhere else can still occur in those countries. These countries can increase their levels of physical capital, human capital, and technology just like the countries that developed before them did. As they do, labor productivity will increase. Of course, textiles still must be made somewhere. But if that location has high labor productivity, the work will be well compensated and have good working conditions. At that stage of world economic development, textile manufacturing in the former Third World will look more like it does in the United States today. Perhaps better. Development is not zero-sum. No nation need be trapped in poverty except by its own misguided policies that impede the process of development.

CONCLUSION

Much of this book has argued that sweatshops are the best alternative available to the people who choose to work in them. That is likely a depressing fact for many readers. Simply being the best bad option for workers might not make you feel much better about buying clothes made in sweatshops. This chapter has argued that sweatshops are more than just the least bad option for workers. Sweatshops are also part of the very process that will ultimately eliminate sweatshops.

Sweatshops are not new. They existed in Great Britain and the United States 150 years ago. Slowly, as our productivity increased, pay also increased and working conditions improved. Eventually the process of economic development eliminated sweatshops in Great Britain and the United States.[20] Sweatshops are part of this development process. They require capital to be created. They often bring in new technology, and workers often build human capital while on the job. Thus, sweatshops bring with them three of the proximate causes of higher productivity that eventually get workers out of sweatshop conditions.

Unfortunately, sweatshops by themselves are not enough to guarantee a rapid developmental path out of poverty. An institutional environment that protects private property and economic freedom is also necessary. Great Britain and the United States had that environment when they went through their transformations. So did East Asian countries that had sweatshops until recently. Some of the countries where sweatshops are located today, such as China and India, have made large strides in improving their economic freedom, but others have not. Sweatshops will be part of their own cure in the countries that embrace economic freedom. In the countries that don't, sweatshops will remain a crutch that is the least bad option for many people.

Let us now examine what role activists might be able to play in improving the lives of workers, at least on the margin, where sweatshops are located today, while not impeding the process of development that ultimately eliminates sweatshops.

---

[20] I'm aware that some people still use the label "sweatshop" when describing some US jobs. However, these cases tend to be categorically different, both in wages and working conditions and in the employment relationship than the type of sweatshops analyzed in this book and that existed in the United States in its earlier stage of economic development.

11

What Good Can Activists Do?

Some readers may likely feel a bit frustrated at this point. You might accept that the sweatshop jobs are better than the available alternatives and that sweatshops are part of the development process that will eventually lead to better jobs. Yet you still feel empathy for the Third World workers who toil making your apparel and want to do something to help them. This chapter is for you. It's time to explore positive steps that activists could take to help Third World sweatshop workers.

First, before moving on to new policies, it's worth considering how your actions should change if you've been an anti-sweatshop activist in the past. Rule number one for helping Third World workers should be "Do No Harm." Using boycotts or advocating for policies that mandate higher minimum wages or better working conditions make Third World workers worse off. They unemploy workers and change their desired mix of compensation for the worse. If you've advocated for these policies, or for trade sanctions against countries that don't have high standards, there is one simple constructive action you can take to help sweatshop workers: Stop. With that in mind, let's take a look at some other constructive steps you might take to help poor workers in the Third World.

SPECIFICALLY TARGET SLAVE LABOR

All the arguments in this book have focused on situations in which workers voluntarily choose to work in a sweatshop. The vast majority of sweatshops that are protested, and appear in the news, fall into this category. There is, however, a minority of cases that could be considered

171

slave labor. These situations could involve a company or government using the threat of violence to get the workers to take the job; fraud in human trafficking, in which after arriving the worker's passport is confiscated, so that they can't leave their employer without risking going to jail; or parents selling unwilling children into bondage. The Chinese government's coercion of the Uyghur population is by far the largest-scale use of slave labor in the apparel industry today. We will explore what is occurring there shortly, but first it is necessary to elaborate why consequences of boycotts and trade sanctions against forced labor sweatshops are different than when these same policies are applied to the types of sweatshops described earlier in this book.

Consumer boycotts of forced labor sweatshops, or the imposition of trade sanctions preventing the importation of goods made in forced labor sweatshops, are fundamentally different from boycotts or sanctions against free labor sweatshops. The very fact that the laborers are forced, with the threat of violence, to perform the job indicates that forced labor jobs are not the best available alternative for these workers. If the jobs were the best available option for workers, they would take the jobs voluntarily, without being threatened. Boycotts and sanctions lower demand for the targeted goods. However, in the case of forced labor sweatshops, if the firms cut back their workforce, because of the decreased demand for their product, these workers are helped, rather than harmed, because the necessity of forcing them to take the job illustrates that workers would be better off in other alternatives. Furthermore, if the targeted firm and/or government capitulates to boycotters demands, that usually means ceasing to use the threat of violence to force workers to perform their jobs. Capitulating to boycotts of forced labor sweatshops usually unambiguously helps all the directly impacted workers, unlike free labor sweatshops, where meeting boycotter demands, such as mandating higher wages or better working conditions, helps some workers and harms others. Even if ineffectual, forced labor sweatshop boycotts aren't likely to create much harm, since decreased demand during a boycott doesn't harm the affected workers. Thus, the key to evaluating the desirability of a boycott or trade sanction involves making sure it is actually targeting forced labor and not indiscriminately impacting free labor firms as well. Let's now turn to examining how the apparel industry is interacting with the coercion of the Uyghur population in China.

In 2016, the Xinjiang Uyghur Autonomous Region (XUAR) experienced a series of policy changes when Chen Quanguo was appointed the region's party secretary.[1] In addition to a surveillance program on citizens' day-to-day activities, Chen's methods of controlling the ethnic minority population include a massive detainment program.[2] This detainment program is under the official guise of Vocational Education and Training Centers. According to several estimations, 61 detainment program facilities were built through government procurement bids in the region in 2017; the camps can hold around one million people.[3]

Once reeducation camp detainees finish "training" of de-extremification, which aims at preventing religious extremism, they are released from camps and sent to manufacturing sites in the region and subjected to forced labor.[4] As indicated by a leaked document from a 2019 *New York Times* article, forced labor is "part of the government's targeted campaign of repression, mass internment, and indoctrination of ethnic minorities in Xinjiang."[5] Former camp detainees testified that the regional government had compelled Uyghurs into forced labor through coercive labor transfers.

Along with transferring former reeducation camp detainees to engage in forced labor, the regional "precise poverty alleviation" program is another source of forced labor. As part of Chinese President Xi Jinping's goal to eliminate absolute poverty by 2020, the region's "war on poverty" pressured each administrative level to achieve poverty alleviation through job creation, which primarily utilized coercive labor transfers.[6]

---

[1] During his tenure in the XUAR, Chen's policies have focused on two subjects: economic development and maintenance of social stability. Linan Peng and Justin Callais, "The Authoritarian Trade-off: A Synthetic Control Analysis of Development and Social Coercion in the Xinjiang Uyghur Autonomous Region," *Contemporary Economic Policy* 41, No. 2 (2023), 370–387, studied the effect of those policies. They concluded that the policies had no substantial impact on economic development, while the impact on social coercion is much larger in the forms of higher public security spending and higher arrest rate.

[2] While the region had established camps since the striking hard campaign in 2014, the scale of those camps reached unparalleled levels since Chen's tenure as the party secretary of the region.

[3] Chris Hayes, "Uncovering China's Secret Internment Camps with Rian Thum," in *Why Is This Happening? The Chris Hayes Podcast,* MSNBC (2019); Adrian Zenz, "Thoroughly Reforming Them towards a Healthy Heart Attitude: China's Political Re-education Campaign in Xinjiang," *Central Asian Survey* 38, No. 1, 102–128, retrieved from https://doi.org/10.1080/02634937.2018.1507997.

[4] Robert Silvers, *Strategy to Prevent the Importation of Goods Mined, Produced, or Manufactured with Forced Labor in the People's Republic of China* (U.S. Department of Homeland Security, 2022).

[5] Silvers, *Strategy to Prevent the Importation,* 11.

[6] Adrian Zenz, *Coercive Labor in Xinjiang: Labor Transfer and the Mobilization of Ethnic Minorities to Pick Cotton* (New Lines Institute, December 14, 2020).

Unlike poverty alleviation programs that provide resources or opportunities to those in poverty, this program forces work on members of poor households. The program established a goal that more than two million poor people, in 3,029 poor villages, must escape poverty by 2020 through forced labor.

The coercive labor program in the region also transferred Uyghurs out of the XUAR to factories across the country. Scholars at the Australian Strategic Policy Institute identified 27 factories in 9 Chinese provinces that used Uyghur labor from the XUAR since 2017.[7] Between 2017 and 2019, they estimated that at least 80,000 Uyghurs were assigned to those factories through the labor transfer program. In addition to constant surveillance, Uyghurs under the program both inside and outside of the XUAR face "the threat of arbitrary detention," which "hangs over minority citizens who refuse their government-sponsored work assignments."[8] In sum, there is ample evidence that the Chinese government, and companies working in conjunction with it, are using forced labor from the Uyghur population. Some of this forced labor is working in the apparel industry.

The XUAR is a major region of cotton production. In 2019, China produced about 23 percent of the world's cotton, and about 85 percent of Chinese production came from the XUAR.[9] The poverty alleviation program made the handpicked cotton production economically viable. Evidence of the utilization of forced labor in cotton picking in the XUAR has been discovered in Chinese government documents and media reports. Under the disguise of the "precise poverty alleviation" program, coercive labor transfers forced workers in rural areas into paid seasonal agricultural work, such as cotton picking, which normally requires physical relocations for the cotton-picking months. Although cotton picking is paid work, it is backbreaking labor, and the average earnings are below the XUAR's minimum wage level. The fact that the Chinese government needs to threaten these workers with violence in order to get them to work is strong evidence that the wages and working conditions being offered are not sufficient to voluntarily attract laborers.

[7] Xu, Vicky Xiuzhong, Danielle Cave, James Leibold, Kelsey Munro, and Nathan Ruser, *Uyghurs for Sale: Re-education Forced Labour and Surveillance beyond Xinjiang* (Australian Strategic Policy Institute, 2020).

[8] Ibid., 3.

[9] Amy Lehr, *Addressing Forced Labor in the Xinjiang Uyghur Autonomous Region: Toward a Shared Agenda* (Center for Strategic and International Studies, 2020).

The textile industry has also been involved in labor transfer programs.[10] Between April 2017 and June 2018, Hotan Prefecture transferred more than 2,000 Uyghur workers to 15 factories of Youngor Group, which supplies textile products to Lacoste, L.L.Bean, Tommy Hilfiger, and Uniqlo.[11] In November 2019, a satellite factory of Jiangsu Guotai International Group hired 3,500 Uyghur workers. The group is a major textile supplier to companies including Abercrombie & Fitch, American Eagle, Anthropologie, Calvin Klein, and Free People.[12] In May 2017, Qingdao Jifa Group, which is a supplier to the Gap and Walmart, announced the opening of an industrial park in Shule County in XUAR.[13] The group helped the local government train potential Uyghur employees and hired 1,200 of them. According to the scholars at the Australian Strategic Policy Institute, 82 major brands had several supply chain exposures to XUAR forced labor.[14] Besides the abovementioned brands, other apparel firms include Adidas, Fila, H&M, Polo Ralph Lauren, Puma, and Zara.[15]

The coercive nature of labor transfer programs and forced Uyghur labor have drawn international attention. In 2020, a coalition of more than 190 organizations in 36 countries called for cutting ties with suppliers implicated in Uyghur forced labor and ending all sourcing from the XUAR within 12 months.[16] Several brands, whose supply chains were exposed to the Uyghur forced labor, raised concern regarding the treatment of Uyghur in the XUAR and began changing sourcing practices. Both H&M and IKEA have stated they will no longer source cotton from the region.[17] Nike, Adidas, Lacoste, and other members of

---

[10] Other industries also utilized the coercive labor transfer program in the region and across the country. The auto industry and electronics industry are two of the other larger employers of forced labor. These industries are included in Linen Peng and Benjamin Powell's analysis in "Sweatshop Boycotts: Can't Live with Them, Can't Live without Them," in press, retrieved from https://papers.ssrn.com/sol3/papers.cfm?abstract_id=4505791.

[11] Retrieved from www.sohu.com/a/243367464_114967.

[12] Xu et al., *Uyghurs for Sale*, 37.

[13] Retrieved from http://news.sina.com.cn/c/2017-05-14/doc-ifyfekhi7615774.shtml.

[14] Xu et al., *Uyghurs for Sale*.

[15] See Xu et al., *Uyghurs for Sale*, for the full list that includes non-apparel firms.

[16] Elizabeth Paton and Austin Ramzy, "Coalition Brings Pressure to End Forced Uighur Labor," *New York Times*, July 23, 2020, retrieved from www.nytimes.com/2020/07/23/fashion/uighur-forced-labor-cotton-fashion.html.

[17] Amber Milne, "Brands Urged to Stop Sourcing from China's Xinjiang over Forced Labour Fears," *Reuters*, July 23, 2020, retrieved from www.reuters.com/article/global-garment-china-xinjiang-idUSL5N2ET3YM.

the Better Cotton Initiative (BCI) also expressed their concerns about cotton produced in Xinjiang.[18]

In 2020, the United States passed the Uyghur Human Rights Policy, which condemns "gross human rights violations of ethnic Turkic Muslims in Xinjiang, and calling for an end to arbitrary detention, torture, and harassment of these communities inside and outside China."[19] That same year, the U.S. Department of the Treasury imposed sanctions on top Chinese Communist Party (CCP) officials in the region. The sanctions froze those officials' assets in the United States. These sanctions were also backed by the European Union, the United Kingdom, and Canada.[20]

The United States also passed the Uyghur Forced Labor Prevention Act (UFLPA) in 2021, which "ensure[s] that goods made with forced labor in the Xinjiang Uyghur Autonomous Region of the People's Republic of China do not enter the United States market."[21] If customs officials identify a product is produced in whole or in part in the XUAR, the law requires importers to provide "clear and convincing evidence" that goods are not made with forced labor.[22] The UFLPA essentially calls for companies to thoroughly investigate their supply chain for any potential exposure to Uyghur forced labor.[23] In

[18] Liz Flora, "Lacoste and Adidas Pledge to Cut Forced Uighur Labor from Supply Chain," *Glossy*, April 27, 2022, retrieved from www.glossy.co/fashion/lacoste-and-adidas-pledge-to-cut-forced-uighur-labor-from-supply-chain/. China immediately retaliated against brands that boycotted. H&M became the first target following its statement to cut ties with cotton from Xinjiang. H&M was pulled from major e-commerce stores in China and blocked by review and rating apps. The first H&M flagship store in Shanghai shut down in 2022. Chinese celebrities terminated promotional work for the brand and cut ties with the brand. Other brands that raised concerns about cotton production also faced backlash from their Chinese market, as Chinese consumers ostracized those brands. Robin Brant, "Xinjiang Cotton: Western Clothes Brands Vanish as Backlash Grows," *BBC News*, March 26, 2021, retrieved from www.bbc.com/news/world-asia-china-56533560.
[19] Uyghur Human Rights Policy Act of 2020, S. 3744, 116th Congress, 2020.
[20] Patrick Wintour, "US and Canada Follow EU and UK in Sanctioning Chinese Officials over Xinjiang," *The Guardian*, March 22, 2021, retrieved from www.theguardian.com/world/2021/mar/22/china-responds-to-eu-uk-sanctions-over-uighurs-human-rights.
[21] Uyghur Forced Labor Prevention Act of 2021, H.R. 6256, 117th Congress, 2021.
[22] Ana Swanson, Catie Edmondson, and Edward Wong, "U.S. Effort to Combat Forced Labor Targets Corporate China Ties," *New York Times*, December 24, 2021, retrieved from https://cn.nytimes.com/usa/20211224/china-uyghurs-forced-labor/dual/.
[23] Both the United Kingdom and European Unions have proposed similar measures to address the forced labor issue regarding supply chains. Lindsay Maizland, *China's Repression of Uyghurs in Xinjiang* (Council on Foreign Relations, September 22, 2022), retrieved from www.cfr.org/backgrounder/china-xinjiang-uyghurs-muslims-repression-genocide-human-rights#chapter-title-0-8.

the fiscal year of 2022, Customs and Border Protection issued six withhold-release orders and detained more than 2,000 shipments under the rebuttal presumption of the UFLPA.[24]

We can trace out some of the theoretical consequences that are likely to result from these boycotts. If well-enforced, both boycotts and sanctions would lower the demand for Uyghur forced labor products. As the demand for the products decreased, the demand for forced labor in sectors that utilize the coercive labor transfer program would also diminish.[25] In the near term, this may lead the Chinese government to force fewer Uyghur people into the forced labor programs, since they do not have the same size market for their products.

The real guesswork in evaluating this forced labor boycott is in attaching probabilities to the potential responses of the Chinese government. In the best-case scenario, the Chinese government abandons the program, and Uyghurs, who were forced to be part of labor transfer programs, would be released to their pre–forced labor situation. The Uyghurs' lives would be improved as a result, since forced labor was not their least bad option. Alternatively, the Chinese government could continue to use forced labor in the same quantities to produce goods exclusively for their domestic market. This domestic production would likely be less profitable, but the Chinese government could counter market forces with state subsidies to keep the program viable. If the Chinese government responds in this manner, the boycotts will not help the workers but they won't harm them either. It's hard to imagine many likely scenarios where the Chinese government's response to the boycotts would make the Uyghur population worse off.

The boycotts of Uyghur forced labor seem sufficiently targeted that they mostly impact only goods made with forced labor. If, instead, boycotts (or sanctions) were imposed on all of China, or the global production of any company that has any exposure to Uyghur forced labor in any one of its products, the evaluation of the boycotts would become more complicated as the boycotts would likely harm many free labor workers

---

[24] Christopher Marquis, *How Companies Are Dealing with the Uyghur Forced Labor Prevention Act* (The China Project, August 17, 2022), retrieved from https://thechinaproject.com/2022/08/17/how-companies-are-dealing-with-the-uyghur-forced-labor-prevention-act/.

[25] For example, it was the labor transfer program that made Chinese cotton production and auto parts manufacturers competitive. See Zenz, *Coercive Labor in Xinjiang*, and Laura Murphy, Kendyl Salcito, Yalkun Uluyol, and Mia Rabkin, *Driving Force: Automotive Supply Chains and Forced Labor in the Uyghur Region* (Sheffield: Sheffield Hallam University Helena Kennedy Centre for International Justice, 2022).

unconnected to the forced Uyghur labor. This is not to deny that there are some harms from these boycotts, to at least some free laborers, whose own outputs are inputs into products made jointly with forced labor outputs. However, based on the targeted nature of the boycotts described, under most plausible scenarios, boycotting forced sweatshop labor from the Uyghur region seems likely to achieve more good than harm for workers and the population of the region on net.

When a factory has to use the threat of violence to keep a worker, it is clearly not the worker's best alternative. Unfortunately, all too often anti-sweatshop activists, such as Jim Keady, blur the line between voluntarily chosen jobs and slavery. Keady, who specifically targets Nike, is known to appear wearing a T-shirt that reads "Slavery" with the "v" turned into a Nike Swoosh.[26] Equating voluntarily chosen low-wage manufacturing jobs with slavery does a tremendous injustice to the millions who have been held in chattel slavery throughout human history. It also confuses the debate about sweatshops today and does an injustice to those who are still forced to toil in a state of involuntary servitude today, such as the Uyghur population in China.

Instead, anti-sweatshop groups should specifically target the rare instances in which slave labor is being used to produce apparel. In these situations, boycotts, sanctions, and pressure for legal changes are appropriate responses.

BUY "MADE IN THE THIRD WORLD"

People need to change their mentality that buying goods from Third World countries harmfully exploits those workers. Buying goods made by Third World labor increases the demand for labor in these countries. More workers can be employed with increased demand, and as long as they are voluntarily choosing the job, they are demonstrating that it is better than their prior employment. Plus, with increased demand, wages can be pushed up. Consciously buying goods made by Third World workers is essentially an anti-boycott.

There is no shortage of advocates for buy "Made in America" or "Buy Local" campaigns. I'm sure there are many union members of the AFL-CIO and UNITE who simultaneously believe in these campaigns while their own unions take actions in the name of helping sweatshop

---

[26] See http://sweatfreeshop.com/sweatshop-videos/jim-keady-exposes-nike/ (accessed August, 31, 2011) for one such video.

workers. But "Buy American" and helping sweatshop workers are conflicting goals. To the extent that "Buy American" programs influence people's purchases, they harm Third World workers by decreasing the demand for their labor.

Therefore, one positive thing people could do is to market their own "Buy Made in the Third World If You Care About Sweatshop Workers" campaigns. Unfortunately, I doubt that such a campaign would become widely popular because it doesn't appeal to the same nationalist instincts that "Buy American" does. But one thing that the anti-sweatshop movement has been successful at is garnering public attention. This type of public awareness campaign would at least be in line with the economic interest of the sweatshop workers, even if it doesn't lead to much of a change in demand. Furthermore, activists themselves could follow the policy in their own shopping decisions. Would activists' purchases alone do much to change the demand for Third World labor? Probably not. But it's a start.

"ETHICAL" BRANDING

I argued in Chapter 8 that it is ethical to buy products from sweatshops, hence the quotations in this section's title. However, I do think there is a role for what activists might label ethical branding, in which companies make voluntary improvements in wages and working conditions as part of their marketing strategy.

Reforms at the level of voluntary company codes can be an inherent part of the market process that both critics of sweatshops and their defenders embrace. Explicit company codes might be voluntarily adopted when firms believe that they will increase consumer demand for their product. In this case, the explicit code and improved wages and conditions are part of a profit-maximizing marketing strategy. A large enough number of consumers would have to place higher subjective valuations on these "ethically" produced goods for the strategy to work. Ethical branding can be successfully pursued for some products but would fail to improve conditions when consumers don't place enough of a premium on such products.

One important caution is in order when reforms come at the company policy level. A company may pursue ethical branding by advertising that its factories have certain minimum wages and working conditions while downplaying the fact that these conditions are met only because their factories are located in relatively richer, higher-productivity countries.

Remember the "Shop with a Conscience Consumer Guide" from Chapter 3? Twenty-nine of the factories are located in the United States and Canada; only 11 are located in Latin and South America, and a single factory is in Asia. Although consumers might feel they are "shopping with a conscience," they are mostly buying products made by wealthy First World union workers while decreasing the demand for products made in poorer countries and thus harming the employment prospects of the poorer Third World workers.

This points to a role that activists should embrace. The average consumer probably isn't going to take the time to know which "sweat-free" or "ethical" brands are actually doing something to help Third World workers and which are merely a sham, or even worse, a fraud like the shop with a conscience guide that transfers wealth to First World workers at the expense of the poor. Anti-sweatshop activists should direct energy to exposing frauds such as the shop with a conscience guide. The National Labor Committee, which is famous for its exposés on sweatshop conditions, should redirect its efforts to exposing false sweat-free branding like this.

At this point, it is also worth remembering that the case for sweatshops does not depend on the claim that the market is necessarily in a perfectly efficient general equilibrium, in which all gains from exchange have been exhausted and all information is known. The market is a dynamic discovery procedure that always tends toward a final state of rest (general equilibrium), but that end point is always moving as new information is discovered, technology changes, and consumer preferences evolve. Therefore, not every voluntary action that employers could take to improve wages and working conditions without unemploying workers has been taken already.[27]

Arnold and Hartman document what they call the "moral imagination" exercised by Adidas-Salomon and Nike management in improving working conditions in their firms and supply chains.[28] For them, moral imagination involves an exploratory function that lets people question the conventional ways of doing things in their own culture as well as utilizing and transforming norms from other cultures. The

---

[27] Both Powell and Zwolinski have commended Arnold and Hartman for their work in documenting some voluntary actions firms have taken. See Powell, "In Reply to Sweatshop Sophistries," and Zwolinski, "Sweatshops, Choice, and Exploitation." We also believe that making these actions more widely known to other companies can help speed the discovery of improvements that can take place without harming workers.

[28] Arnold and Hartman, "Moral Imagination."

exercise of moral imagination helps discover some of the improvements in working conditions that the market has not yet adopted.

However, we should take care not to overgeneralize from anecdotes such as this. The mere fact that ways to improve upon current market conditions always exist does not justify mandating standards at the industry level. Some individual companies may find enhanced consumer demand in response to improved working conditions, whereas others do not. Some companies may find efficiency wages improve productivity, whereas others do not. A filtering process that allows reforms to take place where they help workers, but doesn't mandate them where they do not, is necessary to determine what can work and what would unemploy workers. The market's competitive process is precisely that filter.

The "moral imagination" is precisely the entrepreneurial imagination that generates profits. Although inefficiency exists in the status quo, because profit-maximizing firms have not discovered all information, it is the very undiscovered nature of this knowledge that makes it crucial that reform comes from the bottom up as the knowledge is discovered. The knowledge of the particulars of time and place where particular mechanisms could improve worker welfare without unemploying others is not known to any one mind and thus can't be imposed by regulation without also doing so in other situations in which workers would be hurt.

This is precisely where ethical branding can play a decentralized discovery role. As some firms experiment and succeed or fail, the market discovers information that was previously unknown. Sometimes it is claimed that "defenders of sweatshops tend to ground their arguments in textbook economics, rather than in actual studies of labor markets. Few studies have been conducted of labor markets in which corporations have voluntarily increased wages."[29] Studying some markets in which firms did raise wages, in the manners described here, does nothing to undermine the standard textbook economics. Some businesses, in some markets, will find it profitable to raise wages for marketing purpose, efficiency wages, and so on. Others will not. The assertion that "the claims of sweatshop defenders are undermined by the many corporations, in a variety of industries, that routinely expend substantial corporate resources to help ensure safe and healthy working conditions for workers" is simply false.[30] It's

[29] Arnold, "Working Conditions," 645–646.
[30] Ibid., 642.

precisely the nonuniversal nature of the specific instances and mechanisms that makes the textbook economic defense of sweatshops correct.

Where does this leave a role for activists in the ethical branding process? Firms have a profit incentive to find out when ethical branding will increase profits. But this doesn't mean activists can't help. Activists could undertake market research, and survey consumers, to try to identify where there is a market niche to be served. They could also play a role as certifiers. Many companies or organizations may claim to be practicing ethical branding, but an activist-run nonprofit (or for-profit) could serve as a sort of Good Housekeeping Seal of Approval that certifies the organization is living up to its claims of helping workers. Finally, as mentioned, when discussing the shop with a conscience guide, activists could protest firms making fraudulent claims of ethical branding that don't actually help Third World workers.

Ultimately, however, even where ethical branding can be successful, this is probably a niche market and one in which there will be a lot of room for fraudulent claims, because a lot of consumers want to feel good about themselves but few will actually be willing to do the work to find out if they are actually doing good. As David Vogel put it in another context,

CSR [Corporate Social Responsibility] is best understood as a niche rather than as a generic strategy: it makes business sense for some firms in some areas under some circumstances. Many of the proponents of corporate social responsibility mistakenly assume that because some companies are behaving more responsibly in some areas, some firms can be expected to behave more responsibly in more areas.[31]

TARGETED PROGRAMS FOR CHILDREN

Almost all anti-sweatshop groups are opposed to child labor. Anti–child labor resolutions are among the core labor standards of the ILO. The main cure for child labor is the process of development that raises family incomes, so that children don't have to work. But activists who don't want to wait for the process of development can take actions to help children now.

We don't make sweatshop workers, whether an adult or child, better off by taking their option of sweatshop work away. We make them better off when we give them better alternatives than sweatshop work.

[31] David Vogel, *The Market for Virtue: The Potential and Limits of Corporate Social Responsibility* (Washington, DC: The Brookings Institution, 2005).

The best way to help children attend school rather than work in sweat-shops is to pay them, either with money, food, or some other necessity, to go to school rather than work.

The Progresa program in Mexico is one such program that other countries are increasingly emulating. Under Progresa, transfers to poor households have additional cash incentives for children to go to school. The size of the cash incentive increases as children get older to offset their greater earnings potential. Economist Paul Schultz found that rates of participation in work significantly declined with eligibility for Progresa.[32] He projects that educational attainment will rise from 6.8 years to 7.45 years because of the program. However, as Martin Ravallion and Quentin Wodon found elsewhere, sometimes educational subsidies do more to increase education than they do to decrease child labor, because the two are not necessarily mutually exclusive.[33]

Some caution with these types of programs is in order. Most impor-tantly, when instituted by governments in the countries where the sweatshops are located, these programs must ultimately be financed by taxation. Because taxation stifles capital formation and job growth else-where, such a program would slow the process of economic development that is the ultimate cure for child labor. Furthermore, the redistribution system itself would eat up resources and be at risk of corruption.

However, the basic idea of paying children to go to school rather than work can be an effective one. If First World activists want to do some-thing to decrease child labor, they should work for nonprofits, or form their own, that raise charitable donations for the cause. Their own NGO, with funds raised voluntarily in the First World, could then implement programs in poor countries with sweatshops that pay children to give up their sweatshop job and attend school instead. Schools run by missionary groups could implement similar policies. Raising money from concerned citizens in the First World, and then offering it on a voluntary basis to children in the Third World, in return for their promise not to work, increases the children's options. If they choose to get paid to go to school rather than work in a factory, they demonstrate that the new choice is better than their previous alternative. This, unlike bans on child labor, makes them better off.

[32] Paul Schultz, "School Subsidies for the Poor: Evaluating the Mexican Progresa Poverty Program," *Journal of Development Economics* 74, No. 1 (2004), 199–250.

[33] Martin Ravallion and Quentin Wodon, "Does Child Labor Displace Schooling? Evidence on Behavioral Responses to an Enrollment Subsidy," *Economic Journal* 110 (2000), C158–175.

PROMOTE THE PROCESS OF DEVELOPMENT

The process of economic development has been the greatest cure for poverty in human history. When a country's median income rises, virtually all measures of poverty fall. Development economist Lant Pritchett convincingly argues that broad-based national development, that leads to increases in median incomes, rather than "kinky development" – by which he means targeted anti-poverty programs – is the best way to help the world's poor escape poverty.[34] If activists want to help workers, they should take actions to speed up the process of development in the countries where sweatshops are located. Unfortunately, the development process is complex and difficult to promote from the outside. But that doesn't mean nothing can be done.

Economic development aid is the most common way people think outsiders can help poor countries develop. Unfortunately, it doesn't work. After more than 70 years of World Bank, Organisation for Economic Co-operation and Development (OECD), International Monetary Fund (IMF), and national government programs such as USAID, it is hard to assess them as anything other than a massive failure. Official government aid often goes through Third World countries' national governments. Political graft and outright theft are well-documented problems. In fact, *USA Today* published its list of the 20 worst dictators in the world. All of them received development aid from the United States or OECD.[35] Aid can even increase corruption. But the problems with development aid are more fundamental than bad dictators stuffing their Swiss bank accounts. Economists Jamie Pavlik and Andrew Young studied the relationship between aid flows and corruption across many countries from the mid 1990s through the mid 2010s.[36] They found that, over a 10-year time horizon, sustained increases in foreign aid led recipient countries to become more corrupt. But even if recipient countries are not corrupt, there are more fundamental problems with foreign aid for development.

Economist and former World Bank employee William Easterly has documented that the incentives for donors, recipient governments,

---

[34] See Lant Pritchett's website for a series of papers, blog posts, and lectures on national versus kinky development at: https://lantpritchett.org/national-versus-kinky-development/.

[35] See Benjamin Powell and Matt Ryan, "Stop Aiding Dictators," *Providence Journal,* February 27, 2006, retrieved from www.independent.org/newsroom/article.asp?id=1682.

[36] Jamie Bologna Pavlik and Andrew T. Young, "Sorting Out the Aid-Corruption Nexus," *Journal of Institutional Economics* 18, No. 4 (2022), 637–653.

and private citizens are often perverse and lead well-meaning aid programs to fail.[37] Another fundamental problem is that aid for investment doesn't work like private investment because it takes place outside of the market process and is not subject to the profit and loss test. Thus, even when aid does create capital, it's not the right capital.

Development aid has been a trivial fraction of the economies of almost all the major development successes since World War II. At the same time, the countries that have received large aid flows have failed to develop. As economist Christopher Coyne said about Bono, there is a difference between singing about poor people and actually helping them.[38] Development aid is a soothing song for First World citizens, but it doesn't actually promote development.

We saw in Chapter 10 that an institutional environment that supports private property and protects economic freedom is necessary for the process of development. Although economists have ample evidence that this environment promotes development, they know a lot less about how to create this environment where it doesn't already exist.[39]

Although foreign aid programs have tried tying policy reform to the aid at times, they haven't been successful in promoting an environment of economic freedom. Economist P. T. Bauer spent much of his career arguing that foreign aid "politicizes economic life" and undermines the institutions necessary for development.[40] When large aid transfers can be had from the government, entrepreneurs spend time competing to obtain the aid projects rather than innovating and competing to please consumers. Aid essentially misdirects entrepreneurship from productive activities to unproductive ones. Aid also helps to create a culture in which people believe the economy centers around the state, rather than the private marketplace, and as a result may lead to pressure for

---

[37] See William Easterly, *The Elusive Quest for Growth* (Cambridge, MA: MIT Press, 2001).

[38] Bono was known for encouraging concert-goers to use their cellphones to call their governments to demand greater development aid for poor countries. However, more recently he has stated that "Aid is just a stop-gap. Commerce – entrepreneurial capitalism – takes more people out of poverty than aid." Quoted in Mark Hendrickson, "U2's Bono Courageously Embraces Capitalism," *Forbes*, November 8, 2013, retrieved from www .forbes.com/sites/markhendrickson/2013/11/08/u2s-bono-courageously-embraces-capitalism/?sh=342d52ed575a.

[39] For a survey article on the factors that lead to greater or lesser economic freedom, see Robert Lawson, Ryan Murphy, and Benjamin Powell, "The Determinants of Economic Freedom: A Survey," *Contemporary Economic Policy* 38, No. 4 (2020), 622–642.

[40] See P. T. Bauer, *Dissent on Development* (Cambridge, MA: Harvard University Press, 1971), and *The Development Frontier* (Cambridge, MA: Harvard University Press, 1991), for a couple of examples.

a state-directed economy rather than an environment of economic freedom. There have been numerous studies, with conflicting results, on the
cross-country empirical relationship between foreign aid and economic
freedom. Most of the studies (including an earlier one of my own) strug-
gled to employ plausible identification strategies to establish a causal
relationship between the two.[41] More recently, I conducted a study, with
economists Jamie Pavlik and Andrew Young, that employed matching
methods to better identify the causal relationship between aid and economic freedom.[42] Overall, we found essentially no relationship. Aid
failed to increase economic freedom, but it didn't decrease it either. If,
as I argued in the previous chapter, economic freedom is the environment that best promotes the process of development, foreign aid does not
appear to help foster that environment.

What about military intervention? Can the US armed forces displace
bad governments and then install the right environment for development during reconstruction efforts? Economist Christopher Coyne
studied all US interventions and reconstruction efforts in foreign countries since 1900 to see how successful they were at installing lasting
liberal democratic regimes.[43] He used the Polity IV database to measure
how liberal and democratic regimes were after US military interventions. He didn't set the bar for success high, considering any polity as
good as present-day Iran a success. Of the 25 reconstruction efforts, for
which more than 5 years had passed since the end of occupation, only
7 scored as a well as present-day Iran – a 28 percent success rate. Ten
years after occupation, the rate of success remained the same, and it
rose to only 39 percent 15 years after occupation, and 36 percent after
20 years. Success stories like Japan and Germany after World War II
are the exception rather than the norm.

The problem is that a new constitution establishing the right institutions is still just a piece of paper. A constitution doesn't enforce itself.
If the existing power structure doesn't enforce the rules, it doesn't matter how good they are on paper. Economists Claudia Williamson and
Carrie Kerekes found that the main constraint on state predation is the

---

[41] The first edition of this book reported my findings from my earlier study, Benjamin
Powell and Matt Ryan, "Does Development Aid Lead to Economic Freedom?" *Journal
of Private Enterprise* 22, No. 1 (2006).

[42] Jamie Bologna Pavlik, Benjamin Powell, and Andrew Young, "Does Aid Cause Changes
in Economic Freedom?" *Southern Economic Journal* 89, No. 1 (2022), 90–111.

[43] Christopher Coyne, *After War: The Political Economy of Exporting Democracy* (Palo
Alto: Stanford University Press, 2008).

informal culture rather than the formal rules on paper.[44] Furthermore, for development, the formal institutional rules must be consistent with the ideology and culture of the local population. In other research, Williamson found that the ability of formal institutions to generate beneficial results depends on their mapping onto the informal culture.[45] This doesn't mean that accepting whatever the indigenous culture might be will lead to growth. There are plenty of ways to live but not plenty that result in development. This means the game for development is changing the hearts and minds of people so that informal culture supports markets and private enterprise and forces their governments to respect the formal institutions that support this environment as well.

We must be much humbler about our ability to help a country develop from the outside once we realize that it is citizens' hearts and minds that we must ultimately capture to succeed. But this doesn't mean that activists can't do anything. Circulating ideas supportive of private property and economic freedom in Third World countries is a necessary, though not sufficient, condition for getting the culture and ideology right for economic development.

The Atlas Network is the world leader in spreading the ideas of free markets and individual liberty to intellectual entrepreneurs throughout the world. Sir Antony Fisher founded Atlas in 1981. Fisher had founded the Institute of Economic Affairs, a very influential British think tank, in 1955. After he helped start up a couple of other think tanks abroad, he created Atlas to replicate the process around the world. Atlas's mission is to "discover, develop, and support intellectual entrepreneurs worldwide who share a vision of a peaceful and prosperous society of free and responsible individuals that requires respect for the foundations of a free society: individual liberty, property rights, limited government under the rule of law, and the market order." Atlas now works with more than 500 free market think tanks in more than 100 countries. Economist Matt Ryan and I studied how the spread of these free market think tanks impacted the spread of economic freedom around the globe over the last 40 years.[46] We found that more think-tank activity was associated with larger increases in

---

[44] Claudia Williamson and Carrie Kerekes, "Securing Private Property: Formal versus Informal Institutions," *Journal of Law and Economics* 54, No. 3 (2011), 537–572.

[45] Claudia Williamson, "Informal Institutions Rule: Institutional Arrangements and Economic Performance," *Public Choice* 139, No. 3 (2009), 371–387.

[46] Benjamin Powell and Matt Ryan, "The Global Spread of Think Tanks and Economic Freedom," *Journal of Private Enterprise* 32, No. 3 (2017), 17–31.

economic freedom over both 5- and 10-year time periods. Activists concerned with the plight of workers in countries with sweatshops should consider how they could help Atlas help locals spread the ideas of liberty that are necessary for development.

Think tanks play an important role in disseminating the ideas necessary for development to the general population. But it is also important to educate the future leaders who can help spread those ideas. All too often, schooling in poor countries places little to no emphasis on understanding how market economies operate and what institutions are necessary for them to promote development. Activists could work on educational outreach programs for children. Missionary work could focus on educating in classical liberal ideas.

The most inspiring university I know of is the Universidad Francisco Marroquín. Founded in Guatemala by Manual Ayau in 1971, the university is explicitly committed to educating in the classical liberal ideas that are essential for supporting the environment necessary for economic development. The university now has approximately 3,000 undergraduate students and another 1,500 graduate students. It seeks to educate the intellectual elite of Guatemala in the hope of shaping the ideas of those who will lead the country in the future. Note that the intellectual elite doesn't necessarily mean the financial elite. The university actively recruits students from poor families, some of whose parents might even work in sweatshops, and provides promising students with scholarships to attend. Although economics and law have been the traditional focus of the university, it has schools of medicine, architecture, and psychology, among others. But regardless of major, all students must take one course on the thought of famed classical liberal economists Ludwig von Mises and Friedrich Hayek. If the world had more universities like this one, the chances would be better of changing the hearts and minds of people trapped in the poorer countries around the world.

Forming think tanks and educating students doesn't guarantee that a country's ideology will change in favor of economic freedom, but it's a start. Ultimately, these countries have poor institutions of governance that need to change. When a break occurs in the political equilibrium that is enforcing these bad institutions, it's crucial that the right ideas are on hand and ready to be adopted.

This points to the role that crisis can play in institutional change. The usual development mantra is that aid is necessary to avert crisis. But averting crises in places with poor institutions helps those poor institutions remain in place. Sometimes a crisis provides a break in the political equilibrium that allows for the adoption of good institutions. In recent years, India, Ireland, and New Zealand, to name a few, all embarked on major liberalizations that increased economic freedom as a way to deal with their financial crises.[47] This is not to say that crisis is necessarily good. There has been no shortage of crises that result in no change or worse change. But they do provide a break and, if the right ideas are on hand, an opportunity for real reform.[48]

Agitating for free trade is one final thing activists could do to promote the development of the Third World. Lowering trade barriers to Third World countries increases the wages that the workers who produce the imported goods can be paid. Eliminating tariffs increases the net revenue a firm receives for each good sold, which enables the same physical productivity from a worker to generate more revenue for the firm. As a result, the worker's upper bound of compensation is increased. A lowered trade barrier results in this one-time increase in income, which is reason enough for activists to support free trade. But it gets better.

It turns out that capitalism is contagious. Economists have long contended that free trade promotes the spread of economic freedom. In the 19th century, Richard Cobden and Frederic Bastiat contended that free trade spreads economic freedom abroad by disseminating new ideas. The new ideas might be embodied in the goods themselves, or they might come from how trade affects views toward market exchange compared with isolationist subsistence. It turns out they were right. When a more economically free country trades with a less economically free country, the less economically free country becomes freer. Economists Russell Sobel and Peter Leeson found that countries "catch" approximately 20 percent of their trading partners' levels and changes in economic freedom.[49] Although the impact of any one nation's freedom spreading to a

---

[47] For case studies of the reforms in these three countries, see Benjamin Powell, *Making Poor Nations Rich: Entrepreneurship and the Process of Development* (Palo Alto: Stanford University Press, 2008).

[48] For a book exploring the process of political change see Wayne Leighton and Edward Lopez, *Madmen, Intellectuals, and Academic Scribblers* (Palo Alto: Stanford University Press, 2012). They argue that change occurs when academics have come up with new ideas, intellectuals have popularized them, and then external circumstances change, which makes adopting those ideas in the interests of those ruling society. Also see a book I coedited exploring the relationship between crises and institutional change: Stephen Balch and Benjamin Powell, eds., *Economic and Political Change after Crisis: Prospects for Government, Liberty, and the Rule of Law* (London: Routledge, 2016).

[49] Russell Sobel and Peter Leeson, "The Spread of Global Economic Freedom," in *Economic Freedom of the World 2007 Annual Report*, edited by James Gwartney and Robert Lawson (Vancouver: The Fraser Institute, 2007).

trading partner may be modest, the combined effect of a larger free trade agreement, that includes many trading partners of a less free country, may help to create larger increases in economic freedom. Thus, activists concerned both with the immediate welfare gains for workers in sweatshop countries and with ways to achieve the enabling environment for economic development in those countries should agitate for freer trade between those countries, the United States, and other freer nations.

Economic development is the best way to improve the lives of sweatshop workers. But once we realize that development depends on getting both the correct formal institutional environment and the informal culture and ideology to support it, we must be fairly modest about how much activists, or anyone else, can do from the outside to improve development. The best we can hope for is the spread of ideas supportive of individual liberty, private property, and economic freedom. We can create think tanks, universities, and other educational programs to spread these ideas. We can agitate for freer trade between the United States and countries that use sweatshops, in the hope that some of our free institutions will rub off on them. But ultimately, the local indigenous culture must agitate for the right changes and enforce the right institutions itself. Outsiders in the West can play only a limited role in that.

RELAX IMMIGRATION RESTRICTIONS

Third World countries are poor because they have institutions that do not support an environment of economic freedom. It might be hard to give them that environment from the outside, but an alternative is obvious. Let people move from their country with poor institutions to places like the United States that have better institutions. People who immigrate to the United States from poor countries instantly experience a boost in their productivity and their standard of living. Nothing physical changes about the worker's human capital. But by matching their skills with US capital, technology, complementary labor, and the enabling environment of economic freedom, workers instantly can produce and earn more.

The gains in income that can accrue to a poor Third World worker from emigration dwarf anything that could hope to be achieved by any of the policies advocated by anti-sweatshop groups, even if the laws of economics didn't undermine their favored policies. Take sweatshop-hosting Haiti, for example. Economists Michael Clemens, Claudio Montenegro, and Lant Pritchett documented the wage gap between observably identical Haitians (35-year-old urban males with 9–12 years of education born in Haiti) in the United States and Haiti.[50] They found Haitians living in the United States earned over 1,000 percent more than similar Haitians living in Haiti. This type of gain dwarfs anything that a living wage law could achieve, even if it didn't unemploy workers.

Some might object that when Haitians move to the United States that "Haiti" hasn't developed. That's true of course. But so what? No one walks around wringing their hands worrying that Antarctica hasn't produced enough GDP because no humans permanently live there. We should care about human flourishing, not the amount of economic activity that takes place on a given hunk of land. To continue with the Haitian example, among those living in either the United States or Haiti, 80 percent of Haitians who live on more than $10 per day live in the United States.[51] Allowing more Haitians to move to the United States may do little to raise the incomes of those who remain behind, but there is little evidence that their emigration significantly harms those left behind either.[52] Therefore, emigration would bring a substantial increase in living standards for many, without harming the nonmigrants.

The estimates of the overall gains to the world economy from more emigration are staggering. The estimates vary depending on assumptions but often range between 50 and 150 percent of world GDP if developed countries completely eliminated their policy barriers to immigrants.[53] Obviously, that would entail a huge movement of people, but estimates for smaller movements are also impressive. A worldwide emigration of 5 percent of the population of poor countries would boost world income by more than the gains that could be achieved from eliminating all remaining policy barriers to merchandise trade and capital flows.[54]

The main obstacle to greater emigration is the beliefs of the populations in the receiving countries. Negative opinions of immigrants often stem from misconceptions about economics. People believe that immigrants drag down the economy, steal "our" jobs, and depress our

[50] Michael Clemens, Claudio Montenegro, and Lant Pritchett, "The Place Premium: Bounding the Price Equivalent of Migration Barriers," *Review of Economics and Statistics*, 101 No. 2 (2019), 201–213.
[51] Michael Clemens, "Economics and Emigration: Trillion-Dollar Bills on the Sidewalk?" *Journal of Economic Perspectives* 25, No. 3 (2011), 83–106.
[52] Ibid.
[53] Ibid.
[54] Ibid.

wages. Watching Lou Dobbs's economically uniformed rants about the "war on the middle class" stokes these fears.[55] But all three of these fears are misguided.

Even economists critical of immigration, such as George Borjas, find that immigration brings a net gain to the native-born population.[56] The estimated size of the net gain varies, but all estimates are small relative to the size of the economy. Immigrants also don't, on net, steal jobs from the native-born. It's obvious when an immigrant displaces a worker, and Dobbs and others can put a TV camera on the unemployed worker so that worker can say "I lost my job to an immigrant." This is a classic case of what economist Frederic Bastiat called the problem of that which is seen and that which is not.[57] The guy on the camera who lost is job is seen, but what isn't seen is that another job was created precisely because of the demands for goods and services created by the immigrant. Adding more workers to the labor force simply creates more jobs. Just think of the history of the US labor force since 1950. The size of the labor force has roughly tripled because of the massive entry of women, baby boomers, and immigrants into the marketplace. But the number of jobs has roughly tripled too. Add more workers, and we add more jobs.

Immigrants also don't systematically depress the wages of the native-born. When economists find the wages of native-born workers depressed because of immigration, this is generally true only for those without a high school diploma, and even then, the estimates are often small, temporary, and sometimes nonexistent.[58] Immigration doesn't necessarily depress the wages of the native-born for a few reasons. Immigration increases both the supply of, and the demand for, labor, so which effect dominates is an empirical question. Also, it's often not simply "the" supply of labor that is increased. Immigrants often have skills different from

---

[55] I went on his show once to explain the economics of immigration. Rather than counter my arguments he just called me names. I took it as a compliment. You can see a video of it here: www.youtube.com/watch?v=zoDb3D7B2Zo.

[56] George Borjas, "Immigration," in *The Concise Encyclopedia of Economics*, edited by David Henderson (Indianapolis: Liberty Fund, 2008).

[57] See Frederic Bastiat, *Selected Essays on Political Economy* (1848). Available online at the Library of Economics and Liberty, retrieved from www.econlib.org/library/Bastiat/basEss.html.

[58] For the conflicting sides of the debate, see George Borjas, "The Labor Demand Curve *Is* Downward Sloping: Reexamining the Impact of Immigration on the Labor Market," *Quarterly Journal of Economics* 118, No. 4, (2003), 1335–1374; David Card, "Immigration and Inequality," *American Economic Review* 99, No. 2 (2009), 1–21.

those of the native-born, so they complement the natives' skills rather than substituting for them. As Adam Smith famously noted, specialization and the division of labor are limited by the extent of the market. Greater immigration allows a deeper market with a finer division of labor that can lead to higher living standards.

The most important objection to significantly increasing immigration is not a popular fear but an academic theory that has come to be known as the "new economic case for migration restrictions." This theory, first posited by Paul Collier and George Borjas, asserts that immigrants could bring with them beliefs, behaviors, or characteristics that lower the productivity of destination countries.[59] On its face, the theory is plausible. I have argued that institutions favorable to private property rights and economic freedom are important for economic development and that to get those institutions in poorer countries it is largely dependent on the hearts and minds of people in those countries enforcing them on their governments. If the poor institutions in immigrants' origin countries are, at least in part, the result of the beliefs of these people, might they bring some of these same beliefs with them to the countries they emigrate to and, if enough of them come in mass, might they make their destination country's institutions a little more like their origin country's institutions? If they do, then the wage gains from the place premium shrink, and the massive gain in overall output would shrink or potentially even turn negative.

Let me make this objection concrete. If the Cubans, who fled socialism and escaped to Florida, recreated Cuban socialism in Florida, then both those Cubans and Floridians would be poorer than they are today. Of course, I can think of no more solid anti-socialist voting bloc, in the United States, than Cuban immigrants. The new economic case for migration restrictions is ultimately an empirical question. Do immigrants generally bring with them traits and beliefs that lower productivity or are they like the Cuban immigrants, who bring beliefs in opposition to factors responsible for the low productivity in their origin country? The proponents of the new economic case for migration restrictions have not provided systematic empirical evidence supporting their theory. In another book in this same Cambridge University Press series, *Wretched Refuse: The Political Economy of Immigration and Institutions*, Alex

---

[59] Paul Collier, *Exodus: How Migration Is Changing Our World* (New York: Oxford University Press, 2013); George Borjas, "Immigration and Globalization: A Review Essay," *Journal of Economic Literature* 53, No. 4 (2015), 961–974.

Nowrasteh and I provide the most systematic empirical assessment of the new economic case for migration restrictions.[60] We examine the impact of stocks and flows of immigrants across large numbers of countries and investigate individual case studies of mass migration. Overall, we do not find evidence supporting the new economic case for migration restrictions. In fact, in some cases, we find the opposite. When it comes specifically to economic freedom, we find that greater migration is more likely to be associated with subsequent increases in a destination country's economic freedom, rather than decreases.

Reviewing all the debates about immigration from the native-born perspective is beyond the scope of this chapter.[61] The point here is about emigration. If the welfare of Third World people is your metric, then decreasing the policy barriers preventing them from emigrating is clearly the best action First World countries can take to help these people. As an added bonus, it will also make the world, and the receiving countries, richer. Anti-sweatshop activists should join pro-immigration activists in pushing for lower policy barriers for immigrants. Although I support this as a general policy for all, some activists narrowly concerned only with sweatshop workers could focus on policy reform that targets increased visas for those people with skills in the garment industry in countries that use sweatshops. Just don't hold your breath waiting for union-backed anti-sweatshop groups to join you in that struggle!

CONCLUSION

Just because sweatshops are the best option currently available to workers does not mean that activists can do nothing. But it does significantly change what the anti-sweatshop movement should be doing. Most of their favored policies – boycotts, trade sanctions, minimum wages, and working condition mandates – need to be dropped.

Ethical branding and opposition to slave labor are two areas in which anti-sweatshop activists currently work and can still play a role. Actual slave labor, like that experienced by the Uyghur population in China,

---

[60] This book builds off a series of papers we each wrote with a number of different coauthors. Alex Nowrasteh and Benjamin Powell, *Wretched Refuse? The Political Economy of Immigration and Institutions* (Cambridge: Cambridge University Press, 2020).

[61] For a dated survey of this literature, see Rachel Friedberg and Jennifer Hunt, "The Impact of Immigrants on Host Country Wages, Employment and Growth," *Journal of Economic Perspectives* 9, No. 2 (1995), 23–44. For a more recent survey, see National Academies of Sciences, Engineering, and Medicine, *The Economic and Fiscal Consequences of Immigration* (Washington, DC: The National Academies Press, 2016).

should be vigorously exposed, protested, and punished. Activists can play a role in exposing fraudulent ethical branding, providing seals of approval, and discovering market demand that companies may not be aware of. In addition, activists have been concerned with child labor. Rather than banning it, they should raise funds to pay children to attend school rather than work. Expanding children's options will help, but contracting their options, by banning child labor, will not.

Much of this chapter has argued for anti-sweatshop activists to completely redirect their efforts if the welfare of Third World workers is their goal. The process of economic development leads to the widespread disappearance of sweatshops. Anti-sweatshop activists should become pro-development activists. However, we must realize how limited the ability of outsiders is to create the right environment for development in foreign countries. Despite the difficulties, activists should help spread the ideas of the freer societies to poorer ones through think tanks and other educational efforts. They should agitate for their own governments to adopt freer trade with poorer countries in the hope that trade will provide an avenue for our institutions to be exported abroad.

Finally, anti-sweatshop activists should become pro-immigration activists. A sweatshop worker, or any poor citizen of the Third World, will increase their living standards more by moving to the United States than any policy could ever hope to achieve for them in their own country, at least in the short run.

There is a role for activists. But with an understanding of economics, that role is turned on its head from what much of the anti-sweatshop movement has done since the 1990s. Anti-sweatshop activists should become advocates for free markets in goods, labor, and capital if they want to improve the lives of the poor in countries where sweatshops are located.

12

Conclusion

Thus far, the anti-sweatshop movement hasn't been particularly success-ful in getting their favored policies mandated. Sociologist and activist Jill Esbenshade summarized the progress of the movement as of 2004: "Although this movement has brought the issue of sweatshops into the consuming public's eye, it has had considerably less success in translating this heightened concern into victories for garment workers in their fac-tories."[1] Seven years later, the situation wasn't much different. In 2011, political scientist Shae Garwood wrote,

The anti-sweatshop network has been successful in ... raising awareness and agenda setting. The network as has also influenced the industry's adoption of the discourse of responsibility and workers' rights... As a result of anti-sweatshop advocacy, some targeted corporations have implemented internal social auditing programs... However, the anti-sweatshop network has been unable to achieve ... behavioral change by manufacturers. This means that workers' rights and work-ing conditions, as articulated in the WRC code, remain largely unfulfilled.[2]

Another decade later, with the notable exception of the Accord and Alliance discussed in Chapter 6, the situation remains largely the same. The main message of this book is that the anti-sweatshop movement's failure to mandate policies like minimum wages and working standards is a victory for the sweatshop workers. If the activists had their way, the workers would be worse off.

Straightforward economic reasoning explains why sweatshop jobs are jeopardized by many of the actions taken by First World anti-sweatshop activists. Yet, because workers choose to work at these firms, we know

[1] Esbenshade, *Monitoring Sweatshops*, 202.
[2] Garwood, *Advocacy across Borders*, 184.

that the workers believe the jobs are the best available alternative for them. Agitating for policies that would take the option of sweatshop employment away from these workers makes workers worse off. It throws them into a worse alternative now and it undermines the process of economic development that ultimately leads to better-paying jobs with better working conditions.

The economics surrounding sweatshop employment is simple. But as economist Peter Boettke has often said, simple economics shouldn't be confused with simple minded economics. As he put it,

[it is] the case that economics in the hands of its finest practitioners is little more than applied common sense. As Frank Knight pointed out, "The serious fact is that the bulk of the really important things that economics has to teach are things that people would see for themselves if they were willing to see. And it is hard to believe in the utility of trying to teach what men refuse to learn or even seriously listen to."[3]

Joshua Brown, a sweatshop monitor in the late 1990s, illustrates Knight's insight. He was auditing a Chinese factory. As he describes it,

We find almost every violation in the book. The workers are pulling 90-hour weeks. The place has no fire extinguishers or fire exits, and is so jammed full of material that a small fire could explode into an inferno within a minute. There are no safety guards on the sewing machines, and the first-aid box holds only packages of instant noodles.

With the bosses out of earshot, I fully expect the workers to pour out their sorrows to me, to beg me to tell the consumers of America to help them out of their misery. I'm surprised at what I hear.

"I'm happy to have this job," is the essence of what several workers tell me. "At home, I'm a drain on my family's resources. But now, I can send them money every month."

I point out that they make only $100 a month; they remind me this is about five times what they can make in their home province. I ask if they feel like they're being exploited, having to work 90 hours a week. They laugh.

"We all work piece rate here. More work, more money."

The worst part of the day for them, it seemed, was seeing me arrive. "I don't want to tell you anything because you'll close my factory and ruin any chances I have at having a better life one day," one tells me.[4]

When Joshua left the factory, he told "the owner that she needs to buy fire extinguishers, put actual first-aid supplies in the first-aid kits, install

[3] Peter Boettke, *Living Economics*, 19–20; and Frank Knight, "The Role of Principles in Economics and Politics," *American Economic Review* 41, No. 1 (1951), 1–29, in *Selected Essays of Frank H. Knight*, edited by Ross Emmett (Chicago: University of Chicago Press, 1999), 364.
[4] Joshua Brown, quoted in Esbenshade, *Monitoring Sweatshops*, 212–213.

safety equipment on the sewing machines, and reduce worker hours to below 60 per week."[5] Joshua Brown refused to learn from, and seriously listen to, the sweatshop employees he interviewed.

If you've made it to this point in the book, I appreciate the fact that you have seriously listened to what economics has to say about sweatshops. Economist Henry Simons said, "Economics is primarily useful, both to the student and to the political leader, as a prophylactic against popular fallacies."[6] It is my sincere hope that the second edition of this book will continue to serve as such a prophylactic and will dissuade people from agitating for policies that would jeopardize sweatshop jobs and instead redirect people's efforts toward supporting the free enterprise system that ultimately drives the process of development that will improve the lives of sweatshop workers and their descendants.

[5] Ibid., 213.
[6] Henry Simons, *Simons' Syllabus*, edited by Gordon Tullock (Fairfax: Center for the Study of Public Choice, 1983), 3.

Bibliography

Abadie, Alberto. "Using Synthetic Controls: Feasibility, Data Requirements, and Methodological Aspects." *Journal of Economic Literature* 59, No. 2 (2021): 391–425.

Abadie, Alberto, Alexis Diamond, and Jens Hainmueller. "Synthetic Control Methods for Comparative Case Studies: Estimating the Effect of California's Tobacco Control Program." *Journal of the American Statistical Association* 105, No. 490 (2010): 493–505.

Abadie, Alberto, Alexis Diamond, and Jens Hainmueller. "Comparative Politics and the Synthetic Control Method." *American Journal of Political Science* 59, No. 2 (2015): 495–510.

Abadie, Alberto and Javier Gardeazabal. "The Economic Costs of Conflict: A Case Study of the Basque Country." *American Economic Review* 93, No. 1 (2003): 113–132.

Abadie, Alberto and Jaume Vives-i-Bastida. "Synthetic Controls in Action." *ArXiv*. March 2022: 2203.06279. Retrieved from https://arxiv.org/abs/2203.06279.

Academic Consortium on International Trade. *ACIT Anti-Sweatshop Letter.* July 2000. Retrieved from www.fordschool.umich.edu/rsie/acit/Documents/Anti-SweatshopLetterPage.html.

Academic Consortium on International Trade. *Sweatshop Letter.* July 2000. Retrieved from www.fordschool.umich.edu/rsie/acit/Documents/July29SweatshopLetter.pdf.

Accord. "Quarterly Aggregate Report on Remediation Progress and Status of Workplace Programs at RMG Factories Covered by the Accord." 2020. Retrieved from https://bangladesh.wpengine.com/wpcontent/uploads/2020/02/Accord_Quarterly_Aggregate_Report_January2020.pdf.

Adler-Milstein, Sarah and John M. Kline. *Sewing Hope: How One Factory Challenges the Apparel Industry's Sweatshops.* Oakland, CA: University of California Press, 2017.

Afsar, Rita. "Sociological Implications of Female Labor Migration in Bangladesh." In *Globalization and Gender: Changing Patterns of Women's*

Employment in Bangladesh, edited by Rehman Sobhan and Nasreen Khundker. Dhaka: Centre for Policy Dialogue and University Press Limited, 2001.

Ahmed, Faisal, Anne Greenleaf, and Audrey Sacks. "The Paradox of Export Growth in Areas of Weak Governance: The Case of the Ready Made Garment Sector in Bangladesh." *World Development* 56 (2014): 258–271.

Ahmed, Nazneen and Jack Peerlings. "Addressing Workers' Rights in the Textile and Apparel Industries: Consequences for the Bangladesh Economy." *World Development* 37, No. 3 (2009): 661–675.

Alfaro-Urena, Alonso, Benjamin Faber, Cecile Gaubert, Isabela Manelici, and Jose Vasquez. "Responsible Sourcing? Theory and Evidence from Costa Rica." *NBER Working Paper* No. 30683 (2022). Retrieved from www.nber.org/papers/w30683.

American Center for International Labor Solidarity. Retrieved from www.solidaritycenter.org.

American Federation of Labor-Congress of Industrial Organizations. Retrieved from www.aflcio.org.

Amin, Sajeda. "Responding to Rana Plaza: A Made-in-Bangladesh Boycott Won't Help Girls." *The Guardian.* October 19, 2022. Retrieved from www.theguardian.com/global-development-professionals-network/2014/apr/30/rana-plaza-boycott-bangladesh-garment-factory.

Anner, Mark. *Binding Power: The Sourcing Squeeze, Workers' Rights, and Building Safety in Bangladesh since Rana Plaza.* State College, PA: Penn State College of the Liberal Arts, Centre for Global Workers' Rights, 2018.

Arnold, Denis. "Philosophical Foundations: Moral Reasoning, Human Rights, and Global Labor Practices." In *Rising above Sweatshops: Innovative Approaches to Global Labor Challenges,* edited by Laura Hartman, Denis Arnold, and Richard E. Wokutch. Westport, CT: Praeger, 2003.

Arnold, Denis. "Working Conditions: Safety and Sweatshops." In *The Oxford Handbook of Business Ethics,* edited by George Brenkert and Tom Beauchamp. New York: Oxford University Press, 2010.

Arnold, Denis and Norman Bowie. "Sweatshops and Respect for Persons." *Business Ethics Quarterly* 13, No. 2 (April 2003): 221–242.

Arnold, Denis and Norman Bowie. "Respect for Workers in Global Supply Chains: Advancing the Debate over Sweatshops." *Business Ethics Quarterly* 17, No. 1 (January 2007): 135–145.

Arnold, Denis and Laura Hartman. "Moral Imagination and the Future of Sweatshops." *Business and Society Review* 108, No. 4 (December 2003): 425–461.

Arnold, Denis and Laura Hartman. "Beyond Sweatshops: Positive Deviancy and Global Labour Practices." *Business Ethics: A European Review* 14, No. 3 (July 2005): 206–222.

Arnold, Denis and Laura Hartman. "Worker Rights and Low Wage Industrialization: How to Avoid Sweatshops." *Human Rights Quarterly* 28, No. 3 (August 2006): 676–700.

Asshagrie, Kebebew. *Statistics on Working Children and Hazardous Child Labour in Brief.* Geneva: International Labor Office, 1997.

Associated Press. "Factory in Bangladesh Lost Fire Clearance before Blaze." *New York Times.* December 7, 2012. Retrieved from www.nytimes .com/2012/12/08/world/asia/bangladesh-factory-where-dozens-died-was-illegal.html?_r=0.

Balch, Stephen and Benjamin Powell, eds. *Economic and Political Change after Crisis: Prospects for Government, Liberty, and the Rule of Law.* London: Routledge, 2016.

Barzel, Yoram. "A Theory of Rationing by Waiting." *Journal of Law and Economics* 17, (1974): 73–95.

Bastiat, Frederic. *Selected Essays on Political Economy.* 1848. Retrieved from www.econlib.org/library/Bastiat/basEss.html.

Basu, Kaushik. "Child Labor: Cause, Consequence, and Cure, with Remarks on International Labor Standards." *Journal of Economic Literature* 37, No. 3 (1999): 1083–1119.

Bauer, P. T. *Dissent on Development.* Cambridge, MA: Harvard University Press, 1971.

Bauer, P. T. *The Development Frontier.* Cambridge, MA: Harvard University Press, 1991.

Baumol, William. "Entrepreneurship: Productive, Unproductive, and Destructive." *Journal of Political Economy* 98, No. 5 (October 1990): 893–921.

Berggren, Niclas. "The Benefits of Economic Freedom." *The Independent Review* 8, No. 2 (Fall 2003): 193–211.

Boettke, Peter. *Living Economics: Yesterday, Today, and Tomorrow.* Oakland, CA: The Independent Institute, 2012.

Bologna Pavlik, Jamie, Benjamin Powell, and Andrew Young. "Does Aid Cause Changes in Economic Freedom?" *Southern Economic Journal* 89, No. 1 (2022): 90–111.

Bologna Pavlik, Jamie and Andrew T. Young. "Sorting Out the Aid-Corruption Nexus." *Journal of Institutional Economics* 18, No. 4 (2022): 637–653.

Borjas, George. "The Labor Demand Curve *Is* Downward Sloping: Reexamining the Impact of Immigration on the Labor Market." *Quarterly Journal of Economics* 118, No. 4 (November 2003): 1335–1374.

Borjas, George. "Immigration." In *The Concise Encyclopedia of Economics,* edited by David Henderson. Indianapolis: Liberty Fund, 2008.

Borjas, George. "Immigration and Globalization: A Review Essay." *Journal of Economic Literature* 53, No. 4 (2015): 961–974.

Brant, Robin. "Xinjiang Cotton: Western Clothes Brands Vanish as Backlash Grows." *BBC News.* March 26, 2021. Retrieved from www.bbc.com/news/world-asia-china-56533560.

Brown, Drusilla, Alan Deardorff, and Robert Sten. "Child Labor: Theory, Evidence and Policy." In *International Labor Standards: History, Theories and Policy,* edited by Kaushik Basu, Henrik Horn, Lisa Roman, and Judith Shapiro. Oxford: Basil Blackwell, 2003.

Busse, Matthias. "On the Determinants of Core Labor Standards: The Case of Developing Countries." *Economics Letters* 83, No. 2 (May 2004): 211–217.

Card, David and Alan Krueger. *Myth and Measurement: The New Economics of the Minimum Wage.* Princeton: Princeton University Press, 1995.

Card, David and Andrei Shleifer. "Immigration and Inequality." *American Economic Review* 99, No. 2 (2009): 1–21.

Carson, Kevin. "Vulgar Libertarianism." January 11, 2005. Retrieved from http://mutualist.blogspot.com/2005/01/vulgar-libertarianism-watch-part-1.html.

Cavallo, Eduardo, Sebastian Galiani, Ilan Noy, and Juan Pantano. "Catastrophic Natural Disasters and Economic Growth." *Review of Economics and Statistics* 95 (2013): 1549–1561.

Chartier, Gary. "Sweatshops, Labor Rights, and Competitive Advantage." *Oregon Review of International Law* 10, No. 1 (September 2008): 149–188.

Cheang, Bryan. *Economic Liberalism and the Developmental State: Hong Kong and Singapore's Post-war Development*. London: Palgrave Macmillan, 2023.

Clark, J. R. and Benjamin Powell "Sweatshop Working Conditions and Employee Welfare: Say It Ain't Sew." *Comparative Economic Studies* 55, No. 2 (2013): 343–357.

Clarke, Natalie. "The True Price of the £6 Dress." *The Daily Mail*. September 13, 2007. Retrieved from www.dailymail.co.uk/femail/article-481538/The-true-price-6-dress.html.

Clean Clothes Campaign. Retrieved from www.cleanclothes.org.

Clemens, Michael. "Economics and Emigration: Trillion-Dollar Bills on the Sidewalk?" *Journal of Economic Perspectives* 25, No. 3 (Summer 2011): 83–106.

Clemens, Michael, Claudio Montenegro, and Lant Pritchett. "The Place Premium: Bounding the Price Equivalent of Migration Barriers." *Review of Economics and Statistics* 101, No. 2 (2019): 201–213.

CNN. "Gap: Report of Kids' Sweatshop 'Deeply Disturbing.'" *CNN World*. October 29, 2007. Retrieved from http://articles.cnn.com/2007-10-29/world/gap.labor_1_clothing-retailer-gap-child-labor-gap-kids-stores?_s=PM:WORLD.

Coakley, Mathew and Michael Kates. "The Ethical and Economic Case for Sweatshop Regulation." *Journal of Business Ethics* 117 (2013): 553–558.

Collier, Paul. "Haiti: From Natural Catastrophe to Economic Security." *A Report for the Secretary-General of the United Nations*. January 2009. Retrieved from www.focal.ca/pdf/haiticollier.pdf.

Collier, Paul. *Exodus: How Migration Is Changing Our World*. New York: Oxford University Press, 2013.

Cowen, Tyler and Alex Tabarrok. *Modern Principles: Macroeconomics*. New York: Worth Publishers, 2009.

Coyne, Christopher. *After War: The Political Economy of Exporting Democracy*. Palo Alto: Stanford University Press, 2008.

Deere, Donald, Kevin Murphy, and Finis Welch. "Sense and Nonsense on the Minimum Wage." *Regulation* 18, No. 1 (1995): 47–56.

Donaghey, Jimmy and Juliane Reinecke. "When Industrial Democracy Meets Corporate Social Responsibility – A Comparison of the Bangladesh Accord and Alliances as Responses to the Rana Plaza Disaster." *British Journal of Industrial Relations* 56, No. 1 (2018): 14–42.

Easterly, William. *The Elusive Quest for Growth*. Cambridge, MA: MIT Press, 2002.

Edmonds, Eric. "Does Child Labor Decline with Improving Economic Status?" *Journal of Human Resources* 40, No. 1 (Winter 2005): 77–99.

Edmonds, Eric and Nina Pavcnik. "Child Labor in the Global Economy." *Journal of Economic Perspectives* 19, No. 1 (Winter 2005): 199–220.

Elliott, Kimberly, Gary Hufbauer, and Barbara Oegg. "Sanctions." In *The Concise Encyclopedia of Economics*, edited by David Henderson, 2008. Retrieved from http://econlib.org/library/Enc/Sanctions.html.

Esbenshade, Jill. *Monitoring Sweatshops: Workers, Consumers, and the Global Apparel Industry*. Philadelphia: Temple University Press, 2004.

Fair Labor Association. Retrieved from www.fairlabor.org.

Featherstone, Liza and USAS. *Students against Sweatshops*. New York: Verso, 2002.

Ferman, Bruno, Cristine Pinto, and Vitor Possebom. "Cherry Picking with Synthetic Controls." *Journal of Policy Analysis and Management* 39, No. 2 (2020): 510–532.

Fishback, Price. "Operations of 'Unfettered' Labor Markets: Exit and Voice in American Labor Markets at the Turn of the Century." *Journal of Economic Literature* 36, No. 2 (June 1998): 722–765.

Fishback, Price. *Government and the American Economy: A New History*. Chicago: University of Chicago Press, 2007.

Flora, Liz. "Lacoste and Adidas Pledge to Cut Forced Uighur Labor from Supply Chain." *Glossy*. April 27, 2022. Retrieved from www.glossy.co/fashion/lacoste-and-adidas-pledge-to-cut-forced-uighur-labor-from-supply-chain/.

Forbes Magazine. Retrieved from www.forbes.com/2007/08/13/dangerous-jobs-fishing-lead-careerscx_tvr_0813danger.html.

Friedberg, Rachel and Jennifer Hunt, "The Impact of Immigrants on Host Country Wages, Employment and Growth." *Journal of Economic Perspectives* 9, No. 2 (Spring 1995): 23–44.

Friedman, Monroe. "The Ethical Dilemmas Associated with Boycotts." *Journal of Social Philosophy* 32, No. 2 (2001): 232–240.

Gardner, Bradley. *China's Great Migration: How the Poor Built a Prosperous Nation*. Oakland, CA: The Independent Institute, 2017.

Garwood, Shae. *Advocacy across Borders: NGOs, Anti-Sweatshop Activism, and the Global Garment Industry*. Sterling, VA: Kumarian Press, 2011.

Goldin, Claudia and Larry Katz. "Mass Secondary Schooling and the State: The Role of State Compulsion and the High School Movement." *NBER Working Paper* No. 10075 (2003).

Goodin, Robert E. "Exploiting a Situation and Exploiting a Person." In *Modern Theories of Exploitation*, edited by Andrew Reeve. London: Sage, 1987.

Green, Leslie. *Legal Obligation and Authority*. October 1, 2010. Retrieved from http://plato.stanford.edu/entries/legalobligation.

Grier, Kevin and Robin Grier. "The Washington Consensus Works: Causal Effects of Reform, 1970–2015." *Journal of Comparative Economics* 49, No. 1 (2021): 59–72.

Grier, Kevin, Towhid Mahmood, and Benjamin Powell. "Anti-Sweatshop Activism and the Safety-Employment Tradeoff: Evidence from Bangladesh's Rana Plaza Disaster." *Journal of Economic Behavior and Organization* 208 (2023): 174–190. Retrieved from https://doi.org/10.1016/j.jebo.2023.02.007.

Gwartney, James, Robert A. Lawson, and Joshua Hall. *Economic Freedom of the World Annual Report*. Vancouver: The Fraser Institute, 2011.

Gwartney, James, Robert A. Lawson, Joshua Hall, and Ryan Murphy. *Economic Freedom of the World: 2022 Annual Report*. Vancouver: The Fraser Institute, 2022.

Hall, Joshua and Robert A. Lawson. "Economic Freedom of the World: An Accounting of the Literature." *Contemporary Economic Policy* 32, No. 1 (2014): 1–19.

Hall, Joshua and Peter Leeson. "Good for the Goose, Bad for the Gander: International Labor Standards and Comparative Development." *Journal of Labor Research* 28, No. 4 (2007): 658–676.

Harrison, Ann and Jason Scorse. "Multinationals and Anti-Sweatshop Activism." *American Economic Review* 100, No. 1 (2010): 247–273.

Hayek, Friedrich. "The Use of Knowledge in Society." *American Economic Review* 35, No. 4 (1945): 519–530.

Hayek, Friedrich. "Competition as a Discovery Procedure." In *New Studies in Philosophy, Politics, Economics, and the History of Ideas*. Chicago: University of Chicago Press, 1978.

Hayes, Chris. "Uncovering China's Secret Internment Camps with Rian Thum." In *Why Is This Happening? The Chris Hayes Podcast*. MSNBC, 2019.

Heady, Christopher. "The Effect of Child Labor on Learning Achievement." *World Development* 31, No. 3 (2003): 385–398.

Henderson, David. "The Case for Sweatshops." *Hoover Institution*. February 7, 2000. Retrieved from www.hoover.org/news/daily-report/24617.

Hendrickson, Mark. "U2's Bono Courageously Embraces Capitalism." *Forbes*. November 8, 2013. Retrieved from www.forbes.com/sites/markhendrickson/2013/11/08/u2s-bono-courageously-embraces-capitalism/?sh=342d52ed575a.

Hersch, Joni. "Compensating Differentials for Sexual Harassment." *American Economic Review Papers and Proceedings*. May 2011. Retrieved from http://papers.ssrn.com/sol3/papers.cfm?abstract_id=1743691.

International Labor Organization. *Declaration on Fundamental Principles and Rights at Work*. 1998. Retrieved from www.ilo.org/declaration/lang--en/index.htm.

International Labor Organization. *Every Child Counts: New Global Estimates on Child Labour*. Geneva: ILO, 2002.

International Labor Organization. *Safety and Health at Work*. Retrieved from www.ilo.org/global/topics/safety-and-health-at-work/lang--en/index.htm.

International Labor Organization. "Summary of the Results of the Child and Adolescent Labour Survey in Costa Rica." 2004. Retrieved from www.ilo.org/ipec/ChildlabourstatisticsSIMPOC/Questionnairessurveysandreports/lang--en/index.htm.

International Labor Organization. "Summary of the Results of the Child Labour Survey in El Salvador." 2004. Retrieved from www.ilo.org/ipec/ChildlabourstatisticsSIMPOC/Questionnairessurveysandreports/lang--en/index.htm.

International Labor Organization. "Summary of the Results of the National Child Labour Survey in the Dominican Republic." 2004. Retrieved from www.ilo.org/ipec/ChildlabourstatisticsSIMPOC/Questionnairessurveysandreports/lang--en/index.htm.

International Labor Rights Forum. Retrieved from www.laborrights.org.

Irwin, Doug. *Free Trade Under Fire.* Princeton: Princeton University Press, 2002.

Kates, Michael. "The Ethic of Sweatshops and the Limits of Choice." *Business Ethics Quarterly* 25, No. 2 (2015): 191–212.

Kaufman, Leslie and David Gonzalez, "Labor Standards Clash with Global Reality." *New York Times*, April 24, 2001.

Kleen, Michael. "Sweatshops and Social Justice: Can Compassionate Libertarians Agree?" November 17, 2011. Retrieved from http://c4ss.org/content/8840.

Knight, Frank. "The Role of Principles in Economics and Politics." In *Selected Essays of Frank H. Knight*, edited by Ross Emmett, Vol. 2. Chicago: University of Chicago Press, 1999.

Koenig, Pamina and Sandra Poncet. "The Effects of the Rana Plaza Collapse on the Sourcing Choices of French Importers." *Journal of International Economics* 137 (2022). Retrieved from https://doi.org/10.1016/j.jinteco.2022.103576.

Kristof, Nicholas. "Inviting All Democrats." *New York Times.* January 14, 2004.

Kristof, Nicholas. "My Sweatshop Column." *New York Times.* January 14, 2009. Retrieved from http://kristof.blogs.nytimes.com/2009/01/14/my-sweatshop-column/.

Kristof, Nicholas. "Where Sweatshops Are a Dream." *New York Times.* January 14, 2009.

Krueger, Alan. "International Labor Standards and Trade." In *Annual World Bank Conference on Development Economics 1996*, edited by M. Bruno and B. Pleskovic. Washington, DC: The World Bank, 1997.

Krugman, Paul. "In Praise of Cheap Labor: Bad Jobs at Bad Wages Are Better Than No Jobs at All." *Slate Magazine.* March 1997.

Krugman, Paul. "Reckonings; Hearts and Heads." *New York Times.* April 22, 2001.

Lawson, Robert A., Vincent J. Miozzi, and Meg Tuszynski. "Economic Freedom and Growth, Income, Investment, and Inequality: A Quantitative Summary of the Literature." *Southern Economic Journal* (in press).

Lawson, Robert A., Ryan Murphy, and Benjamin Powell. "The Determinants of Economic Freedom: A Survey." *Contemporary Economic Policy* 38, No. 4 (2020): 622–642.

Lehr, Amy. *Addressing Forced Labor in the Xinjiang Uyghur Autonomous Region: Toward a Shared Agenda.* Washington, DC: Center for Strategic and International Studies, 2020.

Leighton, Wayne and Edward Lopez. *Madmen, Intellectuals, and Academic Scribblers.* Palo Alto: Stanford University Press. 2012.

Leonard, Thomas. "Protecting Family and Race: The Progressive Case for Regulating Women's Work." *American Journal of Economics and Sociology* 64, No. 3 (2005): 757–791.

Levinson, Jeff, ed. *Mill Girls of Lowell.* Boston: History Compass, 2007.

Lindert, Peter and Jeffrey Williamson. "English Workers' Living Standards during the Industrial Revolution: A New Look." In *The Economics of the Industrial Revolution*, edited by Joel Mokyr. Totowa, NJ: Rowman and Allanheld, 1985.

Lindsay, Samuel. "Child Labor in the United States." *American Economic Association* 8 (February 1907): 256–259.

Locke, Richard M. *The Promise and Limits of Private Power: Promoting Labor Standards in a Global Economy.* Cambridge: Cambridge University Press, 2013.

Lopez-Acevedo, Gladys and Raymond Robertson, eds. *Sewing Success?: Employment, Wages, and Poverty Following the End of the Multi-Fibre Arrangement.* Washington, DC: World Bank, 2012.

Lowell Offering, The. 1841.

Lowell Textile Workers Petition. *Voice of Industry.* January 15, 1845.

Mahmood, Towhid and Benjamin Powell. "No Sweat? Living Standards and Sweatshop Wages in Developing Countries." *The Independent Review* (2024).

Maizland, Lindsay. *China's Repression of Uyghurs in Xinjiang.* Council on Foreign Relations. September 22, 2022. Retrieved from www.cfr.org/backgrounder/china-xinjiang-uyghurs-muslims-repression-genocide-human-rights#chapter-title-0-8.

Makioka, Ryo. "The Impact of Anti-Sweatshop Activism on Employment." *Review of Development Economics* 25 (2021): 630–653.

Maquila Solidarity Network. Retrieved from http://en.maquilasolidarity.org.

Marquis, Christopher. *How Companies Are Dealing with the Uyghur Forced Labor Prevention Act.* The China Project. August 17, 2022. Retrieved from https://thechinaproject.com/2022/08/17/how-companies-are-dealing-with-the-uyghur-forced-labor-prevention-act/.

Matsuura, Aya and Carly Teng. *Understanding the Gender Composition and Experience of Ready-Made Garment (RMG) Workers in Bangladesh.* Bangladesh: International Labor Organization, 2020. Retrieved from www.ilo.org/wcmsp5/groups/public/---asia/---ro-bangkok/---ilo-dhaka/documents/publication/wcms_754669.pdf.

Mayer, Robert. "Sweatshops, Exploitation, and Moral Responsibility." *Journal of Social Philosophy* 38, No. 4 (2007): 605–619.

Mayer, Robert. "What's Wrong with Exploitation?" *Journal of Applied Philosophy* 24, No. 2 (2007): 137–150.

McCloskey, Deirdre. "The Industrial Revolution 1780–1860: A Survey." In *The Economics of the Industrial Revolution,* edited by Joel Mokyr. Totowa, NJ: Rowman and Allanheld, 1985.

McCloskey, Deirdre. *Bourgeois Dignity: Why Economics Can't Explain the Modern World.* Chicago: University of Chicago Press, 2010.

McKinsey and Company. *Bangladesh's Ready Made Garments Landscape: The Challenge of Growth.* 2012.

Mencken, H. L. *A Mencken Chrestomathy.* New York: Vintage Books, 1982.

Meyers, Chris. "Wrongful Beneficence: Exploitation and Third World Sweatshops." *Journal of Social Philosophy* 35, No. 3 (2004): 319–333.

Miller, John. "Why Economists Are Wrong about Sweatshops and the Antisweatshop Movement." *Challenge.* January/February 2003.

Milne, Amber. "Brands Urged to Stop Sourcing from China's Xinjiang over Forced Labour Fears." *Reuters.* July 23, 2020. Retrieved from www.reuters.com/article/global-garment-china-xinjiang-idUSL5N2ET3YM.

Mises, Ludwig von. *Economic Calculation in the Socialist Commonwealth.* Auburn: Ludwig von Mises Institute, 1990.

Mises, Ludwig von. *Human Action.* Auburn: Ludwig von Mises Institute, 1998.

Moehling, Carolyn. "State Child Labor Laws and the Decline in Child Labor." *Explorations in Economic History* 36, No. 1 (1999): 72–106.

Mokyr, Joel. *The Enlightened Economy: An Economic History of Britain 1700–1850*. New Haven: Yale University Press, 2009.

Moore, Michael and Kip Viscusi. *Compensation Mechanisms for Job Risks*. Princeton: Princeton University Press. 1990.

Munger, Michael. "Euvoluntary or Not, Exchange Is Just." *Social Philosophy and Policy* 28, No. 2 (Summer 2011): 192–211.

Murphy, David and David Matthew. *Nike and Global Labour Practices: A Case Study Prepared for the New Academy of Business Innovation Network for Socially Responsible Business*. Unpublished. London: New Academy of Business, 2001.

Murphy, Laura, Kendyl Salcito, Yalkun Uluyol, and Mia Rabkin. *Driving Force: Automotive Supply Chains and Forced Labor in the Uyghur Region*. Sheffield: Sheffield Hallam University Helena Kennedy Centre for International Justice, 2022.

National Academies of Sciences, Engineering, and Medicine. *The Economic and Fiscal Consequences of Immigration*. Washington, DC: The National Academies Press, 2016.

National Labor Committee. Retrieved from www.nlcnet.org.

National Labor Committee. *Violation of CAFTA at Sam Bridge SA Guatemala*. October 2007. Retrieved from www.nlcnet.org/alerts?id=0072.

National Labor Committee. *Major Worker Rights Victory in Guatemala*. October 2009. Retrieved from www.nlcnet.org/alerts?id=0022.

National Park Service. *Lowell: The Story of an Industrial City. Official National Park Handbook, Handbook 140*. Division of Publications National Park Service. Washington, DC: U.S. Department of the Interior, 1992.

Neu, Michael. *Just Liberal Violence: Sweatshops, Torture, War*. London: Rowman & Littlefield, 2018.

Neumark, David and Luis Felipe Manguia Corella. "Do Minimum Wages Reduce Employment in Developing Countries? A Survey and Exploration of Conflicting Evidence." *World Development* 137 (2021): 1–23.

Neumark, David and William Wascher. *Minimum Wages*. Cambridge, MA: MIT Press, 2008.

Nowrasteh, Alex and Benjamin Powell. *Wretched Refuse? The Political Economy of Immigration and Institutions*. Cambridge: Cambridge University Press, 2020.

O'Connor, Anne-Marie. "The Plight of Women around the World; Central America; Labor: Sweatshops Meet U.S. Consumer Demand." *The Atlanta Journal Constitution*. September 3, 1995.

Paton, Elizabeth and Austin Ramzy. "Coalition Brings Pressure to End Forced Uighur Labor." *New York Times*. July 23, 2020. Retrieved from www.nytimes.com/2020/07/23/fashion/uighur-forced-labor-cotton-fashion.html.

Pearce, Fred. *The Land Grabbers: The New Fight over Who Owns the Earth*. Boston: Beacon Press, 2012.

Peng, Linan and Justin Callais. "The Authoritarian Trade-off: A Synthetic Control Analysis of Development and Social Coercion in the Xinjiang Uyghur

Autonomous Region." *Contemporary Economic Policy* 41, No. 2 (2023): 370–387.

Pollin, Robert, Justine Burns, and James Heintz. "Global Apparel Production and Sweatshop Labor: Can Raising Retail Prices Finance Living Wages?" *Cambridge Journal of Economics* 28, No. 2 (2004): 153–171.

Powell, Benjamin. "East Asian State Development Planning: Did It Create an East Asian Miracle." *Review of Austrian Economics* 18, No. 3/4 (2005): 305–323.

Powell, Benjamin. "In Reply to Sweatshop Sophistries." *Human Rights Quarterly* 28, No. 4 (November 2006): 1031–1042.

Powell, Benjamin, ed. *Making Poor Nations Rich: Entrepreneurship and the Process of Development.* Palo Alto: Stanford University Press, 2008.

Powell, Benjamin. "Some Implications of Capital Heterogeneity." In *Handbook on Contemporary Austrian Economics*, edited by Peter Boettke. Cheltenham: Edward Elgar, 2010.

Powell, Benjamin. *Out of Poverty: Sweatshops and the Global Economy.* Cambridge: Cambridge University Press, 2014.

Powell, Benjamin. "Sweatshop Regulations: Tradeoffs and Value Judgements." *Journal of Business Ethics* 151, No. 1 (2018): 29–36.

Powell, Benjamin and Ryan Murphy. "Nutritional Efficiency Wages and Unemployment: Where's the Beef?" *American Journal of Agricultural Economics* 97, No. 2 (2015): 405–413.

Powell, Benjamin and Matt Ryan. "Does Development Aid Lead to Economic Freedom?" *Journal of Private Enterprise* 22, No. 1 (Fall 2006): 1–21.

Powell, Benjamin and Matt Ryan. "Stop Aiding Dictators." *Providence Journal.* February 27, 2006. Retrieved from www.independent.org/newsroom/article.asp?id=1682.

Powell, Benjamin and Matt Ryan. "The Global Spread of Think Tanks and Economic Freedom." *Journal of Private Enterprise* 32, No. 3 (2017): 17–31.

Powell, Benjamin and David Skarbek. "Sweatshop Wages and Third World Workers: Are the Jobs Worth the Sweat?" *Journal of Labor Research* 27, No. 2 (Spring 2006): 263–274.

Powell, Benjamin and Matt Zwolinski. "The Ethical and Economic Case Against Sweatshop Labor: A Critical Assessment." *Journal of Business Ethics* 107, No. 4 (2012): 449–472.

Preiss, Joshua. "Global Labor Justice and Limits of Economic Analysis." *Business Ethics Quarterly* 24, No. 1 (2014): 55–83.

Preiss, Joshua. "Freedom, Autonomy, and Harm in Global Supply Chains." *Journal of Business Ethics* 160, No. 4 (2019): 881–891.

Ravallion, Martin and Quentin Wodon. "Does Child Labor Displace Schooling? Evidence on Behavioral Responses to an Enrollment Subsidy." *Economic Journal* 110, (2000): 158–175.

Rawls, John. *A Theory of Justice.* Cambridge, MA: Harvard University Press, 1971.

Reed, Lawrence. "Child Labor and the British Industrial Revolution." *The Freeman* Vol. 41, No. 8 (August 1991).

Reinecke, Juliane and Jimmy Donaghey. "After Rana Plaza: Building Coalitional Power for Labour Rights between Unions and (Consumption-Based) Social Movement Organizations." *Organization* 22, No. 5 (2015): 720–740.

Rodrik, Dani. "A Primer on Trade and Inequality." *NBER Working Paper* No. 29507 (2021).

Rottenberg, Simon, ed. *The Economics of Legal Minimum Wages*. Washington, DC: American Enterprise Institute, 1981.

Sachs, Jeffrey. *The End of Poverty: Economic Possibilities for Our Time*. New York: Penguin Press, 2005.

Sample, Ruth. *Exploitation: What It Is and Why It's Wrong*. New York: Rowman & Littlefield, 2003.

Samuelson, Paul. *Economics*, 9th ed. New York: McGraw Hill, 1973.

Scholars Against Sweatshop Labor. *Statement*. October 2001. Retrieved from www.peri.umass.edu/253/.

Schultz, Paul. "School Subsidies for the Poor: Evaluating the Mexican Progresa Poverty Program." *Journal for Development Economics* 74, No. 1 (2004): 199–250.

Silvers, Robert. *Strategy to Prevent the Importation of Goods Mined, Produced, or Manufactured with Forced Labor in the People's Republic of China*. U.S. Department of Homeland Security: 2022.

Simons, Henry. *Simons' Syllabus*, edited by Gordon Tullock. Fairfax: Center for the Study of Public Choice, 1983.

Skarbek, David, Emily Skarbek, Brian Skarbek, and Erin Skarbek. "Sweatshops, Opportunity Costs, and Non-Monetary Compensation: Evidence from El Salvador." *American Journal of Economics and Sociology* 71, No 3 (2012): 539–561.

Snyder, Jeremy C. "Needs Exploitation." *Ethical Theory and Moral Practice*, 11, No. 4 (2008): 389–405.

Snyder, Jeremy C. "Efficiency, Equality, and Price Gouging: A Response to Zwolinski." *Business Ethics Quarterly* 19, No. 2 (April 2009): 303–306.

Snyder, Jeremy C. "Exploitation and Sweatshop Labor: Perspectives and Issues." *Business Ethics Quarterly* 20, No. 2 (April 2010): 187–213.

Sobel, Russell and Peter Leeson. "The Spread of Global Economic Freedom." In *Economic Freedom of the World 2007 Annual Report*, edited by James Gwartney and Robert Lawson. Vancouver: The Fraser Institute, 2007.

Sollars, Gordon and Fred Englander. "Sweatshops: Kant and Consequences." *Business Ethics Quarterly* 17, No. 1 (January 2007): 115–133.

Sowell, Thomas. *A Conflict of Visions: Ideological Origins of Political Struggles*. New York: William Morrow & Co., 1987.

Stearns, Peter. *The Industrial Revolution in World History*, 3rd ed. Boulder: Westview Press, 2007.

Stern, Robert and Katherine Terrel. "Labor Standards and the World Trade Organization." *University of Michigan, Ann Arbor, RSIE Discussion Paper* No. 499 (2003).

STITCH. Retrieved from www.stitchonline.org.

Stocker, Marshall. "The Price of Freedom: A Fama-French Freedom Factor." *Emerging Markets Review* 26 (2016): 1–19.

Stringham, Edward. "Economic Value and Costs Are Subjective." In *Handbook on Contemporary Austrian Economics*, edited by Peter Boettke. Cheltenham: Edward Elgar, 2010.

Students Against Sweatshops. Retrieved from www.studentsagainstsweatshops.org.uk.

Swanson, Ana, Catie Edmondson, and Edward Wong. "U.S. Effort to Combat Forced Labor Targets Corporate China Ties." *New York Times.* December 24, 2021. Retrieved from https://cn.nytimes.com/usa/20211224/china-uyghurs-forced-labor/dual/.

SweatFree Communities Campaign. Retrieved from www.sweatfree.org.

Tanaka, Mari. "Exporting Sweatshops? Evidence from Myanmar." *The Review of Economics and Statistics* 102, No. 3 (2020): 442–456.

Trebilcock, Anne. "The Rana Plaza Disaster Seven Years On: Transnational Experiments and Perhaps a New Treaty?" *International Labour Review* 159, No. 4 (2020): 545–568.

UNICEF. *The State of the World's Children.* 1997. Retrieved from www.unicef .org/sowc97/.

United Students Against Sweatshops. Retrieved from http://usas.org/.

U.S. Department of Labor. *Bangladesh.* Retrieved from www.dol.gov/ilab/media/reports/iclp/sweat/bangladesh.htm/.

U.S. Labor Education in the Americas Project. Retrieved from www.usleap.org.

Uyghur Forced Labor Prevention Act of 2021, H.R. 6256, 117th Congress. 2021.

Uyghur Human Rights Policy Act of 2020, S. 3744, 116th Congress. 2020.

Valdman, Mikhail. "Exploitation and Injustice." *Social Theory and Practice: An International and Interdisciplinary Journal of Social Philosophy* 34, No. 4 (October 2008): 551–572.

Valdman, Mikhail. "A Theory of Wrongful Exploitation." *Philosophers' Imprint* 9, No. 6 (July 2009): 1–14.

Viederman, Dan. "Any Job Is a Good Job? Think Again." *Huffington Post.* February 18, 2011.

Viscusi, Kip, Joseph Harrington and John Vernon. *Economics of Regulation and Antitrust,* 4th ed. Cambridge, MA: MIT Press, 2005.

Vogel, David. *The Market for Virtue: The Potential and Limits of Corporate Social Responsibility.* Washington, DC: The Brookings Institute, 2005.

War on Want. Retrieved from www.waronwant.org.

Wertheimer, Alan. *Exploitation.* Princeton: Princeton University Press, 1996.

Wertheimer, Alan. "Matt Zwolinski's 'Choosing Sweatshops': A Commentary." Unpublished Manuscript. Presented at the Arizona Current Research Workshop (January 2007).

Whaples, Robert. *Child Labor in the United States.* In EH.Net Encyclopedia. 2005. Retrieved from http://eh.net/encyclopedia/article/whaples.childlabor.

Williamson, Claudia. "Informal Institutions Rule: Institutional Arrangements and Economic Performance." *Public Choice* 139, No. 3 (2009): 371–387.

Williamson, Claudia and Carrie Kerekes. "Securing Private Property: Formal versus Informal Institutions." *Journal of Law and Economics* 54, No. 3 (2011): 537–572.

Wintour, Patrick. "US and Canada follow EU and UK in Sanctioning Chinese Officials over Xinjiang." *The Guardian.* March 22, 2021. Retrieved from www .theguardian.com/world/2021/mar/22/china-responds-to-eu-uk-sanctions-over-uighurs-human-rights.

Wolff, Robert Paul. *In Defense of Anarchism,* 3rd ed. Berkeley: University of California Press, 1970.

Wood, Allen W. "Exploitation." *Social Philosophy and Policy* 12, No. 2 (1995): 136–158.

The Worker Rights Consortium. Retrieved from www.workersrights.org.

World Bank. *World Development Indicators Online.*

Xu, Vicky Xiuzhong, Danielle Cave, James Leibold, Kelsey Munro, and Nathan Ruser. *Uyghurs for Sale: Re-education Forced Labour and Surveillance beyond Xinjiang.* Barton: Australian Strategic Policy Institute, 2020.

Yakovlev, Pavel and Russell S. Sobel. "Occupational Safety and Profit Maximization: Friends or Foes?" *Journal of Socio-Economics* 39, No. 3 (June 2010): 429–435.

Young, Iris Marion. "Responsibility and Global Justice: A Social Connection Model." *Social Philosophy and Policy* 23, No. 1 (January 2006): 102–130.

Zenz, Adrian. "Thoroughly Reforming Them Towards a Healthy Heart Attitude: China's Political Re-education Campaign in Xinjiang." *Central Asian Survey* 38, No. 1 (2018): 102–128. Retrieved from https://doi.org/10.1080/0263493 7.2018.1507997.

Zenz, Adrian. *Coercive Labor in Xinjiang: Labor Transfer and the Mobilization of Ethnic Minorities to Pick Cotton.* New Lines Institute. December 14, 2020.

Zwolinski, Matt. "Sweatshops, Choice, and Exploitation." *Business Ethics Quarterly* 17, No. 4 (October 2007): 689–727.

Zwolinski, Matt. "The Ethics of Price Gouging." *Business Ethics Quarterly* 18, No. 3 (July 2008): 347–378.

Zwolinski, Matt. "Price Gouging, Non-Worseness, and Distributive Justice." *Business Ethics Quarterly* 19, No. 2 (April 2009): 295–306.

Zwolinski, Matt. "Structural Exploitation." *Social Philosophy and Policy* 29, No. 1 (Winter 2012): 154–179.

Index

Printed in the United States
by Baker & Taylor Publisher Services